THE
ALL-AMERICAN
COWBOY
GRILL

D1417369

THE
ALL-AMERICAN
COWBOY
GRILL

Cheryl Rogers-Barnett,
Ken Beck, and Jim Clark

RUTLEDGE HILL PRESS
Nashville, Tennessee
A Division of Thomas Nelson Publishers
Since 1798

www.thomasnelson.com

Published by Rutledge Hill Press, a Division of Thomas Nelson Publishers, P.O. Box 141000, Nashville, Tennessee 37214.

Rutledge Hill Press books may be purchased in bulk for educational, business, fundraising, or sales promotional use. For information, please e-mail SpecialMarkets@ThomasNelson.com.

Design by Harriette Bateman.

Library of Congress Cataloging-in-Publication Data

Rogers-Barnett, Cheryl, 1940–
    The all-American cowboy grill / Cheryl Rogers-Barnett, Ken Beck, and Jim Clark.
      p. cm.
    Includes index.
    ISBN 1-4016-0200-2 (comb-bound pbk.)
    1. Cookery, American—Western style. 2. Motion picture actors and actresses—United States—Miscellanea. I. Beck, Ken, 1951– II. Clark, Jim, 1960– III. Title.
TX715.2.W47R68 2004
641.5978—dc22   2004027671

Printed in Korea

05 06 07 08 09 — 5 4 3 2 1

To
the great American cowboy

CONTENTS

MORNIN' BUSINESS

Lee Henry

Rattlin' of pans in the pre-dawn light
 Signals the end of a cold bitter night.

Jawin' and gratin' of the coffee grinder's song
 Says get up cowboy, it's near breakin' dawn.

A grouchy old figure with pot hook in hand
 Reflects a lifetime of cookin' with his wrinkles and tan.

His breakfast from memory is simple to fix
 It's salt pork, coffee, sourdough, and lick.

His kitchen of canvas, chuck wagon, and hames
 Prances and dances in the flickering flames.

From inside the chuck box the Cookie removes
 A large sack of flour and a bottle of booze.

With his back to the bedrolls from the bottle he takes
 A nip of White Lightnin' to ward off the snakes.

The tools of his trade, a bowl he has kept
 Thru thunder and lightnin' and rustlers he's met.

Washed in streams and scrubbed by the sands
 His large wooden bowl he carved with his hands.

Blendin' the lard in the fixin's so neat
 From the crock pours the sourdough, it's sour but sweet.

The biscuits are cut and then to the Dutch
 Are crowded together by the master's touch.

The coals from the fire on the lid with lip
 Are hot as a Colt drawn from the hip.

The golden brown sourdoughs from his Dutch-oven pan
 Have filled the craw of many a man.

With his back to the cowboys ridin' over the crest
 A nip he will take before attackin' the mess.

With bottle in hand, and the marks from a quirt
 As he toasts, "Thanks, Cookie," cut in the dirt.

THANK YOU, PARDNERS!

Gathering recipes, photographs, and information—even in the age of that virtual corral, the Internet—is no easy task. It just couldn't be done without the help of many folks who love cowboy lore and good food as much as we do.

So first off, we want to say "thanks a million" to the following cowpokes who went the extra mile: Fred Goodwin for sharing many photographs, posters, and lobby cards from his archives; stuntman and historian Neil Summers for the loan of photographs from his archives; historian-journalist Boyd Magers; stuntman Jesse Wayne; Steve Stevens; writer Jonathan Lampley; Brent Baldwin; Peggy Evans; and "Walkin' Talkin'" Charley Aldridge.

A whole passel of others either shared recipes from their cowboy families or helped us make the connection to some cowpokes who were off the beaten trail. Attributions for many of these helpful ranch hands are included with recipes in the book. We tip our Stetsons in honor of others here: Catherine

A meal in the dining room of Roy Rogers and Dale Evans with their children in the 1950s always began with grace. The table was designed and built by western actor George Montgomery.

Bach, Randy Bash, Sherwin Bash, Lisa Beery, Claire Boone, Diane Braga, Sandy Brokaw, Victor Buck, Stephen and Elizabeth Burnette, Marilyn Carey, Laura and John Carter Cash, Donna Chipperfield, Calin Coburn, Mary-Jo Combs, Jeff Connors, Claire Cook, Alisa Cooper, Patsi Cox, Patrick Curtis, Terry Davis, Dennis Devine, Tad Devine, Linda Dotson, Shirley Eaton, Kiki Ebsen, Kathy Edwards, Bud Evans, Karl Farr Jr., Peter Ford, Bonnie Garner, Greta Garner, Daryle Ann Lindley Giardino, Tara Gordon, Vernell Hackett, Diane Hadley, Lisa Hampton, Maxine Hanson, Jay Jenrette, Amanda Joyner, Cheryl Kagan, Fred LaBour, Gail Lander-Kedesh, Marion Carney LaRue, Charlene Lawrence, Dot Leverett, Toni and Brad Light, Ann Lindberg, Maggie Pickens Lindley, Beverly Losey, Ed Lousararian, Bridget Madison, Jim Mahoney, Diane Wills Malone, Sharon Marie, Cherry Martinez, Diane McClure, Wyatt McCrea, Elizabeth Drake McDonald, Melissa Miggo, John Miller, Nikki Mitchell, Dawn Moore, Paige Mudd, Rory Calhoun Nagy, Debbie Nicoletti, Inga Ojala, Jackie Patterson, Joanie Perciballi, Wayne Perryman, Bob Pickard, Tippi Pyle, Richard Renaldo, Amy Richards, Ronnie Robbins, Mark Sissel, Tommie Ritter Smith, Hal Spencer, Beth Steinruck, Paula Szeigis, Vikki Tedford, Bob Terhune, Mindy Tobin, Elizabeth Travis, Marilyn Tucker, Glenda Washam, Guy Williams Jr., and Larryann Willis.

We're also grateful for the publishing version of a "land grant" from Rutledge Hill Press for us homesteading writers. Larry Stone and Bryan Curtis believed in the idea from the start. Trail boss Jennifer Greenstein made sure we had as few stray little dogies as possible during the long drive. We also appreciate the efforts of others at the Rutledge Hill ranch house, including associate publisher Pamela Clements, recipe editor Laurin Stamm, copy editor Janene MacIvor, graphic designers Walt Petrie and Harriette Bateman, and cover designer Brad Talbott.

And we never could have started this book, much less reached the end of the trail successfully, without the love and support of our families. Cheryl thanks her husband, Larry; Ken thanks his wife, Wendy, daughter, Kylie, and son, Cole; and Jim thanks his wife, Mary.

Through the years such stars as Warner Baxter, Cesar Romero, and Gilbert Roland portrayed the Cisco Kid on film, but baby boomers fondly remember the Cisco Kid of TV fame, Duncan Renaldo (right), who rode with trusty sidekick Pancho, Lee Carrillo. (Photo courtesy of Richard Renaldo)

THANK YOU, PARDNERS!

Wagons Ho!

The All-American Cowboy Grill is a collection that celebrates the great American cowboy and cowgirl.

With this cookbook, we have attempted to bring together as many as possible of the filmmakers, actors, singers, and athletes who have enjoyed portraying and sometimes actually living the life of cowboys and cowgirls. They and their families have shared personal recipes and photographs and given us a taste of how much they have loved what they do. We've also rounded up hearty helpings from top modern-day ranches and chuck wagons that

A chuck wagon cook prepares a feast for hungry cowboys beneath the western sky. (Photo by Kevin Green)

carry on cowboy traditions and celebrate the cowboy way of life.

The emphasis in this book is on grilling, always a western favorite, and, in more recent days, an all-American phenomenon. But our contributing cowboys refused to be fenced in by a grill. They have also shared a gamut of favorites from their home larders. You'll find appetizers, salads, soups, breads, desserts, and a couple of libations—all the recipes you'll need to create a complete meal to satisfy even the hungriest cowboy.

Some cowboys in this roundup are also partial to pit barbecuing—and pardner, don't try to tell a serious barbecue cook that barbecuing is the same as grilling. Likewise, the serious grill chefs also appreciate the distinctions of their method. No matter how you like to cook your favorite foods, we think you'll find that this book has some truly sensational recipes that are sure to twang your buds.

This cowboy grill cookbook, a sequel to the original *All-American Cowboy Cookbook*, features photographs and flavors from more than two hundred folks who have gone the cowboy way. The recipes flow from such movie star favorites as Gene Autry, Walter Brennan, Joel McCrea, Robert Mitchum, Paul Newman, Roy Rogers, John Wayne, and even the "shakiest gun in the west," Don Knotts. You'll also find many legendary TV cowpokes, including Richard Boone, Chuck Connors, Clayton Moore, Duncan Renaldo, and Clint Walker. There are cowgirls Gail Davis, Dale Evans, Patsy Montana, and Gloria Winters, plus rodeo stars such as Clay O'Brien Cooper, Donnie Gay, Ty Murray, and Jim Shoulders.

Also corralled here are great recipes from some of the West's best bad guys—men such as Jack Elam, Leo Gordon, and Morgan Woodward. And then there's a whole posse of country and western singers, including Johnny Cash, Don Edwards, Belinda Gail, Riders in the Sky, Dave Stamey, George Strait, and Johnny Western. We are also honored to be able to include a favorite dish from a true horseman and western actor, the late President Ronald Reagan.

As with *The All-American Cowboy Cookbook*, a portion of author royalties from *The All-American Cowboy Grill* will go to the Sunshine Children's Home in Mesa, Arizona, which was suggested as a beneficiary of these books by the late, great western actor and world-champion cowboy Ben Johnson.

So saddle up and let your fingers do the riding as you hit the trail to yesteryear and rendezvous with the world's greatest cowboys. Rustle up a meal for your family and friends, and then enjoy it as you honor the spirited traditions of the American cowboy.

Giddy-up!

WAGONS HO!

EARLY STAGES

Hardie's Hardy Knock on the Noggin Egg Nog

1	dozen eggs
1½	cups sugar
1	quart milk
1	quart whipping cream
1½	quarts club soda
	Fresh ground nutmeg

Separate the egg yolks and whites. Put the whites in the refrigerator. In a bowl, add the sugar to the yolks and whip them. Chill for 30 minutes. In a large bowl, combine the milk, whipping cream, club soda, and yolks. Whip the egg whites, and then fold them into the milk mixture. Sprinkle each serving with nutmeg.

Makes 20 servings, or 40 when doubled.

Dale Robertson, actor

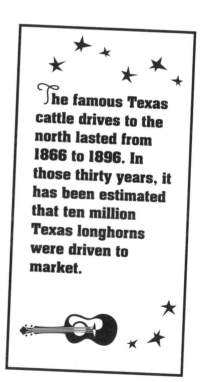

The famous Texas cattle drives to the north lasted from 1866 to 1896. In those thirty years, it has been estimated that ten million Texas longhorns were driven to market.

Stella Stevens played a sheriff in a small town in the 1984 TV movie *West in No Man's Land*. Her other western credits feature *The Long Ride Home*, *The Manitou*, *Honky Tonk*, and *The Ballad of Cable Hogue*.

Hildy's Dandy Boiled Custard

This is an ancient recipe from my grand-mother, Dandy.

1   quart low-fat milk
¾   cup sugar
1   tablespoon all-purpose flour
    Pinch of salt
4   to 6 eggs, well beaten
1   teaspoon vanilla extract
    Dashes of ground nutmeg

Heat the milk slowly in a double boiler until hot, but not boiling. In a separate bowl, mix the sugar, flour, and salt. Add the beaten eggs, and mix well. Add the egg mixture gradually to the milk, stirring constantly until the mixture thickens slightly. Cool for 5 minutes, and add the vanilla. Even when cool, the mixture will be only slightly thick. Serve the custard in glasses so that it may be sipped. Serve warm or cold with a dash of nutmeg on each serving. It goes well with fruit for a low-fat dessert.

Makes 4 to 6 servings.

Stella Stevens, actress

Once-Upon-a-Chili Cheese Dip

This dip is a real winner. It beckons everyone back for more and more. Definitely addicting.

2   pounds lean ground beef
2   pounds Velveeta cheese, cut into cubes
2   (10-ounce) cans Ro-tel green chiles and
    tomatoes, drained
3   teaspoons Worcestershire sauce
1   teaspoon chili powder
¼   cup all-purpose flour
⅓   cup water

In a large pot, brown the beef and drain off the fat. Add the cheese, chiles, Worcestershire sauce, and chili powder. Heat until the cheese melts. In a separate bowl, make a paste with the flour and water. Stir the paste into the mixture in the pot until the mixture thickens. This dip may be stored in the refrigerator for several days. It also freezes well. Defrost overnight in the refrigerator, or thaw in the microwave.

Reheat the dip slowly, and serve hot in a slow cooker set to low. Serve with corn chips.
Makes about 2½ quarts.

Dan Rowan, actor and comedian

Dan Rowan (left) and his comedy partner Dick Martin went West in the 1958 film comedy *Once Upon a Horse.*

BUFFALO BILL
HISTORICAL CENTER

One of the largest and most respected museums and research centers in North America honors the memory of Buffalo Bill Cody, arguably the single most influential figure in shaping the popular image of the Old West—thanks to his phenomenally popular Wild West Shows of the late nineteenth and early twentieth centuries.

The Buffalo Bill Historical Center incorporates five museums:

- The Buffalo Bill Museum focuses on the legendary showman himself through photographs, playbills, and personal items, such as Cody's spectacles.
- The Whitney Gallery of Western Art includes masterworks by such artists as Frederic Remington, Charles M. Russell, and N. C. Wyeth, as well as more recent pieces.
- The Plains Indian Museum preserves and interprets artifacts created and utilized by such tribes as the Lakota, Cheyenne, and Crow Indians, including quilts, artwork, and tools.
- The Cody Firearms Museum is probably the most comprehensive collection of guns and related equipment in the world, particularly for Winchester and Colt products.
- The Draper Museum of Natural History interprets the natural and geographical features of the region using photographs in twenty thousand square feet of exhibit space.

Situated near the eastern entrance of Yellowstone National Park, the Buffalo Bill Historical Center is a tremendous resource for scholars as well. Books, magazines, letters, and original documents are available, including firearm factory records that can be used to trace the history of individual weapons.

The Buffalo Bill Cody Historical Center is located at 720 Sheridan Avenue in Cody, Wyoming. For more information, go to *www.bbhc.org.*

Dueling Fast-Draw Appetizers

Two quick shots that are easy and cheesy.

First Shot:
- 2 (8-ounce) packages cream cheese
- 1 (12-ounce) jar jalapeño jelly (Knotts brand is good, but any will do.)
- 1 box Ritz or Town House crackers

Place the cream cheese on a plate. Spread the jelly over the cream cheese. Serve with crackers.

Makes about 16 to 20 servings.

Second Shot:
- 1 (6-ounce) can crabmeat
  Cocktail sauce
- 2 (8-ounce) packages cream cheese
- 1 box Ritz or Town House crackers

Minced celery and/or green onion (optional)
Couple of drops of Tabasco (optional)

Chill the crab for at least 2 hours in the refrigerator (or in the freezer for 1 hour). Drain the crabmeat, and mix with a small amount of the cocktail sauce. Place the cream cheese on a plate. Pour the crab mixture over the cream cheese. Serve with crackers.

Variations: You may want to add some minced celery and/or green onion to the crab mixture. Or if you want to spice it, try adding a couple of drops of Tabasco.

Makes about 16 to 20 servings.

Eli Wallach, actor

Eli Wallach can cowboy up with the best of them. He slaps leather in such flicks as *Mackenna's Gold, Black Jack,* and *How the West Was Won,* but he is absolutely magnificent as Tuco in The Good, the Bad and the Ugly, and as the bandit leader in *The Magnificent Seven.*

Versatile actress Beverly Garland was a guest star on numerous TV western series, such as *The Lone Ranger, Yancy Derringer, Rawhide, Laramie, Gunsmoke, Laredo, Kung Fu, The Wild Wild West,* and *The Nine Lives of Elfego Baca.* She also starred in her fair share of feature horse operas, such as *Bitter Creek, Two Guns and a Badge, Gunslinger,* and *Badlands of Montana.* Here, she plays a frontier saloon hostess to Robert Horton in TV's *A Man Called Shenandoah.*

Exceptional Bean Dip

This is a great dip to start off a barbecue.

2   (10½-ounce) cans Fritos bean dip
1   cup sour cream
1   (8-ounce) package cream cheese, softened
1   (1¼-ounce) package taco seasoning mix
20 drops (yes, exactly) Tabasco
1   bunch green onions, grated
½   pound sharp Cheddar cheese, grated
½   pound Monterey Jack cheese, grated
    Tortilla chips

Preheat the oven to 350˚. With an electric mixer, combine the bean dip, sour cream, cream cheese, taco seasoning mix, and Tabasco sauce. Spoon into a greased, shallow, 2- quart casserole. Top with green onions and cheeses. May be refrigerated until party time. Bake uncovered for 15 minutes, or until the cheeses are melted. Wrap the casserole in gaily colored napkins and serve with a basket of crisp tortilla chips.

Makes 8 servings.

Beverly Garland, actress

When he was good, marvelous character actor Jack Elam was good; but oh, when he was bad, he was bad. Elam made more than a hundred films and could turn on the charm as easily as a snake can get mean. His films include *High Noon, The Man from Laramie, Jubal, Firecreek, Once Upon a Time in the West, Support Your Local Gunfighter,* and *Support Your Local Sheriff.* Among his TV series were *The Dakotas, Temple Houston,* and *The Texas Wheelers.*

Sassy Salsa

This is an excellent salsa. All our guests rave about it.

4	(28-ounce) cans crushed tomatoes
5	cups chopped green onions
12	jalapeños, finely chopped
½	cup jalapeño juice
1	tablespoon salt
1	tablespoon oregano
5	tablespoons chopped fresh cilantro
4	teaspoons cumin
1½	tablespoons garlic powder

Mix together the tomatoes, green onions, jalapeños and juice, salt, oregano, cilantro, cumin, and garlic powder. Let stand for 24 hours for best results.

Makes 1 gallon.

Grapevine Canyon Ranch
Pearce, Arizona

Jack's Gunfighter Guacamole

1	large avocado, peeled and seeded
1	fresh tomato, finely chopped
1	Mezzetta (yellow) hot chile pepper, finely diced
1	tablespoon Ortega diced green chiles
	Small amount of mayonnaise
	Salt
1	or 2 dashes lemon juice

For very smooth guacamole, put the avocado into a blender and blend on high speed for about 8 seconds. Or run the avocado through a sieve. Add the chopped tomato, chile pepper, green chiles, mayonnaise to taste, salt to taste, and the lemon juice. Serve with tortilla chips.

Note: Leave the avocado seed in the mixture until ready to serve to help prevent discoloration.

Makes 1 to 2 cups.

Jack Elam, actor
Submitted by daughter Jenny Elam

Montana-to-Alabama Grilled Hot Wings

My used-to-be-secret, soon-to-be-famous recipe.

1 fresh pack chicken wings (usually 20 to 30 wings)
Meat tenderizer
Apple cider vinegar
Lemon juice
Honey
Barbecue sauce (I like Kraft original)
Melted shortening
Frank's Hot Sauce (this is key)

Wash the wings thoroughly under running water. Clip off the tips and reserve for making chicken broth. Put the wings in a large casserole dish or dishes, and sprinkle with the tenderizer. Mix enough cider vinegar and lemon juice together in about equal proportions to pour over and coat the wings. Cover and let stand in the fridge for 1 to 2 hours. Mix a small amount of honey into your barbecue sauce. You will probably use 8 to 12 ounces of sauce, depending on the amount of wings and how saucy you like the chicken.

You may use a gas grill or charcoal grill. If you use coals, you may have to add coals at the appropriate time to extend your cooking time to approximately 1 hour. For this reason, I generally prefer a gas grill in this instance. Place the wings bone side down on a hot grill on high for about 5 minutes, being careful not to let them flame up. (Keep a spray bottle of water on hand). Turn them to skin side down for 3 to 4 minutes while still on high heat. Now turn your grill to low (or raise the rack on a charcoal grill or close damper, and turn the wings back to the bone side down and baste with a small amount of melted shortening. (You may substitute vegetable oil, but it will give different results.) I also like to mist the wings with a bit of the water before closing the lid each time. Continue to turn the wings often, about every 5 to 8 minutes, favoring the longer times when they are bone side down, and basting lightly with the shortening. Continue for an additional 30 to 45 minutes on this lower temperature, depending on the temperature and your preference. When you know it is your last round of turns, brush the wings with the sauce onto the bone side, and put them bone side down. Now brush the skin side generously with the sauce, and cook for the remaining minutes. Open the grill, and splash with Frank's Hot Sauce. Present on a large platter in a circular pattern with the wings overlapping.

The only grandson of Patsy Montana, Michael Montana, a musician in his own right, continues to promote his grandmother's music and perform with the guitar she left to him.

Note: You may complement with fresh raw veggies, such as bell pepper, carrot, celery, or green onion, with ranch dressing.
Makes 4 servings, 4 or 5 wings per serving.

Michael Montana, singer

In the early 1800s, there were sixty to seventy-five million buffalo on the Great Plains. From 1871 to 1883, the herds of approximately forty million buffalo were cut down to about one hundred buffalo.

Wild, Wild West Lemon Chicken Wings

6 pounds fresh chicken wings
  Juice of 6 lemons
2 sticks butter
1 tablespoon salt
1 tablespoon pepper
1 tablespoon sugar
2 teaspoons dry mustard
3 ounces Worcestershire sauce
2 tablespoons dried rosemary leaves

Cut the wings into segments at each of the 2 joints. Discard the small bony end, or save for stock. In a saucepan, heat and stir the lemon juice, butter, salt, pepper, sugar, dry mustard, Worcestershire sauce, and rosemary until the butter is melted. Arrange the wing segments on an outdoor grill heated until red hot. Turn the grill to medium, and baste the wings with the lemon-butter mixture. Beware of flare-ups and have a spray bottle of water on hand to put out the flames. Continue to baste often until the wings are slightly blackened, but not dry, about 30 minutes total. Yum! These are great as appetizers, or use chicken breasts with this sauce for a tasty entrée. This recipe has been a family favorite for more than 30 years.

Makes about 20 to 30 servings as an appetizer.

Gail and Red Steagall,
singer and cowboy poet

The Official Cowboy Poet of Texas, Red Steagall is famous for Texas swing dance music and such songs as "Freckles Brown," "Lone Star Beer," and "Bob Wills Music." He has written more than two hundred tunes and recorded more than twenty-five albums. His songs have been heard on movie soundtracks around the world, but he still takes a liking to playing them around a chuck wagon campfire with his best girl, wife Gail.

Lazy Man's Grilled Jalapeños

Fresh jalapeños
Monterey Jack cheese
Cheddar cheese
Bacon strips

Slice the tops off the jalapeños and clean the seeds out (a grapefruit knife works great for this). Rinse the jalapeños and put them in the microwave for about 2 to 3 minutes (just enough to soften them a bit), or blanch them in boiling water for 2 to 3 minutes. Cut the cheeses into strips big enough to fit a strip of each cheese into the jalapeños. Cover each jalapeño with a strip of bacon, and secure it with a toothpick. Place on a grill over medium heat. Cook until done. Enjoy. (And do be sure that you remove the toothpicks before eating.)

Lazy Hills Guest Ranch
Ingram, Texas

Cowboy Hors d'Oeuvres

While we cannot be sure that the cowboys on the trail drives were actually served these "green bullets," we are certain that the Texas cowboys and cowgirls of today enjoy these hot little items.

12 large jalapeños
1 pound Owens pan sausage (regular)

Wash the jalapeños. Slice them in half and remove all seeds. Stuff the jalapeño halves with uncooked sausage. Place in a Dutch oven (or on a flat cookie sheet in a conventional oven), and bake at 350° for 30 minutes. Cool and serve.

Variation: For a spicier version, use Owens picante-seasoned sausage. For a very spicy version, remove only a portion of the jalapeño seeds.
Makes 24 halves.

Barbara and Lonnie Tegeler,
Rocking T Chuck Wagon
Chappell Hill, Texas

Jack Holt, father of actors Tim and Jennifer Holt, made more than 170 films from 1914 to 1951, including a western series for Paramount based on Zane Grey novels. Among his credits are *Across the Wide Missouri, The Strawberry Roan, My Pal Trigger, Trail of Robin Hood,* and *The Thundering Herd.*

Sagebrush Sausage Balls

2   pounds regular Jimmy Dean sausage
2   cups shredded Cheddar cheese
1½ cups dry Bisquick mix
½   tablespoon garlic powder
1   egg

Preheat the oven to 375°. In a large bowl, mix together the sausage, cheese, Bisquick mix, garlic powder, and egg. Form into 2-inch-in-diameter balls. Bake for 20 minutes.
Makes about 16 sausage balls.

Jack Holt, actor
Submitted by grandson Jay Holt
and Sandie Holt

Texas native Don Meredith was dandy as quarterback of the Dallas Cowboys from 1960 to 1968.

Dandy Don's Favorite Stuffed Mushrooms

1   pound Jimmy Dean sausage
⅓   onion, minced
1   garlic clove, minced
      Pinch of ground cinnamon (optional)
2   (8-ounce) packages cream cheese
½   cup minced peeled apple
20   large mushrooms, scrubbed, stems removed, and drained on paper towels

Preheat the oven to 350°. In a large skillet, crumble the sausage, and add the onion, garlic, and cinnamon. Cook until brown, but not crisp. Drain off all the grease carefully. Add the cream cheese to the meat mixture and blend well. Add the apple. Place the mushroom caps in a large ovenproof baking dish, and stuff them with the mixture. Bake for 30 minutes. Serve hot.

Makes approximately 10 servings.

Don Meredith, Dallas Cowboy and actor

Don Meredith played his hand as a cowboy in three TV movies: *Banjo Hackett: Roamin' Free, Kate Bliss and the Ticker Tape Kid,* and *Wyatt Earp: Return to Tombstone.*

The voice rolling behind *Mule Train* and *Rawhide* is full-throated Frankie Laine. He also sang the themes to the films *Blazing Saddles, 3:10 to Yuma, Gunfight at the O.K. Corral, Man Without a Star,* and *Bullwhip.*

Garduna Ma LoVecchio

My mother often made these Sicilian vegetable hors d'oeuvres.

Artichoke stems
Lemons
Eggs, beaten
All-purpose flour
Olive oil

Use small tender artichokes. Cut off the artichoke stems. (Use the artichokes for whatever else you like.) Place the stems between two sheets of waxed paper. Pound them with a mallet until they are flattened and the pithy fibers of the stems are broken down. Rub each stem with a lemon to keep it from turning brown. Dip each pounded artichoke stem into the beaten eggs, and then dredge them in flour. Place each coated stem in a heavy skillet, and fry in hot olive oil until each one is golden brown and crunchy. Place on a platter, and sprinkle with lemon juice. These can be eaten as finger food.

Frankie Laine, singer/songwriter

Sure-Shot
Peanut-Stuffed Celery

1   (3-ounce) package cream cheese
2   teaspoons onion juice
¼   teaspoon curry powder
1½ tablespoons heavy cream
9   ribs celery, cut into 4-inch lengths
⅓   cup chopped peanuts

In a mixing bowl, combine the cream cheese, onion juice, curry powder, and cream. Be sure to add enough cream to spread easily when filling celery. Fill the celery lengths with the mixture. Dip the topsides into the chopped peanuts. Arrange on a platter. Cover with aluminum foil and chill. Serve as an accompaniment to cocktails.

Makes about 24 celery sticks.

Audie Murphy, actor

Audie Murphy starred in more than forty films, most of them westerns, such as *Destry, The Unforgiven, Night Passage,* and *No Name on the Bullet.* The most decorated hero of World War II portrayed himself in *To Hell and Back* and was a Civil War soldier in *The Red Badge of Courage.*

This behind-the-scenes photo on the set of *Ride a Crooked Trail* (1958) shows Audie Murphy with his sons James "Skipper" (left) and Terry.

BEVERAGES AND APPETIZERS

Mom's Pickle Recipe

This is a recipe that my mom and dad used to make tons of pickles throughout my life.

- 7 cups sliced cucumbers
- 1 cup diced onion
- 1 cup chopped bell peppers
- 2 tablespoons sea salt
- 1 cup cider vinegar
- 2 cups sugar
- 2 teaspoons celery seed
- 2 or 3 cloves garlic per jar

In a large bowl, combine the cucumbers, onion, bell peppers, and sea salt. In a separate bowl, mix well the vinegar, sugar, and celery seed. Place the vegetables and 2 or 3 cloves of garlic per jar in sterilized canning jars. Cover with the liquid. These are best if you wait a week to eat. They must be kept in a refrigerator and will keep for up to a year.

Makes about 6 pints.

Shelly Burmeister-Mowery, cowgirl and broadcaster

Shelly Burmeister-Mowery is one of the top equine broadcasters. A former world champion barrel racer, she is an inductee of the National Cowgirl Hall of Fame. Still competing in national cutting horse shows, she and her family own and operate a quarter horse breeding and training facility in Weatherford, Texas.

NATIONAL COWGIRL
MUSEUM AND HALL OF FAME

The women of the West are honored at the National Cowgirl Museum and Hall of Fame in Fort Worth, Texas.

Guests are greeted by an enormous bronze statue, Mehl Lawson's *High Desert Princess*. Four original films introduce visitors to the legacy of female ranchers, farmers, and performers.

Costumes worn by Dale Evans share exhibit space with trophies won by the likes of Vera McGinnis, perhaps the greatest female rodeo champion of all time.

The Hall of Fame includes more than 170 inductees, including Molly Goodnight, the rancher's wife who oversaw efforts to save the Texas buffalo from extinction.

Perhaps the most popular feature of the Cowgirl Museum is a life-size replica of a bucking bronco; patrons can ride the mount (it's tame enough that little kids and senior citizens can participate), while museum staffers videotape the performance, ultimately combining the video with rodeo footage so that it appears patrons are actually participating in a rodeo (these minimovies, ten seconds in length, can be downloaded from the Hall of Fame's Internet site later). The bronco is really more of a life-size rocking horse.

The National Cowgirl Museum and Hall of Fame is located at 1720 Gendy Street in Fort Worth, Texas. For more information, go to *www.cowgirl.net*.

Riding Shotgun

Gloria's Bean Salad

Batch sizes:

Small	Medium	Large	
1	2	3	(16-ounce) cans wax beans (yellow), drained
1	2	3	(16-ounce) cans green beans, drained
1	2	3	(16-ounce) cans red kidney beans, drained and rinsed
1	2	3	(16-ounce cans garbanzo beans, drained
½	1	1½	cups chopped celery
¼	½	¾	cup chopped onion
½	1	1½	cups white vinegar*
½	1	1½	cups sugar
½	1	1½	cups salad oil

Place the beans (after draining), celery, onion, vinegar, sugar, and oil into a big salad bowl, and stir to distribute the ingredients evenly. Refrigerate overnight.

Makes 6, 12, or 18 servings.

*Use distilled white vinegar, not a wine vinegar. Diluted vinegars weaken the sweet and sour flavor and give the salad the "blahs."

Gloria Winters Vernon, actress

Gloria Winters starred as Penny, the niece of cowboy Sky King, who, from his Flying Crown Ranch, used his twin-engined Cessna *(The Songbird)* to bring law and order to a region of 1950s Arizona.

Olympic gold-medal-winning sprinter Dean Smith is a Texas cattle rancher who spent his career in Hollywood as a stuntman in TV and movie westerns. An amateur rodeo enthusiast, Smith worked in the films *The Alamo, Big Jake, Rio Lobo, McLintock!, How the West Was Won, The Stalking Moon,* and *Jeremiah Johnson.* He also doubled Roy Rogers in *Mackintosh and T.J.* and in Roy's two appearances on *The Fall Guy.*

Bar Double Diamond Spinach Salad

Dressing:
- ½   cup sugar
- ½   cup vinegar
- 2   tablespoons oil
- 1   tablespoon chopped green onion
- 1   tablespoon chopped parsley
- 1   tablespoon chives
- 1   teaspoon Worcestershire sauce
- 1   teaspoon prepared mustard
-     Cracked black pepper
- 1   ice cube

Salad:
- 1   pound fresh spinach
- 6   slices bacon, cooked and crumbled
- 2   hard-cooked eggs, chopped

For the dressing, mix the sugar, vinegar, oil, green onion, parsley, chives, Worcestershire sauce, mustard, black pepper, and ice in a plastic container. Shake well and chill. (We like to make this dressing the night before we serve it in order for it to be good and chilled.) Pour the dressing over the spinach, bacon, and eggs. Season to taste with pepper, if desired. Toss well and serve. The dressing keeps well for several days if kept in the refrigerator. This salad goes well with beef.

Makes 6 servings.

Dean, Debby, and Finis Smith,
Bar Double Diamond Ranch
Breckenridge, Texas

William Boyd made nearly 140 films, more than 65 of them as Hopalong Cassidy, the cowboy hero who dressed in black and rode a white horse named Topper. In 1949, he took his silver screen persona to television and became a hit to another generation of buckaroos. His wife, Grace Bradley Boyd, was a film star in her own right, making about 35 feature films.

Bar 20 Ranch Spinach Salad with Sweet Parsley Dressing

1   (10-ounce) package fresh baby spinach
8   bacon slices, cooked and crumbled
½   cup shredded Jarlsberg cheese
½   cup toasted chopped walnuts
    Broccoli florets (optional)
    Dried cranberries (optional)
    Sweet Parsley Dressing (recipe follows)

Place the spinach, bacon, cheese, and walnuts (broccoli and cranberries, if using) in a large bowl and toss. Drizzle with Sweet Parsley Dressing, tossing gently to coat.
    Makes 6 servings.

Sweet Parsley Dressing:
½   cup sugar
½   cup white vinegar*
2   tablespoons vegetable oil
1   green onion, thinly sliced
1   tablespoon chopped fresh parsley
1   teaspoon Worcestershire sauce
1   teaspoon prepared mustard
¼   teaspoon freshly ground pepper

Whisk together the sugar, vinegar, oil, onion, parsley, Worcestershire sauce, mustard, and pepper, and then chill the mixture for about 20 minutes.
    Makes about 1 cup.

*I use ¼ cup white vinegar and ¼ cup orange Moncuit champagne vinegar.

Hopalong Cassidy, actor
Submitted by Grace Bradley Boyd, "Mrs. Hopalong Cassidy"

HOPALONG CASSIDY
COWBOY MUSEUM

The Prairie Rose Chuck Wagon Supper is located fifteen miles northeast of Wichita, Kansas, and boasts wagon rides and an RV park in addition to an old-fashioned chuck wagon supper and cowboy-themed entertainment.

Incorporated into the Prairie Rose attractions is the Hopalong Cassidy Cowboy Museum, the official "home" of the famous movie cowboy created by Clarence E. Mulford and portrayed by actor William Boyd in scores of films between 1935 and 1948 (and still later on TV).

Hoppy's popularity inspired a plethora of merchandising items unequalled by any western character before or since, and the museum includes vintage clothing, toys, and even furniture among the memorabilia contained in ten thousand square feet of display space.

An entire wall is devoted to original one-sheets advertising Hoppy's cinematic adventures. Other displays honor the actual cowboys who rode the Chisholm Trail and such silver screen stars as Roy Rogers, Dale Evans, and Gene Autry, as well as singer and songwriter Johnny Western.

Adjacent to the museum is the Hopalong Cassidy Bar 20 Movie Theater, a two-hundred-seat auditorium where fans of all ages can enjoy Hoppy's movie and TV adventures on the big screen. The attraction is located on SW Parallel Road in Benton, Kansas. For more information, visit *www.prairierosechuckwagon.com/default.htm*.

"HOPPING" FOR MORE?

Hopalong Cassidy fans also can enjoy the annual Hoppyfest, a celebration held the first weekend in May in Cambridge, Ohio, the boyhood home of William Boyd, where the Hometown Museum for Hopalong Cassidy is located at 127 South 10th Street. The museum contains Hoppy fan Laura Bates's collection of the majority of the twenty-four hundred items endorsed by William Boyd over the years.

Big Sky Blue Cheese Salad Dressing

2　(8-ounce) packages cream cheese, softened
1　cup mayonnaise
4　(4-ounce) blocks blue cheese, crumbled
1　or 2 cups half-and-half (depending on desired thickness)
1　teaspoon garlic pepper

In a bowl, mix the cream cheese and mayonnaise until well blended. Add 2 blocks of blue cheese and blend. Add the half-and half, mixing slowly, until the mixture reaches your preferred thickness. Add the remaining 2 blocks blue cheese and the garlic pepper. Mix slowly with a spoon so that you will have chunks of blue cheese. You can keep it refrigerated for up to two weeks.

Makes about 1½ quarts.

Laughing Water Ranch
Fortine, Montana

Southwestern Potato Salad

8　potatoes, cooked and cubed
1　garlic clove, minced, or ⅛ teaspoon garlic powder
3　green onions, diced
½　cup diced green chiles
¼　cup chopped fresh cilantro
1　medium tomato, diced
1½　cups mayonnaise
1　tablespoon Dijon mustard
2　tablespoons lime juice
¼　teaspoon cayenne
　　Salt and pepper

Mix the potatoes, garlic, onions, chiles, cilantro, tomato, mayonnaise, mustard, lime juice, cayenne to taste, and salt and pepper. Chill until served.

Makes 12 servings.

Grapevine Canyon Ranch
Pearce, Arizona

Best Green Salad
for Any Meal

This salad dressing has been the Shoulders family's favorite over any type of green salad.

3   cloves fresh garlic, minced or crushed
     Your choice of greens and vegetables for
     salad
     Salt and pepper

Dressing:
     Olive oil
     Balsamic, red, or cider vinegar

Rub the salad bowl thoroughly with the fresh garlic cloves, leaving some of the small particles of garlic in the bowl. Add the greens and vegetables. Add salt and pepper to taste. To make the dressing, mix 3 parts olive oil to 1 part balsamic, red, or cider vinegar in a jar, and shake well. Add the dressing to the salad. Mix well, scraping the garlic particles from the sides of the bowl into the salad.

Jim Shoulders, rodeo cowboy

Jim Shoulders displays buckles, belts, and saddles won in 1959 when he ruled as world's champion all-around cowboy and world's champion bull rider. The rodeo legend won seven world bull riding championships and four world bareback riding championships. He was five times the all-around champion in a career that spanned twenty-five years.

Baxter Black is known across the U.S.A. as a cowboy poet, humorist, and writer. Formerly a veterinarian, he was a rodeo bull rider in high school and college and today entertains regularly on National Public Radio's *Morning Edition.*

COWBOY VEGETARIAN COOKBOOK

Baxter Black

It should come as no surprise that I can't cook. Furthermore, I'm not a very discriminating diner. Matter of fact, the fajitas in this piece actually sound good.

When beef gets short a lot of cowboys are forced to do without. The cook must come up with meatless meals. The following recipes are from the *Cowboy Vegetarian Cookbook.*

Tennis Shoe Tongue
Select an old one. The price is better, and it may have picked up some natural flavor depending on where it has been worn. Boiling is suggested, but it may also be fried to a crisp and served on a bed of marinated sweatshirt. Garnish with pickled shoestring.

Seed Corn Cap Pizza
Carefully clean with a fish-scaling knife. Remove all metal buttons, rivets, and any plastic tabs. Flatten the cap by soaking in linseed oil, then placing it underneath a doormat that gets heavy use. Once pliable, cover it with lots of cheese and ketchup. Dry kibbles or dust motes may be sprinkled as a topping for variety.

Fan Belt Fajitas
The most succulent fan belts can be found on old farm equipment moldering in your boneyard. It should be sliced into bite-sized chunks. Tenderize before cooking by soaking in fingernail polish remover. Fry in lard along with half a hatful of three-quarter-inch, black plastic hose and shredded playing cards. Serve with beer and jalapeños. It tastes a lot like abalone.

Rawhide Stew
Ever wondered what to do with those old reins, quirts, or saddle tree bark? This recipe has been tried and tested from ancient Mongolians right up through Donner Pass. Place the strips of rawhide in a pot, and boil for as many weeks as the firewood holds out. What you add to the stew depends on what's available—i.e., pine cones, hoof trimmings, iron pyrite, or old hat brims. It's filling, but don't expect much more.

Roasted Kak
Ever eat a saddle? Some parts are edible. Dig a hole big enough to bury a small mule. Burn elm, cottonwood, and old tires to get a bed of coals. Wrap the saddle in a plastic tarp (blue), place it on the coals, and cover with dirt. Cook for hours on end. Dig up and serve with baked faucet washers. Feeds up to two truckloads of hungry cowboys.

That should give you an idea of what you can do when you run out of beef at the ranch. There are many other cowboy vegetarian recipes, like Latigo Jerky, Gunstock Pate, and Smokin' Joe's Copenhagen Torte, but this should get you started.

Female's Favorite Fruit Salad

So named because all the women in the Calhoun clan—as well as family friends—clamor for Smoke's famous fruit salad. We usually serve it with Sweet Sue's Blackened Chicken (see recipe on page 78).

2   medium Haas avocados
2   or 3 bananas
1   cup grapes
1   cup papaya and/or mango
1   cup canned mandarin oranges

Dressing:
½   cup mayonnaise
¼   cup juice from mandarin oranges, or other sweet fruit juice
½   cup grated Parmesan cheese
2   tablespoons The Texan's Garlic Oil Marinade (see recipe on page 177)
1   tablespoon white vinegar
2   teaspoons Smoke's Secret Spice Rub (see recipe on page 177)
    Sugar

Cut the avocados, bananas, grapes, papaya, and oranges into chunks, and place in a large bowl. To make the dressing, in a separate bowl, combine the mayonnaise, fruit juice, Parmesan cheese, The Texan's Garlic Oil Marinade, vinegar, and Smoke's Secret Spice Rub. Add sugar to taste. Fold the dressing into the fruit. Serve chilled.

   Makes 6 to 8 servings.

   Rory Calhoun, actor

Rory Calhoun starred on TV's *The Texan* as Bill Longley, an honest cowboy with a fast gun who helped his friends in need while traveling the Lone Star State. Calhoun made plenty of western films too, such as *Powder River, Domino Kid, Black Spurs,* and *Pure Country.*

Dale Evans was "Queen of the West." The sweetheart and wife of Roy Rogers, she made twenty-nine western films in the 1940s before riding side by side with her husband in *The Roy Rogers Show* on television during the 1950s. She wrote the show's theme song, "Happy Trails."

G-G's Salad

This is one of the best dishes that my grand-mother, Dale Evans, ever made. She originally got the recipe from a family friend and adopted it as her own. This is what her grand-children and the "greats" always wanted her to make for family meals. ("G-G" stands for great-grandmother.)

For every 4 people:
- 1   clove garlic
- 1   rounded teaspoon salt
- ½   teaspoon granulated sugar
- 1   lemon, cut in half
  Leaf oregano to cover lemon juice (see below)
- 1   medium head romaine lettuce
- 1   small bunch green onions, chopped
  Extra virgin cold pressed olive oil

Squeeze the garlic with a garlic press into the bottom of a wooden bowl, and cover it with the salt and sugar. Squeeze the juice from the lemon into the bowl. Cover with the oregano. Let stand for 30 minutes to 1 hour. Tear up (do not cut) the lettuce into bite-size pieces, and drop them on top of the ingredients in the bowl. Sprinkle the green onions over the lettuce. Drizzle the olive oil over the lettuce, starting in the center of the bowl and working outward in circles. Toss the ingredients from the bottom up. Serve with your favorite garlic bread.

Dale Evans, singer and actress
Submitted by grandson Dan Swift

In 1960, Clint Walker (left) starred in the title role of *Yellowstone Kelly*. Supporting him were John Russell (center) of *Lawman* fame and Edd Byrnes, famous as Kookie of *77 Sunset Strip*.

Cheyenne's Favorite Summer Dish

In the summer we enjoy having our whole meal in one dish for easy cleanup. This dinner combines salad, meat, beans, and rice all in one. We have our beans ready in the freezer in small containers that will be adequate for one meal. Brown rice is usually a staple, and we also have that already cooked and in the refrigerator. The salsa also may be made ahead of time and does keep for several days in the refrigerator. We serve this meal in pasta bowls.

 1 cup cooked brown rice
   Black Beans (recipe follows)
 4 or 5 large romaine lettuce leaves broken into bite-size pieces
   Handful of cilantro with stems cut out
   Handful of jicama, sliced in small strips, for each salad
   A few thin sweet onion slices (use the rings); we prefer the red onions
   Cucumber, or any other salad veggies that you like
 1 avocado, sliced in long pieces
 2 large free-range chicken breasts cooked on a grill and broken into bite-size pieces (you may use your favorite marinade)
   Salad dressing of your choice
   Apple cider vinegar (optional, if you want more of a tang)
   Salsa (recipe follows)
   Sour cream (optional)

Place the brown rice in the bottom of the bowls, and then cover the rice with the cooked Black Beans. Add the lettuce, cilantro, jicama, onion slices, cucumber, and avocado. Then add the chicken and the salad dressing. We always add a couple of tablespoons of apple cider vinegar. Finally, add a generous amount of Salsa on the top. Top with sour cream if desired.

Makes 2 servings.

Black Beans:
 2 pounds black turtle beans
 1 large onion, chopped
 2 to 4 ribs celery (use tops, too) chopped
 ⅓ cup chopped fennel root (optional)
 1 to 2 tablespoons cayenne
 2 tablespoons sea salt
 4 or 5 tablespoons Worcestershire sauce
 2 to 3 ounces tamari sauce or Bragg Liquid Amino
 1 ounce apple cider vinegar
 ⅓ bunch cilantro (remove stems)

Wash and clean the beans in a colander, and rinse them thoroughly. Cover the beans in water, and soak them 6 to 8 hours. Rinse again, and place the beans in a pot, cover with water, put on the stove, and bring to a boil. Simmer for a few minutes, pour off the water, rinse again, and start to cook. When the beans begin to boil again, add the onion, celery, fennel root (if using), cayenne, sea salt, Worcestershire sauce, tamari, and vinegar. Cook approximately 1 hour and 30 minutes or until the beans are tender. Add the cilantro after the beans are done cooking, and simmer another 10 minutes.

Salsa:

Make salsa only when tomatoes are in season. No hothouse tomatoes or tomatoes that have been shipped from other regions. If the tomatoes aren't good and sweet, the salsa won't be good. We use only organic Heirloom and sweet organic cherry tomatoes.

3	or 4 large tomatoes, chopped in small chunks
	Small batch of cherry tomatoes, cut in half
2	or 3 cloves garlic, finely chopped
1	large onion (we prefer a red one)
1	large handful cilantro with stems removed and slightly chopped
	Juice of ½ lime
2	tablespoons sea salt
1	to 2 tablespoons cayenne
1	to 2 fresh jalapeño peppers, with seeds removed and finely chopped
2	fresh serrano peppers with seeds removed and finely chopped

In a bowl, combine the tomatoes, garlic, onion, cilantro, lime juice, sea salt, cayenne, and peppers, and mix well.

Susan and Clint Walker, actor

Gentle giant Clint Walker won the hearts of western fans as Cheyenne Bodie in the TV series *Cheyenne* from 1955 to 1963. He also starred in the films *Fort Dobbs, Gold of the Seven Saints, The Great Bank Robbery, Baker's Hawk,* and *The White Buffalo.*

The most famous brand of coffee in the Old West was Arbuckle's. It was made by Arbuckle Brothers in Pittsburgh and had a flying angel as its trademark. The favored beverage of cowboys was boiling hot, black coffee.

Country music outlaw Waylon Jennings sang "Mamas Don't Let Your Babies Grow Up to Be Cowboys," but that's just what he did. He appeared in the 1986 TV movie *Stagecoach* and was a gambler in the 1994 feature film *Maverick*. He also sang on the soundtracks to *Ned Kelly* and *Mackintosh and T.J.*

Cowboy and the Lady's Grilled Salmon Salad

You'll always want way more.
*   This recipe is from the up-and-coming* Cooking Waylon's Way *by Jessi Colter Jennings and Maureen Rafferty.*

2   larges bunches romaine lettuce
1   red bell pepper
1   English cucumber
5   green onions
1   large red onion, sliced and separated
2   tomatoes, chopped
4   (8-ounce) salmon fillets
    Juice of 1 lemon
    Juice of 1 lime
2   teaspoons olive oil
    Paul Prudhomme's Seafood Magic
1   cup honey-mustard dressing
    Fresh black pepper pods

Chop the lettuce, pepper, cucumber, and green onions. Toss the vegetables in a bowl, and place the red onion and tomatoes on top. Wash the salmon fillets, and pat them dry with a paper towel. Squeeze the juices of the lemon and lime on the salmon fillets. Lightly brush each fillet with the oil, and then coat each side with the Seafood Magic. Grill the salmon for 5 minutes per side or until the salmon flakes easily. Cut the fillets into bite-size chunks. Place the salad greens on four large dinner plates. Place the grilled salmon chunks on top of the salad. Drizzle the honey-mustard dressing over the top of the salad and salmon. Grind fresh black pepper over the salad.

   Makes 4 servings.

Jessi Colter and Waylon Jennings,
outlaws and singers

Good Old Days Grilled Shrimp and Scallop Caesar Salad

Caesar Dressing:
- 1 cup mayonnaise (may use reduced-fat mayonnaise)
- ¼ cup freshly grated Parmesan cheese
- 1½ tablespoons freshly squeezed lemon juice
- 1½ teaspoons Worcestershire sauce
- 2 teaspoons freshly minced garlic
- 2 finely chopped anchovy fillets
  Freshly ground black pepper
  Water to thin dressing

Marinade:
- 1 cup olive oil
- ½ cup freshly squeezed lemon juice
- 3 tablespoons freshly minced garlic
  Salt and freshly ground pepper

Salad:
- 1 pound large shrimp, peeled and deveined
- 1 pound sea scallops
- 6 cups (organic) mixed greens, washed and chilled in the refrigerator
  Thinly sliced red onions
- 1 whole avocado, diced
- 1½ cups croutons
- ½ cup freshly grated Parmesan cheese
  Freshly ground pepper

If using bamboo skewers, soak them for 1 hour in water (or use stainless steel skewers). For the salad dressing, combine the mayonnaise, Parmesan cheese, lemon juice, Worcestershire, garlic, anchovy fillets, and pepper to taste in a bowl. Whisk until thoroughly blended. Add (and whisk) the water a little at a time until you achieve your preferred consistency. Refrigerate until chilled.

For the marinade, combine in a bowl the oil, lemon juice, garlic, and salt and pepper to taste. Whisk until well blended. Gently mix the shrimp and scallops into the marinade and refrigerate for 30 minutes.

For the salad, preheat the grill to medium-high. Thread the shrimp and scallops onto separate skewers. Cover the grill and cook approximately 3 minutes per side. Do not overcook. The shrimp should turn pink, and the scallops will be opaque throughout. Put the chilled salad greens in a bowl. Add red onions to taste and the avocado. Toss while adding the salad dressing a little at a time until the greens are coated. Gently remove the shrimp and scallops from the skewers, and place them on top of the salad. Add the croutons and Parmesan cheese and sprinkle ground pepper to taste. This is a meal in itself. Enjoy!

Makes 4 servings.

Clint Black, singer/songwriter

Born in a town named Long Branch in New Jersey, country singer/songwriter Clint Black grew up in Texas, where he idolized his cowboy hero, Roy Rogers. In 1991 he and Rogers recorded the duet "Hold On, Partner." Black composed and sang the theme song for the 1992 TV series *Harts of the West* and played a gambler in the 1994 film *Maverick*. He also played a rodeo star opposite his wife, Lisa Hartman Black, in the 1998 TV movie *Still Holding On: The Legend of Cadillac Jack*. Here Black and Rogers (left) share the stage.

Cowboy Crab Salad

3 ounces (½ can) crabmeat (or fresh if you prefer)
4 green onions, chopped
2 cloves garlic, squeezed
1 rib celery, chopped
1 full tablespoon Vegenaise or other soy mayonnaise
½ cup shredded goat cheese
   Some chopped cilantro
   Creole seasoning

Throw it all together in a bowl and mix it up.

Note: For a very tasty snack, put a long narrow band of crab salad in a flour tortilla, fold it up, and fry it in about ¼ inch of olive oil, turning the tortilla until golden brown. You can dip it in sour cream. Yummm! Enjoy.

Makes 2 to 4 servings.

Peter Brown, actor

Peter Brown appeared in many western TV series before starring as Deputy Johnny McKay to John Russell's Sheriff Troop in *The Lawman*. He returned to TV as Texas Ranger Chad Cooper in the series *Laredo*.

ANDY DEVINE ROOM
(IN THE MOHAVE MUSEUM OF HISTORY AND ARTS)

Kingman, Arizona, was hometown to raspy-voiced actor Andy Devine, who starred in many western films and played sidekick Jingles P. Jones to Guy Madison's Wild Bill Hickok on the 1950s TV series.

An Arizona native, Devine grew up in Kingman, where his family operated the Beale Hotel. Devine's connection to his boyhood home is still there as the city holds Andy Devine Days every October 5. Plus the main street, part of historic Route 66, was named Andy Devine Avenue after him, and recently has been renamed Route 66/Andy Devine Avenue.

The Mohave Museum of History and Arts, which concentrates on honoring Mohave County and its pioneers, pays tribute to the late actor with its Andy Devine Room. The room features memorabilia from Devine's twenty years under contract to Universal Studio as well as his TV days as Jingles. There are photos, movie posters, newspaper clippings, and mementos from *The Adventures of Wild Bill Hickok* series, as well as his jacket, hat, and boots.

There is a model of his dressing room with his actual makeup kit and a gorgeous Bohlin saddle that was made for Devine to ride during the Rose Bowl Parade.

Several blocks from the museum is the Dambar & Steakhouse, which boasts its own Andy Devine Room, filled with posters and lobby cards from the actor's career.

The Mohave Museum of History and Arts and its Andy Devine Room are located at 400 West Beale Street. For more information, go to *www.mohavemuseum.org*.

Where would Wild Bill have been without his Jingles? Jingles was the beloved Andy Devine who rode as Guy Madison's saddle pal on *The Adventures of Wild Bill Hickok* from 1951 to 1958. Devine, the man with the unmistakable voice, was Roy Rogers's sidekick for a time as Cookie Bullfincher and made more than 150 films, including *Stagecoach*, *The Man Who Shot Liberty Valance*, *Two Rode Together*, and TV's *The Over-the-Hill Gang*.

Andy's Game SideDish Devine

1   (16-ounce) can sliced pears
1   (16-ounce) can apricot halves
1   (16-ounce) can purple plums
1   (16-ounce) can black cherries
1   (16-ounce) can peach halves
2   tablespoons softened butter
2   tablespoons packed brown sugar
2   teaspoons cornstarch
1   teaspoon curry powder
½   teaspoon grated lemon peel

Drain the pears, apricots, plums, cherries, and peaches, and mix them together in a 1½-quart casserole. Mix lightly. Blend together the butter, brown sugar, cornstarch, curry, and lemon peel. Sprinkle this mixture over the fruit, cover, and refrigerate 6 to 8 hours or overnight to draw out all of the juices. When ready to use, preheat the oven to 325°. Bake uncovered for 1 hour, basting several times. Serve hot.

Note: You may also use prunes, bananas, papaya, or other fruits. This dish is wonderful with game (deer, goose, pheasant, quail, partridge, or dove), ham, turkey, chicken, or leg of lamb. The recipe may be doubled or tripled with no problem.

Makes 6 servings.

Andy Devine, actor
Submitted by son Timothy "Tad" Devine

A real rootin', tootin' cowboy, Slim Pickens was a teenage rodeo cowboy who became a pro rodeo clown before turning into one of the greatest character actors of all time. A sidekick to Rex Allen in the early 1950s, Pickens made dozens of western films, including such classics as *Rocky Mountain, Will Penny, The Cowboys, Pat Garrett and Billy the Kid,* and *Blazing Saddles.* He's holding the reins here in the 1968 film *Stagecoach.*

Slim's Cowboy Beans

My dad loved these beans. This recipe is sort of by taste—with a pinch of this and a pinch of that—but it's hard to mess up and the beans are great.

1   to 1½ pounds small red beans
1   hambone
1   or 2 pinches of celery seed
    Red chile pepper
1   onion, chopped
    Cloves from cooked ham
    Garlic
    Salt and pepper

Pick over the beans, and rinse them well. Put them in a pot. Cover with water. Bring to a boil, and then reduce the heat. Add the hambone, celery seed, chile pepper, onion, cloves, garlic to taste, and salt and pepper to taste. Cover the pot. Cook all day, adding water as necessary. Stir occasionally.

Makes 4 to 6 servings.

Slim Pickens, actor
Submitted by daughter
Daryle Ann Lindley Giardino

SALADS, VEGETABLES, AND SIDE DISHES

Super Looper's Larrapin' Cowboy Beans

1   pound ground beef
1   large onion, chopped
1   large green bell pepper, chopped
1   cup barbecue sauce
1   cup ketchup
1   cup yellow mustard
1   (16-ounce) can pork and beans
1   (16-ounce) can ranch-style beans

In a large skillet or saucepan, brown the ground beef and drain. Add the onions and bell peppers, and brown slightly. Add the barbecue sauce, ketchup, mustard, pork and beans, and ranch-style beans. Simmer for 20 minutes, stirring frequently. Serve with Crunchy Cowboy Biscuits (see recipe on page 181).
    Makes 10 to 12 servings.

Roy Cooper, rodeo cowboy

"You know, some men got the craving for gold and silver. Others need lots of land with herds of cattle. And there's those that got the weakness for whiskey and for women. When you boil it all down, what does a man really need? Just a smoke and a cup of coffee."

—Sterling Hayden in *Johnny Guitar* (1954)

Nicknamed "Super Looper," Roy Cooper holds eight world titles and is considered one of the greatest tie-down ropers in the history of American rodeo. The "World's Ropingest Cowboy" notched two million bucks in career earnings in 2000. He wrote *the* book on roping: *Calf Roping: The World Champion's Guide for Winning Runs.*

World Champion Beans

1   pound bacon, diced
3   large white onions
1   green bell pepper
1   red bell pepper
1   sweet orange or yellow pepper
1   (16-ounce) can navy beans, drained
1   (16-ounce) can butter beans, drained
1   (16-ounce) can pork and beans with sauce, drained
2   (16-ounce) cans Boston-style baked beans with sauce
1   (9-ounce) package frozen lima beans
1   cup packed dark brown sugar
1   cup barbecue sauce
2   tablespoons Worcestershire sauce (or more)
8   ounces dark molasses
    Your favorite red wine

In a large skillet, brown the bacon, and drain on paper towels. Peel and dice the onions, and cook in the reserved bacon grease until they turn golden. Drain the onions, reserving the grease. Cut the peppers, and remove the veins and seeds. Dice the peppers, and then sauté them in the bacon grease. Drain the peppers. In a large Dutch oven, combine the beans, bacon, onions, peppers, brown sugar, barbecue sauce, Worcestershire sauce to taste, molasses, and red wine to taste. Cook at medium-high heat, watching closely until the mixture starts to boil, and then turn the heat down to simmer for at least 4 hours. This dish just gets better the longer it cooks. If it's too soupy, turn the heat up and let some of the liquid bubble away until the broth thickens. The broth is good on biscuits.

Makes about 16 servings.

Don Collier, actor

Don Collier (left) was Deputy Marshal Will Foreman to Barton MacLane's Marshal Frank Caine in the TV series *The Outlaws*. He played Sam Butler on *The High Chaparral*. Collier worked in many John Wayne flicks and was in such TV productions as *The Sacketts, How the West Was Won,* and *The Young Riders.* He is a frequent guest on the Tucson radio show *Out West.*

Gail Davis starred as TV's sharpshooting Annie Oakley in the 1950s and was a guest on the series *The Lone Ranger, The Cisco Kid,* and *The Gene Autry Show.*

Annie Oakley's Baked Beans

½ pound bacon, diced
1 to 2 bell peppers, diced
½ onion, diced
2 (16-ounce) cans B&M baked beans
1 (16-ounce) can drained kidney beans
½ bottle maple syrup

Brown the bacon in a skillet. Add the bell peppers and onion. Sauté. Transfer to a hanging pot over an open fire or to a slow cooker. Add the beans and maple syrup, and cook slowly.

Makes 8 servings.

Gail Davis, actress

Baked Beans Breckenridge

1 (16-ounce) can kidney beans
1 (16-ounce) can pork and beans
1 (16-ounce) can green lima beans
½ cup packed brown sugar
1 teaspoon dry mustard
1½ tablespoons Worcestershire sauce
6 strips bacon, diced
¾ cup chopped onion
¾ cup chopped bell pepper
2½ cups grated Cheddar cheese

Preheat the oven to 325°. Combine the beans, brown sugar, dry mustard, Worcestershire sauce, bacon, onion, and bell pepper in a baking dish, and bake for 3½ hours. For the last 5 minutes of baking, cover with the cheese.
    Makes 10 servings.

Dean, Debby, and Finis Smith,
Bar Double Diamond Ranch
Breckenridge, Texas

Lazy Hills Bean Medley

1 pound chopped bacon
1 onion, chopped
1 (12-ounce) bottle chili sauce
⅓ cup sugar
1 (16-ounce) can French-style green beans, drained
1 (16-ounce) can pork and beans
1 (15-ounce) can Boston-style baked beans
1 (16-ounce) can kidney beans
1 (16-ounce) can pinto beans

In a large pot, brown the bacon, and leave a little of the drippings in the pot along with the browned bacon. Add the onion, chili sauce, sugar, and beans, and cover and simmer 3 hours, or put the mixture in an ovenproof casserole dish and cook in the oven at 325° for 3 to 4 hours. These are very good and different.
    Makes 15 to 20 servings.

Lazy Hills Guest Ranch
Ingram, Texas

Walter Brennan won three Oscars during his lengthy career and earned his spurs in such films as *The Westerner, Red River, Rio Bravo, My Darling Clementine,* and *Three Godfathers.* He also starred in the TV series *The Guns of Will Sonnett.*

East-Meets-West Boston Baked Beans

This is a favorite recipe, not only of Walter Brennan's, but of the whole family.

4 cups navy beans
8 ounces salt pork or bacon pieces
2 teaspoons salt (or more)
2 tablespoons molasses
3 level teaspoons dry mustard
½ teaspoon dry ginger
½ teaspoon pepper
⅓ to ½ cup ketchup (optional)
   Water

In a large pot, boil the beans in enough water to keep them covered until the skins crack, about 10 minutes. Preheat the oven to 300°. Put half the meat and then half the beans in a 3-quart casserole dish. Repeat with the rest of the meat and beans. In a bowl, mix the salt, molasses, dry mustard, ginger, pepper, and ketchup. Pour the mixture over the beans. Add enough water to barely cover. Do not stir. Bake for about 6 hours. After a couple of hours, stir and check the beans. Add more water, if necessary, but do not make the beans too wet.

Walter Brennan, actor
Submitted by son Andrew Brennan

Whiplash Baked Beans

1   (55-ounce) can B&M Brick Oven beans
1   (31-ounce) can pork and beans
1   (15-ounce) can Dennison limas with ham
     (use liquid)
1   (15¼-ounce) can dark red kidney beans,
     drained
1   (15-ounce) can black-eyed peas, drained
1   piece salt pork, approximately 3 x 4-
     inches, parboiled for 10 minutes, cooled,
     and cut into ½-inch cubes
4   medium onions, quartered
1   cup loosely packed dark brown sugar
2   tablespoons Worcestershire sauce
½   (8-ounce) jar Grey Poupon mustard
6   to 8 shakes Tabasco
½   cup blackstrap molasses

Preheat the oven to 350°. Combine the four cans of beans, the peas, pork, onions, sugar, Worcestershire, mustard, and Tabasco in an ovenproof container of at least 6-quart capacity, and stir to blend. The mixture will be quite runny. Pour the molasses over the top in a spiral pattern. Bake uncovered for 1 hour, and then reduce the heat to 200° to 225°. Continue cooking for about 6 hours until thickened.

Makes about 20 servings.

Peter Graves, actor

Famed for *Mission: Impossible* and hosting A&E's *Biography,* Peter Graves was a cowboy in such films as *The Ballad of Josie, Texas Across the River, Rogue River, Fort Defiance, Wichita,* and *Fort Yuma.* He starred in two TV western series, *Fury* and *Whiplash.* The latter aired in the United States in 1961 but was shot in Australia in 1960. It was about an American, Christopher Cobb, who started a stage line Down Under. Graves is pictured on the set with a local critter.

Grin and Lariat Grilled Vegetables

2   zucchini squash
2   summer squash
1   bunch broccoli
1   red bell pepper
1   yellow bell pepper
1   fresh jalapeño pepper
3   to 4 new or small red potatoes
6   cloves garlic
    Any other fresh vegetables you prefer

Marinade:
8   ounces any Italian dressing (I prefer one containing balsamic vinegar)
1   teaspoon soy sauce
1   teaspoon Worcestershire sauce
    Garlic salt
    Pepper

Rinse and cube the squashes, broccoli, peppers, and potatoes. Leave the garlic cloves whole. In a large bowl, combine the Italian dressing, soy sauce, and Worcestershire sauce to make the marinade. Pour the marinade over the vegetables. Cover and marinate in the refrigerator all day. Before grilling, drain the marinade, and pour the vegetables into a grilling dish. Season with the garlic salt and pepper to taste. Place the grilling dish on a barbecue rack. Grill until the vegetables reach the desired softness, tossing often. This goes great with steak or chicken and French bread.

Makes 6 servings.

Will Rogers, humorist and actor
Submitted by great-granddaughter
Jennifer Rogers Etcheverry

WILL ROGERS
MEMORIAL MUSEUM AND RANCHES

One of the most beloved westerners of the early twentieth century was undoubtedly Will Rogers (1879–1935), who first delighted vaudeville audiences with his rope tricks and humorous anecdotes before finding fame as the star of fifty silent and twenty-one talking pictures. In addition to his stage and screen performances, Rogers made his mark as a newspaper columnist and radio commentator, cracker barrel philosopher, and philanthropist.

The Will Rogers Dog Iron Ranch & Birthplace Home in Oologah, Oklahoma, preserves the 1875 home where the performer made his debut on November 4, 1879. Influenced by the Greek Revival style, the birthplace is one of the few buildings that date back to Oklahoma's territorial days.

In 1993 a period-style barn was erected to house a classroom and to continuously play a video about Rogers. The four-hundred-acre site is still a working ranch.

In 1911, Will Rogers purchased a twenty-acre farm in Claremore, Oklahoma, where he intended to someday retire, but his tragic death in a 1935 plane crash negated that plan. Today the site contains the Will Rogers Memorial Museum (172 West Will Rogers Boulevard in Claremore, Oklahoma), which was built in 1938 by the state of Oklahoma.

The 16,652 square-foot museum features nine galleries, three theaters, and a special children's museum. Various exhibits interpret Rogers's activities as a performer, writer, and philosopher. Vintage photographs depicting Rogers performing his legendary rope tricks are on display, as are Rogers memorabilia and his saddle collection.

A substantial art collection includes works by Charles Russell and other distinguished artists. More than two thousand volumes line the shelves of the library.

The archives contain letters, contracts, manuscripts, and more than fifteen thousand photographs. The Rogers family tomb is on the grounds as well.

The Will Rogers Santa Monica Ranch, at 1603 Will Rogers Road in Pacific Palisades, California, is now owned by the state. Among the items on display at the Santa Monica ranch is the typewriter Rogers used to compose his columns, books, and stories. The original polo field and stables are intact.

For more details on these sites, go to *www.willrogers.org.*

One of the most beloved Americans of the first half of the twentieth century was cowboy and roper Will Rogers, who left Oklahoma to become a star of radio and film, and a popular syndicated newspaper columnist. He's riding his horse off a porch in this scene from his film *Cupid the Cowpuncher*.

Pancho's Grilled Portobello Mushrooms

Portobello mushrooms
Olive oil
Seasoned salt
Pepper

Scrape the backside of each mushroom cap. Rub each mushroom with approximately 3 tablespoons olive oil, and then season with seasoned salt and pepper. Place on a hot grill for 4 to 5 minutes. Enjoy the mushrooms as a complement to grilled steak or pork chops or by themselves.

Lazy Hills Guest Ranch
Ingram, Texas

"With the life we're following, we're going to get a belly full of lead for breakfast sooner or later."
—Raymond Hatton in *Law and Order* (1932)

Stuart Whitman starred as Marshal Jim Crown in TV's *Cimarron Strip* from 1967 to 1968 and was also in the feature films *Rio Conchos, The Comancheros,* and *The White Buffalo.* He is the spokesman for Kalamazoo Grills.

Jim Crown's Grilled Vidalia Onion

1   Vidalia onion
     Rock salt
     Ground pepper
     Granulated brown sugar
     Olive oil
     Spices, including paprika, chili powder, and cloves

Cut thick slices of the onion, and marinate them in rock salt, ground pepper, and brown sugar to taste, and enough olive oil to form a sufficient marinade. Add the paprika, chili powder, cloves, and other spices if you choose. Put the onions in the marinade in a large tray, and let them marinate for 1 hour. Grill the onions over an open fire, basting frequently with the marinade, until the onions are an amber-brown with streaks of gold. Excellent by themselves, or put the onions over a tender T-bone, Kansas City strip, or any other meat.

Makes about 2 servings.

Stuart Whitman, actor

Deadwood Vegetables on the Grill

1   large tomato
1   medium green bell pepper
1   medium red bell pepper
1   medium white onion
1   (14-ounce) can sliced potatoes
     Olive oil
1   tablespoon lemon juice
2   tablespoons melted butter
     Salt and pepper

Slice the tomato, peppers, and onion into bite-size pieces. Put in a large bowl. Add the sliced potatoes. Drizzle the olive oil over the vegetables. Stir until all the pieces are coated with the oil. Add the lemon juice and melted butter, and stir. Add several dashes of salt and pepper. Place a large piece of heavy-duty aluminum foil on the grill. Let it heat a minute or two. Dump the vegetables onto the aluminum foil. Cook for about 12 minutes, stirring and tossing frequently.

Makes 3 to 4 servings.

William Sanderson, actor

Mighty fine character actor William Sanderson has played lots of western characters in such productions as *Lonesome Dove, Andersonville, Crossfire Trail, Gods and Generals,* and *Monte Walsh.* Most recently, he has been E. B. Farnum in the HBO series *Deadwood.*

Singer and guitar picker supreme Glen Campbell (right) has sold more than forty million records, which include such hits as "Gentle on My Mind," "Wichita Lineman," "Galveston," and "By the Time I Get to Phoenix." He starred opposite John Wayne and Kim Darby as a Texas Ranger in the film classic *True Grit* (shown here) and had a major hit with his tune "Rhinestone Cowboy."

Rhinestone Cowboy Brussels Sprouts

Fresh Brussels sprouts
Virgin olive oil
Minced garlic (from a jar is fine)
1 jar julienne-cut, sun-dried tomatoes in olive oil
Pine nuts (you decide the quantity)
Kosher salt (very important; kosher salt tastes better)

In a pot of water, boil the Brussels sprouts for 5 minutes. Drain and cut the sprouts in half. In a large frying pan, heat the virgin olive oil and minced garlic. Toss in the Brussels sprouts. Add the sun-dried tomatoes and pine nuts. Sprinkle with the kosher salt. Sauté over medium-high heat. When the sprouts begin to brown and the tomatoes start to get crispy, it's done.

Variation: Slice up some red cabbage. (You can also add in asparagus tips, if you like.) Sprinkle with the kosher salt. In a skillet, sauté the cabbage in virgin olive oil over medium-high heat until it begins to brown and get crispy.

Servings depend on the number of sprouts you choose to cook and your diners' appetites.

Glen Campbell, singer and actor

Kedesh Carrots and Zucchini with Onions

- 3 pounds carrots, sliced
- 1 small onion, sliced and separated into rings
- 6 small zucchini, sliced
- 4 teaspoon dried basil
- 1 teaspoon salt
- 1 teaspoon pepper
- 4 tablespoons butter
- ¼ cup packed brown sugar

Put the carrots, onion, and zucchini on a piece of heavy-duty aluminum foil. Add the basil, salt, pepper, butter, and brown sugar. Fold the foil up and around the vegetables to seal so the juices won't leak out. You can make 2 or 3 of these pouches. Put the pouches on a grill with medium heat for about 1 hour. Check every once in a while, and stir the vegetables around to make sure that they are cooking evenly. Add more butter if needed. Open and serve while hot.

Makes 12 servings.

Terri "Cookie" Doty, Kedesh Ranch Shell, Wyoming

Ol' Sweet Toes' Old West–New Age Rice Diet

This recipe once saved my life. It's the basis of the macrobiotic diet.

- 2 cups bottled water
- 1 cup organic short-grain brown rice
  A pinch or two o' sea salt
  A small pawful of Adzuki beans
  A few slices o' onion

In a pot, boil the water. Add the rice, sea salt, beans, and onion. Set your stove flame low. Cook for an hour with the pot lid ajar. Stir occasionally. Serve piping hot with a dash o' soy sauce if you like. For your beverage I suggest mo' tea.

My friends, eat this tasty devil for ten days, and you'll be a man, my son, unless, of course, you're a woman. It's good for what ails you. Be sure to chew each bite thoroughly. At first, this delight may bore you. Push on into the breach, dear friends. After three days or so, your taste buds will sharpen, and if you cheat (as I did) and indulge in a glass of iced tea, you'll think you're downing vintage champagne. If you're diligent and stay

Lanky and witty Will Hutchins was a cowboy tenderfoot in the 1957 to 1961 Warner Bros. series *Sugarfoot.* He also walked the West in the film *The Shooting.*

the course, you'll reach a higher realm of consciousness. You'll welcome a new, brighter body, mind, and spirit. You'll be more aware, inside and out, and that, folks, is what the wise, wizened, bearded gent on the mountaintop will tell you is the Magic Secret.

Back in the experimental epoch of the flower child '60s I experimented with this dish—I lost all excess weight. I weighed less than my ex-spouse, and I got a job on Elvis's *Clambake*—what fun! Elvis took one look at me and told me to chow down in the commissary at lunch. To make him happy, I did so and put back a few pounds. The flick continues to this day to amuse, astound, to confuse, confound. I get letters. Recently, I heard tell that Elvis considered Bill Bixby and me to be his favorite all-time second bananas. In fact, Elvis wanted to make one more flick to remove the bad taste of *Change of Habit,* and he wanted me for his compadre. He had a 'change of mind,' and the rest is history. Hi-Ho—and so it goes.

The bottom line (as they say in the show biz) is that I owe the Magical Elvis Clambake experience to bowls of steamy, hot brown rice for ten days. Selah!

Makes 2 servings.

Ol' Sweet Toes, Will Hutchins, actor

Horseman's Hash-Brown Bake

1   (24-ounce) bag shredded hash browns
¾   cup sour cream
¾   cup cream of mushroom or cream of
    chicken soup
4   green onions, chopped
¾   cup cooked, crumbled bacon
¾   cup grated Cheddar cheese
1   teaspoon course ground pepper
1   teaspoon salt
½   cup bread crumbs

Preheat the oven to 350°. In a large bowl, mix together the hash browns, sour cream, soup, onions, bacon, cheese, pepper, and salt. Spread into a well-greased 13 x 9-inch baking dish. Sprinkle with the bread crumbs, and bake until golden brown, about 1 hour.
    Makes 6 to 8 servings.

Laughing Water Ranch
Fortine, Montana

Posse Potatoes

6   to 8 large potatoes, peeled and cubed
1   stick butter
½   teaspoon garlic powder
1   teaspoon Cavender's Greek seasoning
    Salt and pepper
2   teaspoons olive oil
½   cup finely chopped onions
1   cup finely chopped green cabbage

Preheat the oven to 350°. Boil the potatoes until done, drain off the water, and place the potatoes in a mixing bowl. Mash the potatoes, and then add the butter, garlic powder, Cavender's seasoning, and salt and pepper to taste. Mix well. In a skillet, add the olive oil, onions, and cabbage. Sauté until the onions are translucent and the cabbage is tender. Add the skillet ingredients to the mashed potatoes, and stir well. Place in a baking pan in the oven, and cook for 20 minutes.
    Makes 6 to 8 servings.

Donnie Gay, rodeo cowboy

Donnie Gay is an eight-time PRCA World Champion Bull Rider. He was inducted into the Pro Rodeo Hall of Fame in 1979 and into the PBR Ring of Honor in 1997. He is currently the voice of TV's *Mesquite Rodeo* and PBR events on cable at CBR and on RodeoNetwork.com. He is also the chute boss at the National Finals Rodeo.

Bar E Easy Mexican-Fried-Potatoes Technique

Cut some red potatoes with the peeling on in wedges or flat slices. Coat the potatoes in olive oil, and sprinkle with McCormick's Montreal Grill seasoning. Put the seasoning on heavy if you like it hot. Coat the potatoes with all-purpose flour, and fry in a Dutch oven.

Tom Bob and Cheryle Elliott, Bar E Ranch
Clinton, Arkansas

PRO RODEO HALL OF FAME
AND MUSEUM OF THE AMERICAN COWBOY

The Pro Rodeo Hall of Fame, founded in 1979, is located in Colorado Springs, Colorado, and is right next door to the National Headquarters of the Professional Rodeo Cowboys Association. The facility is the only heritage center in the world devoted exclusively to professional rodeo, America's original sport.

The first thing visitors to the hall will spy as they approach the Hall of Fame on Interstate 25 is *The Champ,* a larger-than-life bronze statue of the legendary rodeo cowboy Casey Tibbs as he rides the infamous saddle bronc Necktie.

A nine-time world champion, Tibbs has an exceptional exhibit at the hall of fame. It features nine of his championship saddles and other memorabilia from his cowboy career.

The museum, dedicated to the more than 190 honorees and Hall of Famers, is divided into sections by rodeo events. Each section features a lighted kiosk with a bronze statue depicting the rodeo events: bareback riding, steer wrestling, saddle bronc riding, calf roping, and bull riding.

There are two theater presentations, one on the history of rodeo and the other on contemporary rodeo. A sculpture garden blooms with half-life-size bronzes of all rodeo events, while the museum has a gallery that shows the evolution of rodeo gear with a great variety of cowboy hats, boots, chaps, and other rodeo equipment.

The hall of fame is not only for the cowboys. Retired rodeo stock is kept on the grounds, usually a couple of broncs and an occasional bull that has been put out to pasture.

It is located at 101 Pro Rodeo Drive in Colorado Springs, Colorado. For more information, go to *www.prorodeo.org/hof.*

Plain Good Potatoes Grilled in Foil

3   large potatoes, peeled and sliced
    Salt and pepper
4   or 5 slices bacon, crisply cooked and
    crumbled
1   large onion, sliced
½   cup (1 stick) butter or margarine, sliced
2   cups cubed sharp American cheese
    (optional)

Place the potatoes on a large sheet of heavy foil, and sprinkle with the salt, pepper, and bacon. Top with the onion and butter or margarine. Seal the foil, and grill about 1 hour (give or take eight seconds) until the potatoes are tender, turning the packet occasionally.

To make cheese potatoes, you can add the cubed cheese to the packet before grilling.

Makes about 4 servings.

Jim Shoulders, rodeo cowboy

The first real western novel was Owen Wister's *The Virginian*, published in 1902.

Mom's Black-Eyed Peas

This was Dad's favorite of Mom's recipes.

1   pound black-eyed peas (dry sack of peas)
2   ham hocks or 2 cottage hams or 1 hambone and juice or 1 rolled ham
½   dozen cloves garlic
1   heaping tablespoon regular sandwich mustard
3   heaping tablespoons brown sugar
1   whole large onion
3   ribs celery, cut up
1   pound sausage (optional)
3   or 4 carrots
1   turnip, cut up
    (Mom's recipe calls for 1 green bell pepper, but she never adds it.)

Wash and soak the black-eyed peas in a pot overnight or at least for several hours. In a large pot, cook the meat with water by itself for 1 hour. Add the black-eyed peas, garlic, mustard, brown sugar, and onion. Cook for at least 2 hours. Then add the celery, sausage, carrots, and turnip. Continue cooking until the sausage and added vegetables are the desired doneness.

Makes 10 to 12 servings.

Stuart Hamblen,
actor and singer/songwriter
Submitted by daughter
Lisa Hamblen Jaserie

Texas singer, songwriter, and all-around entertainer Stuart Hamblen, seen here with wife Suzy, was first known on Hollywood radio as "Cowboy Joe." A member of the original Beverly Hillbillies, one of radio's first popular western singing groups, he later scored with his own radio shows *King Cowboy and His Woolly West Review, Stuart Hamblen and His Lucky Stars,* and *Covered Wagon Jubilee.* As an actor he was in the western films *In Old Monterey, The Arizona Kid, King of the Cowboys, The Plainsman and the Lady, The Sombrero Kid,* and *Flame of the Barbary Coast.*

Stuart Hamblen composed many western songs and the classic "This Ole House." In 1945, he became the first man to fly a horse when he transported his racehorse, El Lobo, from Los Angeles to Bay Meadows on the Flying Tiger Airlines. His early 1950s radio show, *The Cowboy Church of the Air,* was syndicated nationally.

"I'm only asking you to remember one thing. In every gunfight, there's one who walks up to the bar and buys the drinks. And there's the other who gets his name carved into a tombstone."

        —Robert Taylor in
        Saddle the Wind (1958)

Red-haired star Rhonda Fleming was perfectly matched with many leading men in western films such as *The Last Outpost, Abilene Town, Pony Express, Gunfight at the O.K. Corral, Bullwhip, Alias Jesse James,* and *The Redhead and the Cowboy.*

Cowboy Caviar

1 (16-ounce) can shoe-peg corn, drained
1 (16-ounce) can black-eyed peas
1 to 2 avocados, cubed
⅔ cup chopped cilantro
⅔ cup chopped green onions
1 tomato, seeded and chopped

Dressing:
¼ cup olive oil
¼ cup red wine vinegar
2 cloves garlic, minced
¾ teaspoon salt
⅛ teaspoon pepper
1 teaspoon cumin

Mix together the corn, peas, avocados, cilantro, green onions, and tomato. For the dressing, mix the olive oil, vinegar, garlic, salt, pepper, and cumin together. Pour the dressing over the vegetables, and toss to mix. Chill. Serve with chips or on a bed of lettuce. If you can't find shoe-peg corn, use cooked fresh white corn. Enjoy!

Makes 6 to 8 servings.

Rhonda Fleming, actress

SALADS, VEGETABLES, AND SIDE DISHES

Noah Beery Jr., known as Pidge to his pals, was the son of actor Noah Beery and nephew of Wallace Beery. He made scores of westerns such as *Jubal, 20 Mule Team, Red River, The Daltons Ride Again,* and the serial *Riders of Death Valley.* On TV he was in the westerns *Circus Boy, Riverboat, Hondo,* and *The Yellow Rose,* and was Rocky, James Garner's father, in *The Rockford Files.*

Frontier Frijoles

2 cups dried pinto beans
¼ pound salt pork, slashed
1 large onion, chopped
1 clove garlic, crushed
1 tablespoon chili powder
¼ teaspoon ground cumin
½ teaspoon oregano

In a large pot of water, soak the beans overnight. Remove the beans from the water. Pour out the water and any dirt, stems, and other unwanted debris. Put the beans back in the pot, and cover with fresh water, about 1 inch over the beans. Add the salt pork, onion, garlic, chili powder, cumin, and oregano. Simmer on low heat, stirring occasionally, for 4 hours, or until the mixture is thick.

Makes about 8 servings.

Noah Beery Jr., actor

CHEYENNE FRONTIER DAYS
OLD WEST MUSEUM

Home to Cheyenne Frontier Days, the world's largest outdoor rodeo (which rolls along for ten full days in late July), Cheyenne is also host to the Cheyenne Frontier Days Old West Museum.

The museum opened July 8, 1978, with the goal to preserve, promote, and perpetuate the history and meaning of the Cheyenne Frontier Days celebration as well as the history, values, and culture of the American West.

The Old West Museum specializes in items and exhibits that interpret Wyoming's history. There is a large collection of photographs and postcards that date back to the late 1800s.

The museum boasts 60,000 catalogued items in all, including over 140 wagons, carriages, and primitive automobiles (50 of which are on display at any given time). Another exhibit interprets the history of Cheyenne Frontier Days.

Probably the most notable item is Chris Navarro's statue of Lane Frost, the legendary young rodeo star who died in competition at the 1989 Frontier Days event.

The museum includes a large collection of contemporary western art and sponsors two major art shows. The Western Spirit Art Show is held each spring, and the Cheyenne Frontier Days Art Show takes place every July.

The Cheyenne Frontier Days Old West Museum is located at 4610 North Carey Avenue in Cheyenne, Wyoming. For more details, go to *www.oldwestmuseum.org.*

King of the Cowboys
Corn on the Cob

Since Dad was from Ohio, he considered himself a corn aficionado. He said that the best way to fix corn for a barbecue was to get a big pot of cold water. Take a couple of dozen ears of corn. Take off the tough outer husks, leaving the tender inner ones—take out the silks—close up the husks and put the corn in the pot. Set the pot on a high flame, either on the grill or on the stove. When the water comes to a boil, the corn is done. Run under cold water, remove the remaining husks, and then butter and season the corn to taste.

Dad used to have corn-on-the-cob eating contests with his fishing and hunting buddies. He almost always won.

Roy Rogers, singer and actor
Submitted by Cheryl Rogers-Barnett

Roy Rogers and Dale Evans, as a husband and wife team, made about twenty-eight films together, beginning with *The Cowboy and the Señorita* in 1944.

ROY ROGERS–DALE EVANS
Museum & Happy Trails Theater

After many years in Victorville, California, the Roy Rogers and Dale Evans museum relocated to Branson, Missouri, where it continues to draw thousands of visitors every year.

There are thousands of Rogers family items and memorabilia in the gigantic museum (the gift shop alone takes up three thousand square feet), but undoubtedly the most popular artifact is Trigger, Roy's beloved horse, who is mounted on display.

Several vehicles can be seen, as well as original clothing, jewelry, and costumes worn by Roy and Dale. The Rogers's gun collection is on display, as are hundreds of toys, books, and other vintage merchandise.

Several interactive displays and a laser shooting gallery are popular with visitors. The Happy Trails Theater costs extra, but it allows patrons to meet a member of the Rogers clan. Roy "Dusty" Rogers Jr. performs with the High Riders in the 325-seat auditorium. Dusty sticks around after the show to meet fans, sign autographs, and appear in photographs. Indeed, the museum is unusual among western-themed attractions in that it is owned and operated by the family of the celebrity cowboy it honors.

The Roy Rogers–Dale Evans Museum is located at 3950 Green Mountain Drive in Branson, Missouri. For more information, go to *www.royrogers.com*.

ROY ROGERS
RIDERS CLUB RULES

Be neat and clean.

Be courteous and polite.

Always obey your parents.

Protect the weak and help them.

Be brave, but never take chances.

Study hard, and learn all you can.

Be kind to animals and care for them.

Eat all your food and never waste any.

Love God and go to Sunday school regularly.

Always respect our flag, and country.

Cowboy Corn
Grilled in the Husk

Something extra to add to the barbecue.

Dampen the husks of your corn with salted water. Place the ears in their husks directly on hot coals, which should be well burned down and without any flames. Turn the corn often so that the husks are not burned through. Corn cooks in 8 to 10 minutes if the fire is good and hot.

Dirk London, actor

Dirk London hit the streets of Tombstone as Morgan Earp, brother Wyatt's law and order partner, in *The Life and Legend of Wyatt Earp*, which ran on ABC from 1955 to 1961. His western films include *The Lonely Man* and *Ambush at Cimarron Pass*.

Johnny Mack Brown rears back on his horse, Wheezer, while filming *Desperate Trails* for Universal in 1939. Brown starred in more than a hundred B-westerns from the 1930s into the 1950s, often playing Nevada Jack McKenzie or Johnny Mack Brown. He was famous for how well he threw a good punch.

'Bama Cowboy's Corn Goodie

Johnny Mack Brown's favorite dish.

1   large onion
1   clove garlic
    Butter (and oil)
1   (8½-ounce) box Jiffy corn muffin mix
1   (15-ounce) can cream-style corn
1   large egg, partially beaten
1   (16-ounce) container sour cream
1   (8-ounce) mild or sharp Cheddar cheese brick

Chop the onion into approximately ½-inch cubes. Mince the garlic clove. In a large skillet, sauté the onions and garlic in some butter (or half butter and half oil) until limp or slightly brown around the edges. In a large mixing bowl, pour in the corn muffin mix, cream-style corn, and egg. Mix well. Add the sautéed onion and garlic to the bowl mixture and stir well. Grease or oil a 9-inch square or round pan, and add the mixture to it. Spread evenly. (The pan should never be more than 2 inches deep, and mixture should be about 1½ inches deep.) Stir the sour cream in its own container to soften, and then spread it with a knife over the corn and onion mixture to make a layer on top. Grate the cheese, and sprinkle to cover the sour cream. Be generous and cover well. Preheat the oven to 425°, and bake the mixture for 25 to 30 minutes. Place some foil underneath the pan in case the contents should boil over. Look in the oven to see if the cheese is turning brown around the edges. The consistency is like a bread pudding.

Note: It might be better for some to double the recipe and have some leftovers that you could cut into portion-size quarters and freeze for future meals. In that case use a 13 x 9-inch pan. It's yummy.

Makes 4 to 6 servings.

Johnny Mack Brown, actor
Submitted by the family
of Johnny Mack Brown

Mexican Fiesta
Corn Casserole

6   (14½-ounce) cans cream corn
3   sleeves soda crackers, crushed
6   eggs
3   (4-ounce) cans chopped green chiles
1   (4-ounce) jar pimientos

In a large bowl, combine the corn, crackers, eggs, chiles, and pimientos, and mix well. Preheat a very large Dutch oven, and add the mixture. Place the Dutch oven over medium-low coals on the grill with more coals on top than on the bottom, and cook for about 1 hour. Rotate the Dutch oven and lid often.
   Makes 20 to 25 servings.

Donna and Dennis Williams,
Circle Double D Chuck Wagon
Neosho, Missouri

Carrot Delectable
Casserole

3   plus 4 tablespoons butter or margarine
½   cup chopped onion
¾   cup shredded Cheddar cheese
1   (10¾-ounce) can cream of celery soup
4   cups cooked carrots or 1 (24-ounce)
     package frozen, sliced carrots
2   cups Pepperidge Farm herbed stuffing

Preheat the oven to 350°. Melt 3 tablespoons butter or margarine in a large skillet. Add the onion, and sauté until tender. Add the cheese, soup, and carrots, and mix well. Pour the mixture into a 2-quart casserole. Top with the stuffing. Melt the remaining 4 tablespoons butter, and pour over the stuffing. Bake for 20 minutes.
   Makes 12 servings.

Ruth Terry, actress

Ruth Terry made seven western films, including three with Roy Rogers and one with Ernest Tubb. Her biggest and best was *Pistol Packin' Mama,* while many fans love *Heart of the Golden West.*

Debbie Reynolds can sing and dance in the rain, but she truly sang and danced up a storm out West in *The Unsinkable Molly Brown*. The native of El Paso, Texas, also shone brightly in *How the West Was Won,* as seen here on the left, with director Henry Hathaway behind the camera, actor Karl Malden at right, and Carroll Baker sitting in the tent.

Molly Brown's Favorite Cheese Enchiladas

¼   cup vegetable oil
1   medium onion, chopped
2   tablespoons all-purpose flour
1   (16-ounce) can tomato sauce
1   cup water
     Salt
     Pepper
     Chili powder
1   dozen tortillas
½   pound longhorn cheese, grated medium
½   pound Monterey Jack cheese, grated medium

Preheat the oven to 350°. In a saucepan, heat the oil, and sauté the onion until translucent. Add the flour, then the tomato sauce, and enough water to make a gravy-like sauce. Add the salt, pepper, and chili powder to taste. Warm the tortillas, and then dip each one into the sauce. Fill the tortillas with the cheese and roll. Place the rolled tortillas in a casserole dish, and top with the rest of the sauce and cheese. Bake for 15 minutes.

     Makes 1 dozen.

Debbie Reynolds, actress

GIL: "Partner, you know what's on the back of a poor man when he dies? The clothes of pride. And they're not a bit warmer to him dead than they were when he was alive. Is that all you want, Steve?"
STEVE: "All I want is to enter my house justified."

—Randolph Scott and Joel McCrea in *Ride the High Country* (1962)

Wide Country Green Chile and Cheese Enchiladas

2   (8-ounce) packages cream cheese
1   cup shredded Monterey Jack cheese
1   cup shredded mozzarella cheese
1   (7-ounce) can diced Ortega green chiles, drained
½   cup chopped green onion (tops only)
     Coarse salt
     Pepper
1   dozen corn tortillas

Sauce:
1   (12-ounce) can tomatillos, drained
1   cup chicken broth
1   cup whipping cream
2   eggs

Andrew Prine starred in the TV series *The Wide Country* and *The Road West* and has been in western films *Texas Across the River, Chisum, Bandolero!, The Winds of Autumn,* and *Gettysburg.*

Mix the three cheeses together in a large bowl. When well mixed, add the chiles, green onion tops, and coarse salt and pepper to taste. Soften the tortillas (they can be placed in a covered container in the microwave for 1 minute, or put one at a time on a hot frying pan or griddle until soft enough to roll up without breaking). Spray a 13 x 9-inch baking pan with vegetable spray. Take a tortilla, and place the cheese mixture down the middle. Roll up and place seam side down in the pan. Repeat with the remaining tortillas.

Preheat the oven to 350°. To make the sauce, place the tomatillos, chicken broth, and cream in a blender, and purée until smooth. Add the eggs and pulse only until blended. Do not overblend or the eggs will cook. Pour the sauce over the enchiladas, and cook in the oven for 35 minutes, or until the cheese is melted and the top is bubbly. Serve immediately.

Note: This is a great side dish, but you can make it a main dish by adding cooked-and-pulled-apart chicken to the enchiladas. Sliced black and/or green olives are also delicious in the enchiladas. Neufchatel cheese can be substituted for cream cheese, if you are cutting fat from your diet.

Makes a dozen enchiladas.

Andrew Prine, actor

Kelo Henderson starred as Arizona Ranger Clint Travis in the TV series *26 Men,* from 1957 to 1959. He is also a trick-gun artist and trained many actors in the use of firearms for their western roles.

Cheesy-but-True Grits

4   cups boiling water
1   teaspoon salt
1   cup grits
½   cup butter (do not use margarine)
2   eggs plus enough milk to make 1 cup
1   cup grated Cheddar cheese
     Pepper

Preheat the oven to 350°. In a large saucepan, boil the water. Add the salt and grits. Lower the heat, and cook for about 4 minutes. Remove the saucepan from the heat, and stir in the butter, the egg-and-milk mixture, cheese, and pepper to taste (about 1 teaspoon is a good rule of thumb). Stir well. Pour into a buttered, 2-quart casserole. Bake for about 45 minutes.

Makes 6 to 8 servings.

Kelo Henderson, actor and trick-gun artist

O.K. Pasole

But it's really far more than just O.K. around our corral.

6   (16-ounce) cans hominy or 1 large package pasole
3   pounds pork roast, cut into chunks
2   tablespoons red chili powder
1   (8-ounce) can chopped green chiles (fresh-roasted green chiles, peeled are preferred)
1   small onion, chopped
1   garlic clove, minced
     All-purpose flour

If pasole is used, put it in a large kettle with 6 to 8 cups water, and boil for about 2 hours or until the pasole pops. Drain the water, and add fresh water along with the pork. If hominy is used, just drain the liquid from the can, and place in a kettle with 6 to 10 cups of water and the cut-up pork. Cook for about 2 hours. Then add the chili powder, green chiles, onion, garlic, and a little all-purpose flour to thicken, if desired.

Makes 12 to 16 servings.

Dale Robertson, actor

SALADS, VEGETABLES, AND SIDE DISHES

BRANDED MEALS

Calhoun's Flavorsome Filet Mignon

For best flavor, use a charcoal grill instead of gas.

4   (6 to 8-ounce) filet mignons
    Smoke's Secret Spice Rub (see recipe on page 177)
    The Texan's Garlic Oil Marinade (see recipe on page 177)

Rub the filet mignons with a generous amount of Smoke's Secret Spice Rub. In a glass dish or plastic bag, marinate the steaks in The Texan's Garlic Oil Marinade at least 4 hours in the refrigerator, or overnight if possible. Turn once. Get the charcoal fire going. Remove the steaks from the marinade, and lightly pat off the excess oil. Place the steaks on the grill over high heat to get a good sear and to seal in the juices. For a rare steak, grill for 5 minutes on each side, or until the juices start to run. For medium steaks, cook an additional 5 minutes per side. For well done, remove the steaks when rare, and plate up an old boot or bologna sandwich.

Makes 6 to 8 servings.

Rory Calhoun, actor

The original chuck wagon was probably adapted from a surplus Civil War army wagon by Charles Goodnight in 1867.

When he was president of the United States, his Secret Service code name was Rawhide. As an actor Ronald Reagan was host of TV's *Death Valley Days* from 1965 to 1966. He starred in the western films *Santa Fe Trail*, *The Bad Man*, *The Last Outpost*, *Law and Order*, and *Cattle Queen of Montana*.

Rancho del Cielo Tri-Tip

President Reagan was fond of grilling and barbecuing at his ranch, Rancho del Cielo. He would serve this beef roast with fresh salsa, beans, and maybe even a personal favorite, macaroni and cheese.

1   teaspoon garlic powder
1   teaspoon onion powder
    Salt and freshly ground black pepper
1   (1½ to 2-pound) tri-tip roast

Mix the garlic powder, onion powder, and salt and pepper together, and rub all over the roast. Place the roast in a large plastic bag, and refrigerate for several hours. When ready to cook, lightly brush your grill grate with vegetable oil to prevent the roast from sticking. Grill the roast over medium heat, turning occasionally, for 30 to 35 minutes, or until the roast reaches the desired doneness. Remove from the heat, and cover with foil for 10 minutes. Slice the roast across the grain into thin slices. Serve with fresh salsa.

Makes 4 servings.

President Ronald Reagan
Submitted by the Office of Ronald Reagan

MAIN DISHES FOR THE GRILL, BARBECUE PIT, AND SMOKER

NATIONAL COWBOY & WESTERN HERITAGE
MUSEUM

The National Cowboy & Western Heritage Museum in Oklahoma City is a fabulous showplace of the Old West. Formerly known as the Cowboy Hall of Fame, the museum sits atop Persimmon Hill and overlooks a portion of the Old Chisholm Trail and historic Route 66.

A national treasury of western art and history, the museum brings reality and romance together with a look at the true Old West as well as an entertaining look at the mythical West, mostly created by Hollywood film and TV shows.

The awesome collection of art and artifacts is sure to cheer any cowboy lover's heart. One of the most impressive works is James Earl Fraser's eighteen-foot-tall sculpture *End of the Trail,* a monument to Native Americans. This masterpiece depicts an exhausted Indian brave slumped on his weary pony.

The National Cowboy & Western Heritage Museum contains galleries that pay tribute to specific areas of western history and its people. The American Cowboy Gallery explores the culture and history of the working cowboy. It features clothing and equipment used by cowboys. The American Rodeo Gallery salutes the history, people, and events of the true-blue sport of the West. More than four hundred artifacts cover such themes as rodeo history, women in rodeo, trick riders, fancy ropers, and rodeo clowns.

The Art of the American West Gallery presents more than two thousand exemplary paintings, sculptures, and other artwork. These include Gerald Balciar's eighteen-foot-tall marble *Canyon Princess,* Albert Bierstadt's *Emigrants Crossing the Plains,* and William R. Leigh's *The Leader's Downfall.* The cornerstone of the museum's historical collection of western art is in a group of paintings and sculptures by Charles M. Russell and Frederic Remington.

The Native American Gallery opened October 20, 2000 and honors the spiritual, social, economic, and cultural influences embodied in Native American art.

The Hambrick Gardens contains the Trail of the Great Cow Ponies, which is the final resting place of the infamous rodeo bull Tornado and bucking broncos Midnight and Five Minutes to Midnight. The gardens are also host to the *Legend of the Westerner* sculpture of William F. "Buffalo Bill" Cody, which looks down at Deep Fork Creek, a place where cowboys once watered their cattle on the trail to market in Kansas.

The Weitzenhoffer Gallery of Fine American Firearms takes aim at the mechanical and decorative arts of domestic arms from the second half of the nineteenth century. On display are more than one hundred firearms as functional sculpture. The products of such gun makers as Colt, Remington, Smith & Wesson, Sharps, Winchester, Marlin, and Parker Brothers fill the gallery.

The Western Performers Gallery allows visitors to investigate how the West has been interpreted in literature and film. It honors western performers who have contributed to the making and preservation of the stories and legends of the West. This gallery features the museum's extensive collection of memorabilia, such as John Wayne's collection of personal firearms and kachina dolls, Walter Brennan's saddle and cowboy hat, and portraits of such TV cowboy stars as James Arness, James Garner, Clayton Moore, and Amanda Blake.

The National Cowboy and Western Heritage Museum is located at 1700 NE 63rd Street in Oklahoma City, Oklahoma. For more information, go to *www.nationalcowboymuseum.org.*

L. Q. Tips

My theory about cooking . . .
Simple, that's the way it should be.
Simple, kinda' like me.
Hey—poetry.
Enough.

Roll a tri-tip roast in coarse kosher salt. Tip: Moisten the roast so a bunch of salt sticks to it. Toss on an outdoor grill. Flip once. Cook about 30 minutes—the center will be pink. Tastes more like Texas barbecue than the law allows.

L. Q. Jones, actor

Moonlight Mesquite Pit-Barbecued Brisket

A great brisket! We have shipped it all over the United States.

1	bottle Fiesta Brisket Rub with tenderizer
4	(15-pound) briskets, packer cut
	Heavy foil
	Plenty of dry mesquite firewood

Wash the briskets. Rub all the briskets with Fiesta Brisket Rub until dark red. Put on a preheated, medium fire in a pit (about 275°) for 4 hours, fat side up. Do not open the lid. After 4 hours, double wrap the meat in heavy foil. Put the meat back in the pit, fat side up. Keep the heat at 275° for 4 more hours. Do not open the lid. Pull off and stack the briskets in a large steel pan. Let cool for 2 hours. Open the foil, and slice. Caution: meat will still be hot.

Makes about 20 servings per brisket.

The Moonlight Ranch Shed and Bed
Valley Mills, Texas

Texan L. Q. Jones was Cheyenne's partner Smitty for a time in the TV series and later joined the cast of *The Virginian*. He's well-known for his roles in a passel of great western flicks including *Warlock, Nevada Smith, Ride the High Country, Major Dundee, The Ballad of Cable Hogue*, and *The Wild Bunch*. The busy cowboy was also in *Love Me Tender, Hang 'Em High*, and *Lightning Jack* and was a guest star in the TV westerns *Annie Oakley, The Rebel, Laramie, Rawhide, Gunsmoke*, and *The Yellow Rose*.

Gail Davis was Gene Autry's leading lady in about a dozen films and starred with Roy Rogers, here, in the 1948 film *The Far Frontier* .

On-Target Beef Brisket

It's a bull's-eye.

⅓ cup molasses
⅓ cup hot sweet mustard
½ cup packed brown sugar
¾ cup wine vinegar
½ cup pineapple juice
¼ teaspoon hot sauce
1 tablespoon minced onion
3 tablespoons Worcestershire sauce
1 teaspoon chili powder
1 (4 to 6-pound) beef brisket

In a bowl, combine the molasses, mustard, brown sugar, vinegar, pineapple juice, hot sauce, onion, Worcestershire sauce, and chili powder to make a marinade. Mix well. Place the beef in a heavy plastic bag, and pour the marinade over it. Squeeze the air from the bag and tightly fasten. Place in a 13 x 9-inch baking dish, and set in the refrigerator for at least 4 to 6 hours, or it can also marinate overnight. Once the roast has marinated, pour the contents of the bag into a foil-lined baking dish. Preheat the oven to 325°. Cover the top of the dish with foil, and bake in the oven for 2½ hours. Then transfer the beef to a grill or smoker for an additional 2 hours and 30 minutes to 3 hours. To serve, slice in thin diagonal slices. For those rainy days, this dish can be oven-baked for the full 5 hours.

Makes 8 to 10 servings.

Gail Davis, actress

Texas Bix Bender's Smoked Brisket

1   (2-pound) brisket

Marinade:
- 3   cloves garlic, minced
- ¼   cup red wine vinegar
- ¼   cup olive oil
- 1   medium onion, diced
- 1   tablespoon chili powder
  Freshly ground pepper (about 1 tablespoon)
- 1   teaspoon turmeric (I put this stuff in everything; a cowboy scientist at M.I.T.—The Montana Institute of Technology—says it's good for you.)
  Several dashes Worcestershire sauce (Let yourself go; this one's hard to overdo.)
- ¼   habanero chile pepper, diced as fine as your patience allows (Be very careful here. This is the hottest pepper known to man.)
  Juice of ½ lime

The day before you smoke the brisket, trim all the fat off your brisket and set it aside while you make the marinade. In a large bowl, stir up good the garlic, red wine, oil, onion, chili powder, pepper, turmeric, chile pepper, and lime juice, and then pour this marinade over the meat. Cover and refrigerate until you get up and get the smoker going the next morning. Smoke the brisket for 8 hours. Make sure you've got water under the meat and that your fire stays ideal. Once you close your smoker, don't open it until those 8 hours have gone by. When the brisket is done, slice it thinly against the grain. Serve it up with some pinto beans, coleslaw, corn on the cob, and sourdough bread. Shiner Bock is a faithful companion. And always remember, "Don't squat with yer spurs on."

Makes 4 to 6 servings.

Texas Bix Bender, writer

Texas Bix Bender hangs his cowboy hat at a small chile pepper ranch on the outskirts of Nashville. A former writer for *Hee Haw,* he puts pen on paper for Riders in the Sky and is a million-selling author of little humor books, such as *Don't Squat with Yer Spurs On!* and *Hats and the Cowboys Who Wear Them.*

"I guess folks and horses are a lot alike. It all depends on how they're saddle-broke, whether the good or bad crops out. And the thing that counts most ought to be how they finish the race."

—Allan "Rocky" Lane in *Stagecoach to Denver* (1946)

Newman's Own Saddle-Up Steak with Mucho Garlic

- 2 large bulbs garlic
- 1 cup Newman's Own Balsamic Vinaigrette or Lighten Up! Light Balsamic Vinaigrette
- 1 teaspoon dried basil
- 1 teaspoon dried oregano
- ½ teaspoon ground black pepper
- 2 (1-inch-thick) boneless beef rib-eye steaks or sirloin steaks, trimmed (about 1½ pounds)

Using a sharp knife, cut ½ inch off the top of each garlic bulb to expose the tops of each individual clove. Leaving the garlic bulbs whole, remove any loose, papery outer layers. Fold a 20 x 18-inch piece of heavy foil in half crosswise. Trim into a 10-inch square. Place the garlic bulbs, cut side up, in the center of the foil square. Place a large zipper-seal plastic bag into a large, shallow dish. Into the bag, put the vinaigrette, basil, oregano, and pepper. Seal the bag. Massage gently to combine the ingredients. Drizzle 3 tablespoons of the vinaigrette mixture over the garlic. Bring up the opposite edges of the foil. Pinch and fold the foil closed. Add the steak to the bag and seal. Marinate both the steak and the garlic in the refrigerator at least 4 hours or overnight. Occasionally turn the steak. Remove the garlic, and grill or roast it for 30 minutes over indirect heat until the garlic bulbs are soft. Remove the steak, discarding the marinade. Grill or broil the steak directly over medium heat until you have the desired doneness, 10 to 15 minutes, turning once halfway through the cooking time. To serve, remove the garlic from the foil. Squeeze the garlic pulp from each clove onto the steaks. Mash the pulp slightly with a fork, spreading it over the steaks.

Makes 4 servings.

Paul Newman, actor

Paul Newman has played cool-handed cowboys in the westerns *The Left Handed Gun, Hud, Hombre, Pocket Money, Butch Cassidy and the Sundance Kid, The Life and Times of Judge Roy Bean,* and *Buffalo Bill and the Indians.*

Branded Chuck Roast

1 (3-pound) chuck roast, 1½ to 2 inches thick
1 teaspoon Accent
⅓ cup wine vinegar
¼ cup ketchup
2 tablespoons cooking oil
2 tablespoons soy sauce
1 tablespoon Worcestershire sauce
1 teaspoon prepared mustard
1 teaspoon salt
¼ teaspoon pepper
¼ teaspoon garlic powder

Sprinkle both sides of the roast with the Accent. Place in a shallow baking dish. In a bowl, thoroughly combine the vinegar, ketchup, oil, soy sauce, Worcestershire sauce, mustard, salt, pepper, and garlic powder. Pour the mixture over the roast, and marinate it for 2 to 3 hours, turning once or twice. Place the roast on a grill, and cook about 6 inches from the heat. Turn the roast, and baste with marinade every 10 to 15 minutes. Cook for a total of 35 to 45 minutes for a medium-rare roast or until desired doneness.

Note: This dish can also be prepared in the broiler.

Makes 6 to 8 servings.

Chuck Connors, actor

Chuck Connors, who could twirl rifles with the best of 'em, also cowboyed in such feature films as *The Big Country* and *Old Yeller*. A former two-sport professional athlete, he saw action with the Brooklyn Dodgers and Chicago Cubs in baseball and the Boston Celtics in basketball.

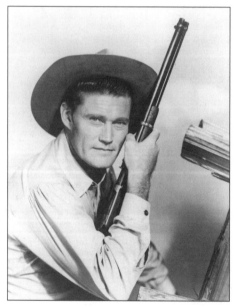

One of TV's tallest western stars, Chuck Connors starred in four western series: *The Rifleman,* *Branded, Cowboy in Africa,* and *The Yellow Rose.*

Nicknames for trail-drive and bunkhouse cooks included cookie, biscuit shooter, gut robber, greasy-belly, dough-boxer, bean-master, belly-cheater, and Sallie. (What . . . no Wishbone or Hop Sing?!)

MAIN DISHES FOR THE GRILL, BARBECUE PIT, AND SMOKER

Tuck's
Peanut Butter Steak

Steaks (the best cut to use is Spencer or rib-eye)
Adolph's tenderizer (or Accent)
Black pepper
Liquid smoke
Worcestershire sauce
Creamy peanut butter

Rub both sides of the steaks with Adolph's tenderizer (or Accent) and black pepper. Splash both sides with a few drops of liquid smoke and Worcestershire sauce. Rub each steak all over with about 1 tablespoon creamy peanut butter. Grill for about 5 to 8 minutes on each side over hot coals or flame for medium-rare to medium.

Forrest Tucker, actor

Forrest Tucker starred as Sergeant Morgan O'Rourke on the 1960s TV western comedy *F Troop*. In this episode, his wife Marilyn Tucker played an Indian maiden. A few of his many western films include *The Westerner, Pony Express, Chisum, Coroner Creek,* and *Cat Ballou*.

Wild Bill Hickok's Hickory-Smoked Steaks

2   tablespoons chili powder
2   tablespoons packed brown sugar
½   teaspoon finely minced garlic
2   teaspoons olive oil
4   New York strip steaks, about 1 inch thick
    Salt and pepper

In a bowl, mix together the chili powder, brown sugar, and garlic. Add the olive oil, and stir into a consistent mixture. Season the steaks with the salt and pepper. Rub the spice mixture into both sides of the steaks. Smoke the steaks for approximately 8 to 10 minutes. To smoke, heat one side of the grill, adding hickory, mesquite, or other wood chips that you like. Be sure to soak the wood chips in water for at least 30 minutes before using so that the chips smoke rather than burn away. Then squeeze the water out, and place the chips in an aluminum pan on the coals. Once the coals are hot, place the steaks on the grid so as not to be directly over the heat. Put the cover on the grill down. After smoking the steaks, remove the wood chips, and place the steaks directly over the hot coals. Grill the steaks for approximately 4 minutes per side or until done to your taste.

Makes 4 servings.

Guy Madison, actor

From 1951 to 1958, handsome Guy Madison starred in TV's *The Adventures of Wild Bill Hickok.* His films include *The Charge at Feather River, Drums in the Deep South,* and *The Last Frontier.*

WILD BILL HICKOK'S
DEPUTY MARSHAL'S CODE OF CONDUCT

I will be brave, but never careless.
I will obey my parents. They do know best.
I will be neat and clean at all times.
I will be polite and courteous.
I will protect the weak and help them.
I will study hard.
I will be kind to animals and care for them.
I will respect my flag and my country.
I will attend my place of worship regularly.

Ben's Honey
of a Grilled Steak

2   tablespoons crushed red pepper
1   teaspoon black pepper
2   cloves garlic, squeezed
1   onion, thinly sliced
1   cup honey
6   large sirloin steaks

In a large pot, combine the red and black pepper, garlic, onion, and honey. Marinate the steaks for 6 to 8 hours. Remove the meat from the marinade, and grill 'em like you like over a fire.

Makes 6 servings.

Ben Johnson, actor and rodeo cowboy

Ben Johnson rode lead in director John Ford's *Wagonmaster* (1950). The Oscar-winning, world-champion rodeo cowboy made as many great westerns as anybody. Among his credits are *Rio Grande, Shane, Will Penny, One-Eyed Jacks, Chisum, Junior Bonner, The Wild Bunch, Hang'Em High,* and *Oklahoma.*

She Wore A Yellow Ribbon (1949)
John Wayne & Ben Johnson

Ben Johnson is Sergeant Tyree to John Wayne's Captain Brittles in John Ford's 1949 classic cavalry film *She Wore a Yellow Ribbon.*

One of the great western stars of the golden era of Hollywood, handsome Joel McCrea played valiant cowboy heroes in more than two dozen westerns, including the 1944 film *Buffalo Bill,* shown here. One of his best was one of his last, *Ride the High Country.*

Joel McCrea's Hand-Rubbed Steak

My grandfather always preferred to use either sirloin steak or filet mignon for this recipe, although you could probably use any type of steak. Make sure your steak is top quality beef and that it is freshly cut. Steak should be cut thick, approximately 1 to 1½ inches. Take each steak and hand-rub both sides with rock salt until the entire steak is covered with salt. Then sprinkle each steak very lightly with garlic salt or just plain pepper if preferred. Then quickly sear (approximately 10 to 15 seconds) both sides of the steak on the grill over a very hot fire. This will seal in the natural juices of the steak. Then continue to cook the steak slowly over a low heat until done to your taste. The cooking process will absorb most of the salt so that the steak will be flavorful, but not taste overly salty.

Joel McCrea, actor
Submitted by grandson Wyatt McCrea

Chuck's T-Bone Technique

Sprinkle steaks on both sides with Lawry's seasoned salt. Put plastic wrap over the top, and keep them in the refrigerator until grilling time. The longer the steaks marinate, the better. Twelve hours or overnight to marinate is best. Throw the steaks on the grill, salt and pepper to taste, and cook to preference or until the cow quits mooin'.

Chuck Lander, Kedesh Ranch
Shell, Wyoming

CATTLE RAISERS MUSEUM

The Cattle Raisers Museum preserves the heritage of the southwestern livestock industry. The history of cattle barons, rustlers, cowboys, longhorns, and ranches is told here, often with the assistance of interactive computers, talking mannequins, and dioramas.

The eight-thousand-square-foot museum is the repository of the Joe Russell Spur Collection (fifty-two sets), the Ken Spain Saddle Collection, and the Leonard Stiles Branding Iron Collection which includes the Spanish branding iron once owned by Texas founder Stephen F. Austin and irons registered to such celebrities as Nolan Ryan and John Wayne.

The W. T. Waggoner Memorial Library contains thousands of books and historic photographs. The letters and other documents contained in the Captain John T. Lytle Manuscript Collection provide insight into the challenges faced by trail bosses and their crews in the late nineteenth century.

The Cattle Raisers Museum is located at 1301 West Seventh Street in Fort Worth, Texas. For more details, go to *www.cattleraisersmuseum.org*.

Hidden Valley Ranch Ultra Steak Prep for Grilling

3   to 4 dried red chile peppers (ancho, pasilla, chiles de ristra, or the like)
½   bulb garlic
½   teaspoon cumin
1   teaspoon Mexican oregano
¼   teaspoon ground nutmeg
¼   cup olive oil
¼   cup dried onion flakes
5   center-cut New York steaks

Heat a burner on your stove to medium (electric or gas). Scorch the dried chiles by either pressing the chiles onto the burner element (if electric) or roasting carefully over the gas flame, being careful not to burn the dried meat of the chile. Don't inhale the smoke.

Tear the top of the chiles off, empty the seeds, and scrape the webbing off the inside of the chiles. Tear the chiles into strips, and place them in enough hot water to cover the strips. Let sit for an hour or so until the meat of the chiles has absorbed enough water to be easily scraped off. Do not discard the water.If you are sensitive at all to hot chiles, wear industrial strength gloves. The seed and web portion of the chile contains most of the capsaicin. Scrape the meat of the chile by either holding the chunks meat side up and then scraping with a dull knife and depositing the scrapings in a bowl, or by rubbing the chunks against the screen of a frying pan splatter shield to scrape the meat off, or some other method I have not thought of. Peel and press the garlic. Place the chile meat (it will be thick and pasty) in a bowl, and add the cumin, oregano, nutmeg, olive oil, and onion flakes. Adjust the consistency, if necessary, to a paste (pesto viscosity) with the water you soaked the chiles in. Mix well.

Have your butcher prepare (ideally) five center-cut New York steaks, 1 to 1¼ inches thick. Smear the paste on both sides of the steaks, and let them marinate at room temperature for at least 3 hours before grilling or barbecuing. Throw the steaks on the barbecue, and cook to your desired doneness. Note: I like to buy a whole New York strip (ask your butcher) and cut and trim the steaks myself. (Your guests will think you're cool if you do that.)

The basic recipe makes enough marinade for five steaks. Adjust accordingly for more. If you have leftover marinade, it makes a great enchilada sauce.

Bruce Coe, Hidden Valley Guest Ranch
Cle Elum, Washington

Singer and songwriter Sheb Wooley was an Oklahoma cowboy who could play good guys and bad, but played mostly good guys. He starred on TV's *Rawhide* as trail scout Pete Nolan. His movie credits include *High Noon, Rocky Mountain, Little Big Horn, The Lusty Men, Johnny Guitar, The Outlaw Josey Wales,* and *Silverado.*

Ol' West Cowboy Slab o' Meat

Us cowboys know what grillin' out on the open range means—some danged bad food, unless we get lucky enough to have a halfway decent cook like ol' Wishbone on Rawhide. *Sometimes he couldn't much more 'n boil water without scorchin' it, but he did have a mean way of tenderin' up a slab of just 'bout any kind of meat us boys could round up. Doesn't matter if it was wild jackrabbit, elk, deer, pig, buffalo, or plain ol' cow meat. He was kind enough to teach this cookin' trick that I am passin' on to you.*

½ teaspoon rock salt, ground up (table salt will do)
4 big garlic cloves
2 cups chopped onions (scallions, wild, white Vidalia . . . doesn't matter)
1 tablespoon whole fresh black pepper
1 cup oil (olive oil, sesame . . . whatever you like to cook with)
½ cup chopped cilantro
½ cup chopped parsley
¼ cup chopped mint
½ cup apple cider vinegar
¼ cup packed brown sugar
1 cup cold, day-old coffee left over from breakfast
2 pounds (big ol' slab) of whatever kind of meat you've got

Mix up all your ingredients in a big bowl. You need to make sure the bowl is big enough so that all the ingredients get covered well with the spices. Lay your meat in the bowl so all of it will get marinated well on the bottom and top. Pour the seasonings over your meat. Cover with a lid of some kind to keep in all the flavor, and put it up (in the refrigerator) overnight so the meat can get all the good flavors locked inside. You can cook this meat over a roarin' fire on the grill until it's tender. It doesn't take a long time because it has marinated overnight. Just check it until you get it cooked to your likin'. (Now if it's pork, cook the stuffin's out of it so you won't get that kinda' worm that lives in pork . . . phooey!) Or if you have an oven or gas cookin' stove, cook it on top of the stove in a big heavy grillin' pan or skillet, same as if you're doin' it on the open flame.

You can save some of the spice marinade for grilled chunks of carrot, pineapple, whole cherry, or Roma tomatoes, potatoes, green pepper, eggplant, or whatever you like to go along with your meat. Add some good homemade bread and salad, and you're sittin' pretty. There's nothin' like the taste of fresh, open-range grillin'. Enjoy!

Makes 4 servings.

Sheb Wooley, actor and singer/songwriter

MAIN DISHES FOR THE GRILL, BARBECUE PIT, AND SMOKER

Don Edwards is known as the minstrel of the range. A pure cowboy singer, his influences include B-westerns and the writing of Will James. His albums include *Guitars & Saddle Songs* and *Songs of the Cowboy.* Edwards was featured in the film *The Horse Whisperer.*

Balladeer's Grilled Steak with Salsa

2   pounds flank steak or 4 rib-eye steaks (½ pound each)
1   yellow onion
2   cloves garlic, finely chopped
2   teaspoons ground cumin
2   teaspoons freshly ground pepper
½   cup fresh lemon juice

Spicy salsa:
2   avocados, pitted, peeled, and cut into chunks
4   to 6 Roma tomatoes, peeled and cut into small chunks
1   to 2 teaspoons finely minced jalapeño chiles (or to taste)
1   teaspoon finely minced garlic
¼   cup finely chopped green or red bell pepper
3   tablespoons finely minced red onion
2½ tablespoons red wine vinegar or fresh lemon juice
3   tablespoons minced fresh cilantro
½   cup olive oil
    Salt and pepper

Arrange the steaks in a shallow dish. In a food processor or blender, combine the onion, garlic, cumin, pepper, and lemon juice, and pulse a few times to combine. Pour over the steaks, cover, and let stand for 1 hour at room temperature. Or cover and refrigerate for 2 hours. For the salsa, combine the avocados, tomatoes, chiles, garlic, bell pepper, onion, wine vinegar or lemon juice, cilantro, olive oil, salt, and pepper. Mix well. Set aside at room temperature. Heat the grill. Remove the steaks from the marinade, brush lightly with olive oil, and sprinkle with salt. Place on the grill rack, and grill, turning once. Cook for 3 minutes on each side for rare, or until done to your liking. Slice the steaks across the grain, spoon the salsa over the steaks, and serve with black beans and tortillas.

Makes 4 servings.

Don Edwards, singing cowboy

Cury-Favored Grilled Flank Steak

1½ to 2 pounds flank steak
4 or 5 cloves garlic (remove green center and cut into slivers)
½ onion, cut into slivers
4 or 5 sprigs parsley with stems removed
½ to ¾ cup soy or tamari sauce (regular or low sodium)
Olive oil

Wash the flank steak and pat dry. Cut a 1-inch pocket into the flank steak about 1 inch from the end of the steak, and insert a sliver of garlic, a sliver of onion, and 1 or 2 small leaves of parsley. Continue this procedure, cutting pockets about 1 inch apart across the entire flank steak (about 20 pockets). Place the prepared steak in a shallow dish, and pour soy sauce or tamari sauce over it. Turn the steak over every 5 or 10 minutes for about 20 minutes. Prepare the grill. The fire is ready when the coals turn from flame to white hot embers, about 15 to 20 minutes. Remove the steak from the sauce, and pat it dry with paper towels. Brush it with olive oil. This helps char the outside and seal in the flavor. Grill the steak on one side for about 4 or 5 minutes. (If you can adjust the grill, sear each side of the steak for the first minute of the grilling. Then raise the grill and continue grilling at a medium setting.) Turn and grill for another 4 or 5 minutes, depending on the thickness of the cut and the degree of "rare" you like. Let the steak rest for 10 minutes, and then cut thin slices to serve.

Makes 4 to 6 servings.

Ivan Cury, radio cowboy

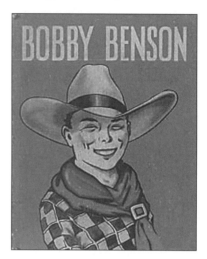

When radio's *Bobby Benson Show* of the 1930s was reincarnated in 1949, the voice behind the Cowboy Kid was Ivan Cury, who held down the fort until 1951.

Denny Miller played cowboy Duke Shannon in the TV series *Wagon Train* and was in the film *Buck and the Preacher*.

Duke Shannon's Stuffed Flank Steak

1 (2½ to 3-pound) flank steak
1 cup Worcestershire sauce
4 slices aged Swiss cheese
½ pound mushrooms, sliced
1 small bell pepper, thinly sliced

Cut a large pocket in the flank steak. Marinate the steak in Worcestershire sauce in the refrigerator overnight. Stuff the pocket with the Swiss cheese, mushrooms, and bell pepper. Close the pocket, and seal with toothpicks. Season to taste. Grill on a medium-hot fire to desired doneness. Cut the meat diagonally into thin slices.

Makes 4 servings.

Nancy and Denny Miller, actor

Diamond Farnsworth is a top Hollywood stuntman and stunt coordinator for the TV series *JAG* and *Navy: NCIS*. He was a guest on *Walker, Texas Ranger.* His list of movie credits is as long as your arm. He learned the trade from one of the best—his father, the late Richard Farnsworth (right).

Western Territory Teriyaki Flank Steak

Prepare this dish on an open or covered grill. The cooking time is about 12 minutes. Typical seasonings for Japanese teriyaki give a special flavor to this flank steak.

½   **cup soy sauce**
1   **clove garlic, minced or pressed**
1   **teaspoon ground ginger**
2   **tablespoons firmly packed brown sugar**
2   **tablespoons lemon juice**
2   **tablespoons salad oil**
1   **tablespoon instant minced onion**
¼   **teaspoon pepper**
1   **flank steak (about 1½ pounds)**

In a bowl, combine the soy sauce, garlic, ginger, brown sugar, lemon juice, oil, onion, and pepper. Pour over the steak, cover, and refrigerate for 6 hours or until the next day. Lift the steak from the marinade and drain briefly. Reserve the marinade. Place on a lightly greased grill 4 to 6 inches above a solid bed of glowing coals. Cook, turning once and basting with the reserved marinade for about 6 minutes on each side, or until done to your liking when slashed. To serve, cut the meat across the grain into thin, slanting slices.

Makes 4 servings.

Diamond Farnsworth, stuntman

Jack Ging starred as Beau McCloud on *Tales of Wells Fargo* in 1961 and was in the films *Mosby's Rangers* and *Hang 'Em High.* He was a guest on many TV westerns, such as *Bonanza, Gunsmoke,* and *Bat Masterson.* (Photo courtesy of *Wildest Westerns* magazine)

Ging-Grilled Stuffed Veal Chops

8   thick veal chops, well trimmed
8   thick slices Italian fontina cheese
8   thin slices, prosciutto
    Garlic pepper
    Lawry's seasoned salt
    Store-bought steak sauce (your choice)

Preheat the grill to high. Cut a pocket in the veal chops, and stuff each with 1 slice fontina cheese and 1 thin slice prosciutto. Seal with a toothpick. Season the chops with garlic pepper and salt. Place on a hot grill and sear about 3 or 4 minutes. Rotate once in between to achieve grill marks. Then flip the chops, and do the same on the other side. Remove from the direct heat, and put the chops on the shelf of the barbecue. Baste with the steak sauce and close the lid. After about 5 minutes, flip and baste the other side. Close the lid for 4 or 5 minutes, or until the chops are fully cooked, when the internal temperature reaches 140°. Let rest for 3 to 5 minutes in a warm spot. Then serve immediately.
    Makes 8 servings.

Apache and Jack Ging, actor

Rodeo Top Sirloin on Skewers

Nothing beats a good piece of "cow meat" thrown on the grill just until the blood stops running out, and seasoned with a little salt and pepper.

8   tablespoons butter
2   garlic cloves, minced
1   teaspoon paprika
    Salt and pepper
1½   to 2 pounds boneless beef sirloin
1   red bell pepper
8   large fresh mushrooms, if desired

In a small pan, melt the butter. Add the garlic, paprika, salt, and pepper. Simmer 1 minute. Remove from the heat. Cut the sirloin and the bell pepper into 1½-inch pieces. Skewer the beef, peppers, and mushrooms. Brush with the butter mixture. When the grill is ready, cook the skewers, turning and basting often. May be grilled with cover closed.
    Makes 4 servings.

Jim Shoulders, rodeo cowboy

Vaqueros was the Mexican term for the men who worked with cows. Texan Anglos turned the word into buckaroos.

Country music star Lynn Anderson has been competing at rodeos since the age of ten. The champion horsewoman has won at cutting competition and is a breeder of quarter horses and paints.

Wapiti Meadow Fajitas

4   onions, very thinly sliced
1   green bell pepper, julienned
1   red bell pepper, julienned
    Butter
1   marinated flank steak (try Flint's Flank-Steak Marinade on page 177)
8   flour tortillas
    Shredded Monterey Jack cheese (or other if preferred)

In a pan, sauté the onions and peppers in the butter until soft and tender. Grill the flank steak rare. Warm the tortillas on the grill. Cut the flank steak on the diagonal into very thin slices. Place the steak pieces on the tortillas. Spoon generous helpings of the onion/pepper mixture over the meat. Layer on some shredded cheese, fold the tortilla, and enjoy.
    Makes 4 servings.

Diana Bryant, Wapiti Meadow Ranch Cascade, Idaho

Carburetor Burritos

Using a different kind of cowboy horsepower. This is a specialty in New Mexico—preferably with the help of a "chopped and channeled" '57 Chevy.

    Meat
    Chopped onion
    Chopped garlic
    Minced cilantro
    Flour tortillas
    Grated Monterey Jack cheese

Use any leftover meat, such as chopped beef, chicken, pork, shrimp, or fish. Just put it in a bowl, and add some chopped onion, a little chopped garlic, and a teeny bit of fresh minced cilantro. Soften the flour tortillas for 30 seconds on an open gas burner or a real comal. (That's a black iron skillet.) Once you've seasoned the meat (you can use veggies instead), place about 2 tablespoons of the mix along the middle of a flour tortilla. Add some Monterey Jack cheese and roll it up like a cigar. Then wrap each burrito in foil, and place the burritos on the hottest part of your car's engine. By the time you get to wherever you're going, lunch will be hot and ready.

Lynn Anderson, singer and horsewoman

Cattle-drive cooks would call the trailhands to breakfast with such shouts as "Roll out! Roll out! While she's hot!" "Wake up, snakes, and bite a biscuit!" and "Grubpile! Come a-runnin', fellers!"

Dobe's Skewered Steak and Mushrooms

Here's a recipe that Dobe cooked for our youngest daughter, who's now in her fifties, when she had her birthday dinners. It was a "must" even when it was raining. It's a good recipe and quite easy—we usually double it.

—Mrs. Harry Carey Jr.

½   cup Burgundy
1   teaspoon Worcestershire sauce
1   clove garlic, peeled and sliced
½   cup salad oil
2   tablespoons ketchup
1   teaspoon sugar
½   tablespoon vinegar
    Marjoram and rosemary or a grilling
    mixture
1½ pounds sirloin steak
12 or more large mushrooms

Mix the Burgundy with the Worcestershire sauce, garlic, salad oil, ketchup, sugar, vinegar, marjoram, and rosemary. Cut the meat into squares. Wash the mushrooms. Marinate the steak and mushrooms in the wine mixture in the refrigerator for 2 hours or more. Alternate the meat and mushrooms on skewers. Grill and enjoy!

Makes 4 servings.

Harry Carey Jr., actor and author

Harry Carey Jr. was born to be a cowboy, seeing as how his dad was one of the silver screen's finest. Nicknamed Dobe, Harry Carey Jr. starred in such classics as *3 Godfathers, The Searchers, She Wore a Yellow Ribbon, The Rare Breed, Big Jake,* and *The Undefeated.* And he was in *The Mickey Mouse Club*'s serial *Spin & Marty* as ranch foreman Bill Burnett. His book *Company of Heroes,* about his career as a member of the John Ford stock company, is a must for any western film admirer.

Red Ryder Kebabs

1   cup favorite barbecue sauce
½   teaspoon garlic powder
½   teaspoon salt
    Juice of 1 lime
½   cup tequila
1   to 2 pounds thick-cut steak, cut into 1 to 2-inch cubes
1   pound mushrooms, washed, and stems trimmed
1   pound cherry tomatoes, washed
2   or 3 large zucchini, sliced into 1-inch pieces
2   large onions, cut into wedges
3   or 4 ears of corn, cut into 3 to 4-inch pieces

Mix the barbecue sauce, garlic powder, salt, lime juice, and tequila together. Place the steak cubes in the marinade, and make sure all the meat is covered. Refrigerate 8 to 10 hours or overnight. Take the meat from the refrigerator, and thread onto skewers with the mushrooms, tomatoes, zucchini, onions, and corn. Place on the grill, and baste with the leftover marinade. Grill, turning occasionally so they don't burn, and cook until done.

Makes 4 to 6 servings.

Don "Red" Barry, actor

Karl Farr (pictured here) and his brother Hugh joined the Sons of the Pioneers in 1934. The group sang in three Gene Autry films, twenty-eight Charles Starrett westerns, and thirty-nine films with cowboy pal Roy Rogers.

Don "Red" Barry made about a hundred western films from the 1930s to the 1970s. He picked up his nickname from the 1940 Republic serial *Adventures of Red Ryder*. He played such characters as Jesse James, Billy the Kid, the Tulsa Kid (seen here), the Cyclone Kid, and the Pecos Kid. Later film credits include *Rio Lobo, Bandolero, Shalako,* and *Junior Bonner.*

Campfire Grilled Meatballs

1   pound ground beef
¼   cup dry bread crumbs
1   egg, slightly beaten
¼   cup water
¾   teaspoon garlic salt
¼   teaspoon pepper
2   medium zucchini, cut into ½-inch slices
2   cups prepared spaghetti sauce
    Parmesan cheese, grated
    Garlic breadsticks (optional)

In a medium bowl, combine the ground beef, bread crumbs, egg, water, garlic salt, and pepper, mixing lightly but thoroughly. Shape into 24 (approximately 1¼-inch) meatballs. Cut four 18 x 12-inch-long sheets of heavy-duty aluminum foil. Place equal amounts of meatballs and zucchini in the center of each. Top each with ⅓ cup spaghetti sauce. Bring shorter edges of the foil together over the center; and fold down loosely to seal, allowing room for heat expansion and circulation. Fold in the open ends to seal. Place the packets on the grill over medium ash-covered coals. Grill, uncovered, for 16 to 18 minutes, or until the meatball centers are no longer pink and the zucchini is tender, turning packets over once. To serve, carefully unfold the ends and tops of the packets. Sprinkle Parmesan cheese over the meatballs. Serve with garlic breadsticks for dipping into the remaining ⅔ cup sauce.

Makes 4 servings.

Karl Farr, Sons of the Pioneers

High Chaparral's Famous Cowboy Chili-Grilled Bunkhouse Burgers

Just a taste will keep the cowboys happy and hoppin'.

3 pounds ground beef
¼ cup chili sauce
3 teaspoons jalapeño mustard
3 teaspoons regular horseradish
4 teaspoons Worcestershire sauce
3 tablespoons finely chopped onion
10 hamburger buns

In a mixing bowl, combine the ground beef, chili sauce, mustard, horseradish, Worcestershire sauce, and onion. Mix well. Form into patties and grill the burgers over medium-hot coals for about 5 minutes to seal in the flavor. Turn the burgers over, and grill till desired doneness, approximately 3 to 4 minutes longer. Serve on hamburger buns split and toasted.

Makes hamburgers for 10 hungry cowboys.

Bob Hoy, stuntman and actor

Bob Hoy has been a stuntman and actor since the 1950s with credits in the films *River of No Return, Nevada Smith, 5 Card Stud, The Outlaw Josey Wales,* and *Bronco Billy.* He played Joe Butler on *The High Chaparral.* Hoy was a stunt double for Charles Bronson and Audie Murphy, among others.

PONY EXPRESS
NATIONAL MUSEUM

The Pony Express was founded by William H. Russell, William B. Waddell, and Alexander Majors. It opened for business on April 3, 1860.

The idea was to set up a relay system by which men on horseback, carrying saddlebags of mail, would gallop at top speeds for a stretch of miles and then pass the mail to the next rider over a 2,000-mile trail. That first trip from St. Joseph, Missouri, to Sacramento, California, took nine days and twenty-three hours, while riders coming the opposite direction took eleven days and twelve hours. The horsemen rode about 250 miles in twenty-four hours.

Before its short history was over, the Pony Express had more than a hundred stations, eighty riders, and more than four hundred horses. The business went under after nineteen months, hitting the end of the trail on October 24, 1861. Its demise was tapped out with the rise of the telegraph.

During the 1950s, a portion of the neglected Pikes Peak Stables in St. Joseph, Missouri, was saved from extinction and became the Pony Express National Museum. The museum underwent dramatic renovation in 1993.

About 75 percent of the museum's exhibits are interactive. Visitors can touch the Mochila (backpack) saddles. There is also a life-size replica of a relay station.

An eighty-foot interactive diorama depicts terrain across the trail from Kansas to California. It is motion sensored with a built-in rolling thunderstorm. Meanwhile, an entire children's play area re-creates an experience similar to life as it was during the mid- to late 1800s.

Among the museum's displayed artifacts are a number of guns used during the period, one of the only surviving envelopes carried by the Pony Express, an example of a Bible carried by riders, and a jacket worn during the Buffalo Bill Wild West shows.

The Pony Express National Museum is located at 914 Penn Street in St. Joseph, Missouri. For more information, go to *www.ponyexpress.org.*

The Lone Ranger (Clayton Moore) and Silver share the arena spotlight with Dale Evans and Roy Rogers at this mid-twentieth-century cowboy gala. (Photo courtesy of Dawn Moore)

Lone Ranger's Beefy Onion Cheeseburgers

My father was the most gracious "eater." Really, he would eat anything put in front of him—praising the cook no matter how simple or unremarkable the meal was. While he was growing up as the youngest son of a real estate developer in Chicago, his family enjoyed the talents of a German cook, and he always fondly remembered her (and her meals). I imagine this was the foundation of his easy-to-please palate. Or perhaps he was just displaying polite good manners. In either case, he was a delight to cook for—always finishing everything, and I do mean everything, on his plate. And sometimes everything on yours!

He loved to barbecue (barbecue—the grandfather of grills). Hamburgers and steaks were his specialty. While this recipe is not particularly sophisticated, most of you will recognize and lovingly remember this hamburger recipe from your youth. Comfort food at its finest and one of Dad's favorites.

—Dawn Moore

2   pounds ground beef
1   envelope Lipton onion soup mix
1   egg (can substitute ½ cup water)
1   cup shredded Cheddar cheese, shredded Monterey Jack cheese, or crumbled Roquefort

In a large bowl, combine the ground beef, soup mix, and egg. Divide and shape the mixture into 12 kind-of-flat patties. Place 2 tablespoons of cheese in the center of 6 patties. Top with the remaining patties, and seal the edges tightly. (If you're not careful with this part, you'll have cheese oozing all over your grill.) Put aside the remaining cheese for the top of the burgers. Grill, barbecue, or broil until desired doneness. Serve with fresh, fluffy hamburger buns, cold crisp lettuce, thick slices of tomatoes, and lots of condiments. Enjoy!

Makes 6 servings.

Clayton Moore, actor
Submitted by daughter Dawn Moore

THE LONE RANGER CREED

I believe that to have a friend, a man must be one.

That all men are created equal and that everyone has within himself the power to make this a better world.

That God put the firewood there, but that every man must gather and light it himself.

In being prepared physically, mentally, and morally to fight when necessary for that which is right.

That a man should make the most of what equipment he has.

That "this government of the people, by the people, and for the people," shall live always.

That men should live by the rule of what is best for the greatest number.

That sooner or later . . . somewhere . . . somehow . . . we must settle with the world and make payment for what we have taken.

That all things change but the truth, and the truth alone lives on forever.

I believe in my Creator, my country, my fellowman.

The Lone Ranger finally unmasked: a grinning Clayton Moore, the man who portrayed the Lone Ranger, does a little backyard grilling (or is that burning?), in 1949. (Photo courtesy of Dawn Moore)

John Schneider (left) rode high in the 1986 TV movie *Stagecoach,* as seen here with Johnny Cash, and he was Davy Crockett in the 1994 film *Texas.* For one season he played Daniel Simon on *Dr. Quinn, Medicine Woman.*

Viola Slaughter's Grilled Weenies

Hot dogs (use the best quality, all-beef weenies you can find; I prefer Oscar Mayer)
Longhorn cheese
Bacon
Hot dog buns

Start your grill. If you're using charcoal, wait to put the hot dogs on the grill until the coals are fairly coated with white ash. (You can also cook the hot dogs on a broiler in an indoor oven at 375°.) Cut each hot dog lengthwise, but not all the way through. Insert a strip or two of longhorn cheese into the crease of each hot dog. Wrap a strip of bacon tightly around each hot dog and secure with two toothpicks. Place the hot dogs, cheese side up, on the grill, and cover the grill, leaving an opening for ventilation. After about 5 minutes of cooking, place the hot dog buns, inner side down, on the grill to toast them lightly. (If your grill is flaming up at all from the bacon drippings, be careful not to torch the buns.) When the bacon is cooked, the hot dogs should be ready to serve. Serve with your favorite condiments and side dishes. Be sure to remove the toothpicks before eating.

Betty Lynn, actress

Before she became Barney Fife's sweetheart Thelma Lou on *The Andy Griffith Show,* Betty Lynn portrayed Viola Slaughter, wife to Tom Tryon's Texas John Slaughter in the late 1950s TV series. Lynn also was a guest on the western TV series *Sugarfoot, Bronco, Wagon Train,* and *Lawman.*

Riding-Shotgun
Captain Crunch Burgers

2 pounds lean hamburger meat
1 large egg
1 cup Captain Crunch cereal, crushed in a
   bag and pounded with your hands
1 teaspoon Tony Chachere's Cajun spices

In a bowl, mix the meat, egg, cereal, and spices together, and make eight ½-pound burger patties. Grill or cook as desired. Yee-ha! Enjoy!

Variation: Captain Crunch meat loaf is almost the same, but double the recipe and add 1 can Hunt's tomato sauce on the top as you bake at 375° for 1 hour and 45 minutes.
   Makes 8 servings.

John Schneider, actor and singer

Across-the-Border
Grilled Tequila Chicken

2 shots José Cuervo Gold tequila
   Juice of ½ lemon
2 teaspoons Worcestershire sauce
4 fresh garlic cloves, smashed
½ cup finely chopped cilantro
1 (3-pound) chicken, cut in half
1 bottle F. McIntoc's pineapple barbecue
   sauce
   Great American Land and Cattle Cajun salt
   for chicken

Combine the tequila, lemon juice, Worcestershire sauce, garlic, and cilantro in a deep dish, and mix for at least 1 minute. Brush the chicken halves and cover. Let them marinate 6 to 8 hours or overnight. Just before cooking, add the pineapple sauce, and then sprinkle both sides of the chicken halves with the Cajun salt. Grill on medium-high until done, about 30 to 45 minutes.
   Makes 6 servings.

Steve Stevens Jr., rodeo cowboy

Steve Stevens Jr., son of cowboy talent agent Steve Stevens, is a rodeo bronc rider in the Pro Rodeo Cowboy Association and a horse trainer. He has also written and produced the film *Skinwalker: Curse of the Shaman.*

Johnny's Grilled Chicken Breasts Western

Plump chicken breasts, as many as you need
Kraft Free Caesar Italian dressing, enough to marinate the amount of chicken you choose

Remove the skin from the chicken breasts. Parboil the chicken for 10 minutes and drain. Place the chicken in a dish. Cover with the dressing. Cover the dish. Refrigerate for 4 to 5 hours. Grill on medium-high because the dressing burns easily. Grill about 30 minutes.

Makes as many servings as you choose.

Johnny Western,
singer/songwriter and actor

One of the top balladeers of western tunes for the past fifty years is Johnny Western, the singer and songwriter behind "The Ballad of Paladin," theme for TV's *Have Gun, Will Travel*. Western is also a member of the Country Music DJ Hall of Fame and has recorded dozens of western albums.

Sweet Sue's Blackened Chicken

This is a delicious sweet 'n' sour chicken with crispy, charred skin.

3   pounds chicken pieces (breasts, legs, and thighs; leave skin on)
Smoke's Secret Spice Rub (see recipe on page 177)
1   (16-ounce) can sweet 'n' sour sauce (such as Contadina)
¼   cup The Texan's Garlic Oil Marinade (see recipe on page 177)

Rub the chicken with Smoke's Secret Spice Rub. Combine the sweet 'n' sour sauce and The Texan's Garlic Oil Marinade. Pour this over the chicken, and marinate for at least 4 hours in the refrigerator, or overnight if possible. Get a banked fire going in a charcoal grill. Cook the chicken over the coals to crisp the skin, and then finish off over direct heat until the internal temperature is 180°.

Note: Dark meat takes longer than breast meat.

Makes 4 servings.

Rory Calhoun, actor

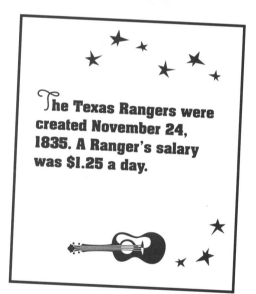

The Texas Rangers were created November 24, 1835. A Ranger's salary was $1.25 a day.

Rodeo champion Ty Murray shows his style while on his way to winning the Calgary Stampede in 1998. He was a cowboy millionaire by age twenty-three. Murray has been nine times the Professional Rodeo Cowboy Association's world champion and was seven times world champion all-around cowboy. (Photo by Mike Copeman)

Ty's Swiss Grilled Chicken

6　pieces boneless, skinless chicken breast
6　slices thick Swiss cheese
2　large tomatoes
2　avocados

Cook the chicken on the grill. When almost done, lay one Swiss cheese slice over each piece of chicken to melt. Slice the tomatoes. Peel and slice the avocados. Take the chicken off the grill when done. Top each piece of chicken with one slice of tomato and two slices of avocado. Serve immediately.

Makes 4 to 6 servings.

Ty Murray, rodeo cowboy

Knob Creek
Saloon Chicken

While we were living in New York City (during one of the Annie runs), we were invited to submit recipes to a benefit, "big deal" charity reception. I believe it was in the lobby of the Plaza. Harve submitted this recipe. A week later, while Harve was walking on Park Avenue past some big bank, a fellow ran out of the bank, caught up with Harve, grabbed his arm and said, "That was the best chicken I've ever eaten. We're trying to make it at home this weekend." The man then turned and trotted back into the bank. So I guess that's a positive testimonial.

The first time Harve created this was while he was "holding the fort" during the days I had jury duty in Independence, California.

—Veeva Presnell

Harve Presnell sang "They Call the Wind Maria" in *Paint Your Wagon* and battled Apaches in the film *The Glory Guys.*

4   **split and skinned chicken breasts**
1   **cube real butter**
3   **shots Knob Creek whiskey**
1   **Reynolds Wrap cooking pouch**
1   **(12-ounce) jar orange marmalade**

Basting Preparation:
3   **tablespoons orange marmalade**
1   **shot Knob Creek whiskey**

Remove all the "white stuff" (fat chunks, etc.) from the chicken breasts. Put the chicken breasts, butter, 3 shots of the whiskey into the cooking pouch. Place the pouch on a hot grill, close the grill, and cook the pouch for 15 minutes. Remove the pouch from the grill. Saving the juice, remove the chicken from the pouch. For the Basting Preparation, mix 3 tablespoons of marmalade with 1 shot of whiskey. (The ratio of marmalade to whiskey is 3 to 1. To make more Basting Preparation, increase proportionally.) Mix the Basting Preparation with the saved juice. Place the chicken pieces on the grill. Cook until done, turning and basting with the mixture until crispy and done. If you don't want the chicken, you can drink the basting juice.

Makes 4 servings.

Harve Presnell, singer and actor

Harve Presnell was Johnny "Leadville" Brown in *The Unsinkable Molly Brown,* both on Broadway and in the feature film.

MAIN DISHES FOR THE GRILL, BARBECUE PIT, AND SMOKER

As a kid growing up in Texas and going to the movies, Barry Corbin idolized the Durango Kid and Sunset Carson and dreamed of playing cowboys on the silver screen. His dream came true. He is featured in the films *Honkytonk Man* and *Urban Cowboy,* and his work can be seen in the TV movies *Conagher, Crossfire Trail,* and *Monte Walsh* as well as in the miniseries *Lonesome Dove.*

Chicken Corbin Skew

I ain't much of a cook, but this is a recipe everybody seems to like.

> Boneless chicken breasts (or cubed sirloin steak)
> Italian salad dressing
> Green bell pepper, sliced
> Cherry tomatoes
> Onions, quartered
> Jalapeño peppers (optional)

Marinate the chicken breasts (or cubed sirloin steak) in the Italian dressing in the refrigerator for 6 to 8 hours or overnight. When ready to cook, preheat the grill. Skewer the meat, alternating it with the bell pepper, cherry tomatoes, and onions. Cook the chicken on the grill until it's done (about three beers). Slide it onto a plate and serve hot. If you like it spicier, you can slide on a few jalapeños between the tomatoes and onions. It ain't fancy, but it's filling. With some good conversation, everybody'll feel like they've had a night at Delmonico's. Good luck and best wishes!

Barry Corbin, actor

Tenderfoot Chicken Kebabs

Marinade:
- ¾ cup vegetable oil
- ¼ cup soy sauce
- ¼ cup red wine
- 2 tablespoons Worcestershire sauce
- 4 tablespoons Tenderfoot Chicken Rub

Chicken and Vegetables:
- 2 pounds boneless, skinless chicken breast, cut into 1-inch cubes
- 12 ounces small fresh mushrooms
- 1 green bell pepper, cut into 1-inch pieces
- 1 medium onion, cut into 1-inch pieces
- 1 (20-ounce) can pineapple chunks, drained.

For the marinade, in a large bowl or plastic bag, mix the oil, soy, wine, Worcestershire sauce, and rub. Add the chicken, mushrooms, green pepper, onion, and pineapple chunks. Marinate in the refrigerator at least 6 hours or overnight. Drain and discard the marinade. Thread the chicken, vegetables, and pineapple alternately on skewers. Grill with the lid closed over medium coals for 15 to 20 minutes, or until juices run clear, turning frequently.

Variation: This is also good using shrimp with, or instead of, the chicken.
   Makes 8 servings.

Lee Henry, Rockin' L-H Chuck Wagon Eufaula, Oklahoma

The average age of cowboys on the trail was twenty to twenty-five and they made from twenty-five dollars to forty dollars a month in salary.

Herb's "Buckaroo" Chicken Breasts

6 skinless chicken breasts
1 whole garlic, sliced into slivers
½ cup Worcestershire sauce

Make small pockets in the chicken breasts. Insert the slivers of garlic in each pocket, approximately 12 slivers per breast. Place in a saucepan or other container with a top, cover with the Worcestershire sauce, place the top on the container, and refrigerate 6 to 8 hours or overnight. When ready to grill, wrap the chicken in aluminum foil, and cook on the grill for approximately 30 minutes or until cooked through. Unwrap the chicken, and lay the breasts directly on the grill for approximately 2 minutes per side. Serve with brown rice.

   Makes 6 servings.

Herb Jeffries, actor and singer

"The Bronze Buckaroo," Herb Jeffries starred in four westerns in the late 1930s, including *Harlem on the Prairie* and *Harlem Rides the Range*. But this cowboy is one heck of a jazz singer and is the voice behind the standard "Flamingo," which he recorded in front of Duke Ellington and his orchestra. (Photo by Ralph F. Merlino)

BLACK AMERICAN WEST
MUSEUM & HERITAGE CENTER

Paul Stewart founded the Black American West Museum & Heritage Center as a hobby in 1971, after vowing to find material that told the stories of the African American westerners. Today, it is one of the most comprehensive sources of material about African Americans in the West.

   In spite of their scarcity in mainstream Hollywood westerns, black cowboys were very common in the Old West. In fact, historians estimate that at least a third of all cowboys were of African descent. The museum also commemorates the contributions of other black settlers, including farmers, barbers, teachers, and politicians.

   Featured exhibits include a display on black miners, complete with original prospecting equipment, and an exhibit interpreting the role of African Americans in the settlement of Colorado. Perhaps the most notable display commemorates the Ninth and Tenth U.S. Cavalry Regiments—the famous "Buffalo Soldiers" who built forts and pursued Apaches in the years following the Civil War. Uniforms, guns, and other items belonging to the Buffalo Soldiers are included in the exhibit.

   The museum is located in a National Historic Landmark—the Victorian home of Dr. Justina Ford, the first black female licensed to practice medicine in Colorado. Dr. Ford used the home as a hospital to treat blacks, Indians, and whites who were turned away from conventional hospitals.

   The Black American West Museum & Heritage Center is located at 3091 California Street in Denver, Colorado. For more information, go to *http://www.coax.net/people/lwf/bawmus.htm*.

South Texas Barbecued Chicken

2 cups apple cider vinegar
1 cup water
1 cup Worcestershire sauce
¾ cup barbecue sauce
½ cup maple syrup
½ cup margarine
1 small to medium onion, chopped
2 tablespoons minced garlic
2 tablespoons lemon pepper
1 tablespoon sweet basil
1 tablespoon coarse black pepper
1 teaspoon salt
1 teaspoon red pepper
1 teaspoon dill weed
4 to 5 chickens, cut up or cut in half

In a large pot, mix together the vinegar, water, Worcestershire sauce, barbecue sauce, maple syrup, margarine, onion, garlic, lemon pepper, basil, black pepper, salt, red pepper, and dill weed. Bring to a rolling boil. Reduce the heat to low, and simmer for 20 minutes. This is a baste to be mopped onto chicken while it is cooking; it is not a marinade or a barbecue sauce. Place the chickens on a hot pit. Be sure the coals have burned down and you are cooking with hot coals and not with flames; have a water bottle handy to spray flames. Turn the chicken over every 15 to 20 minutes, and mop with the basting sauce, using a barbecue mop. Total cooking time is about 1½ hours. The secret to this great-tasting chicken is that it is slow-cooked over hot coals, not flames, and is turned and basted often to seal in the juices. Eat with fingers and enjoy.

Makes 8 to 10 servings.

*Dee Gibbs, Laughing Water Ranch
Fortine, Montana*

Ty Hardin starred as Bronco Layne, an ex-Confederate officer who wandered the West in the 1958–1962 TV series *Bronco.*

Bronco's Spicy Mexican Chicken

1 (8-ounce) can tomato sauce
1 tablespoon finely chopped cilantro
1 tablespoon sugar
Juice of ½ lime
½ teaspoon chili powder (or to taste)
1 teaspoon salt
⅛ teaspoon pepper
⅛ teaspoon Tabasco (or to taste)
2 broiler-fryer chickens (2 to 2½ pounds each), split in half

In a bowl, combine the tomato sauce, cilantro, sugar, lime juice, chili powder, salt, pepper, and Tabasco to make a sauce. Brush the chicken halves with the sauce, and place bone-side down on a grill about 5 inches from medium coals. Cook 20 to 30 minutes. Turn the chicken, and cook 30 to 40 minutes longer, turning and brushing frequently with the sauce. Garnish with cilantro sprigs and lime wedges, and serve with hot tortillas or cornbread and garbanzo bean salad.

Makes 4 servings.

Judy and Ty Hardin, actor

Claude Jarman Jr. won a special Oscar as a boy for *The Yearling* and played cowboys with Joel McCrea, Randolph Scott, John Wayne, and Fess Parker in such films as *Rio Grande, Hangman's Knot, The Outriders, Roughshod,* and *The Great Locomotive Chase,* and in the miniseries *Centennial.*

Marin County Grilled Chicken

It's golden.

Now that I reside in Marin County, north of the Golden Gate Bridge, my recipe for grilling is quite different. My family and I prefer chicken on a regular basis. I begin by mixing a glass of Chardonnay wine with a half stick of butter. I then put in Lawry's seasoned salt, garlic powder, and an herb of choice. I then turn on the stove burner and heat the mixture until the butter has melted, all the while stirring as the wine mixes with the butter and the other ingredients. After that is completed, I baste the chicken and put it on the grill and cook it. Several times during the cooking process I continue the basting. The results are quite delicious. The chicken is not burned or overcooked.

Claude Jarman Jr., actor

Moonlight Drunken Chicken

1   medium-size whole chicken
    Lemon pepper or barbecue rub
1   (12-ounce) can good beer or soda

Wash the chicken thoroughly. Drain. Do not dry. Rub heavily with the lemon pepper or barbecue rub inside and out. Open the can of beverage and drink half. Place the chicken on the can with the remaining half of liquid inside. Make the chicken stand upright on the can. Place in a closed barbecue pit at average heat (325°) for 2 to 2½ hours or until a wing test* shows it is done.

Note: We use mesquite wood, but you can use whatever is available. You can use a gas grill or cook it in your oven. In the oven, adjust the heat to 350°, and be sure to place the chicken in a pan that is deep enough to handle any overflow of the beverage.

Makes 2 servings.

*Wing Test: Pick up a wing with your fingers. If it breaks off, and the meat is done inside, the chicken is done.

The Moonlight Ranch Shed and Bed
Valley Mills, Texas

Maverick's
Chili Jam Chicken

- 4 chicken breasts
- ¼ cup Heinz chili sauce
- 4 ounces peach preserves or jam
- ¼ cup soy sauce
- 2 tablespoons crystallized ginger (I use Trader Joe's)
- 1 tablespoon packed brown sugar
  Splash of balsamic vinegar
- 4 pineapple rings

Rinse the chicken breasts in cool water, and then pat dry. In a large bowl, mix the chili sauce, preserves, soy, ginger, brown sugar, and vinegar together very well to make a marinade. Place the chicken in the marinade in the refrigerator for 6 to 8 hours or overnight. Grill on high until completely cooked. Cut open to check for doneness. Throw the pineapple rings on the grill for the last few minutes of cooking. Use the leftover marinade to baste the pineapple rings, and use them as a garnish on top of the chicken.

Note: This recipe has no garlic or onions, because Mr. G. doesn't like them, but you can be a maverick and add them if you like.

Makes 4 servings.

James Garner, actor

Although most TV fans recollect James Garner as a roving gambler in his classic *Maverick* series, one of his personal favorites was his role as sheriff in 1914 Nichols, Arizona, in the short-lived *Nichols* (1971). In the first western (*Maverick*), he rode a horse; in the second (*Nichols*) he rode a motorcycle and drove a car. Garner also starred in the western films *Duel at Diablo, Hour of the Gun, Support Your Local Sheriff!, Support Your Local Gunfighter,* and *Maverick* (1994).

John Pickard starred from 1958 to 1959 as Captain Shank Adams in the TV series *Boots and Saddles,* set in the Arizona territory of the 1870s. Pickard also played the role of Frank Ross, Kim Darby's father who is killed in the opening of *True Grit.* Other film credits include *Little Bighorn, Arrowhead, Chisum, and Charro!,* and lots of episodes of TV westerns.

Chicken Pickard

- 4 cloves garlic, mashed
- 1 leaf basil
- 3 tablespoons soy sauce
  Juice of 1 lemon
- 2 tablespoons vinegar
- 1 tablespoon packed brown sugar
- 4 tablespoons orange and/or apple juice (use more or less to taste)
- 4 tablespoons white wine (optional)
  Salt and pepper
- 1 whole chicken

In a large pot, for the marinade combine the garlic, basil, soy, lemon juice, vinegar, brown sugar, juice, wine, and salt and pepper. Add the chicken to the marinade. Let the chicken marinate for two hours or more in the refrigerator. Then grill until your heart's content.

Note: I would use the same marinade, without the vinegar and brown sugar, to marinate hamburgers. When I make the patty, I include onions, and then marinate. I usually add barbecue sauce after cooking, but while the burgers are still warming on the back of the grill.

John Pickard, actor
Submitted by nephew Bob Pickard

Rodeo Kate's Dijon and Lemon Chicken

This is an easy recipe, and I have yet to see anyone not be able to do it.

- 2 tablespoons cooking oil
- 1 tablespoon Dijon mustard
- 1 tablespoon lemon juice
- 1½ teaspoons lemon-pepper seasoning mix
- 1 teaspoon dried oregano, crushed
- ⅛ teaspoon ground red pepper for more bite (optional)
- 2 to 2½ pounds chicken (meaty pieces work best)

Combine the oil, mustard, lemon juice, seasoning mix, oregano, and red pepper, and mix well. After the grill has heated up, grill the chicken 5 minutes. Turn the chicken, and grill another 5 minutes. Brush the chicken with the glaze, and then turn and brush the other side with the glaze. Grill each side 10 minutes longer. (Be sure to brush the glaze on each time you turn the chicken.) Brush the glaze on one more time, and cook about 5 minutes more, or until the chicken is cooked through.

Well, that is all there is. The total cooking time is about 25 minutes. It leaves plenty of time to do chores and so on after cooking and eating.

Makes 4 to 5 servings.

Rodeo Kate, Texas Trailhands

Rodeo Kate is the top hand for fiddlin' with the Texas Trailhands.

MAIN DISHES FOR THE GRILL, BARBECUE PIT, AND SMOKER

Country singer Tracy Byrd hails from Beaumont, Texas, and favors cowboy hats, shirts, boots, and jeans. As he sings in his hit song, "A cowboy ain't no ordinary man."

Tracy Byrd's Grilled Game Hens

2   whole Rock Cornish game hens, dressed
5   jalapeño pepper slices
5   slices bacon

Marinade:
¾   cup oil
¾   cup honey
½   cup Tracy's Sweet and Tangy Marinade (found at select Kroger stores and Wal-Mart Supercenters nationwide)
⅓   cup lemon juice
⅛   teaspoon black pepper

Clean the birds well, rinse, and pat dry. Wrap the jalapeño slices in bacon, and place them in the body cavity of each bird. Place the birds in a glass baking dish. Combine the oil, honey, marinade, lemon juice, and black pepper for the marinade, and pour over the birds. Marinate in the refrigerator for at least 8 hours. Place heavy-duty aluminum foil on a grill grate, and grill the birds slowly over low heat, turning and basting often until done, about 40 minutes to 1 hour.

Note: On charcoal, hens cook for nearly an hour, but a gas grill might cook a little faster.

Makes 2 servings.

Tracy Byrd, singer
From Eat Like a Byrd, *published by Interactive Blvd*

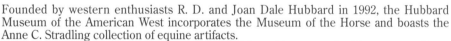

HUBBARD MUSEUM
OF THE AMERICAN WEST

Founded by western enthusiasts R. D. and Joan Dale Hubbard in 1992, the Hubbard Museum of the American West incorporates the Museum of the Horse and boasts the Anne C. Stradling collection of equine artifacts.

The institution's mission is to preserve, exhibit, and interpret significant art, artifacts, and information related to horses and the American West.

Visitors to the museum are greeted by Dave McGary's *Free Spirits at Noisy Water,* an elaborate display of seven larger-than-life statues commemorating such popular horse breeds as the Morgan and the Appaloosa. Other items on display include bits, bridles, saddles, and an impressive collection of horse-drawn conveyances, including stage-coaches, wagons, and carriages.

A Smithsonian affiliate, the Hubbard Museum sponsors numerous exhibits of art and photography. Works by noted western artists Gordon Snidow and Gary Morton are on permanent display, and every November the Fall American Photo Show offers prizes for the best western-themed photographs.

The annual Lincoln County Cowboy Symposium is held at the Hubbard every October and features programs devoted to western music and lifestyles as well as art.

Located at 841 Highway 70 West in Ruidoso Downs, New Mexico, the museum is adjacent to Ruidoso Downs racetrack and the Billy the Kid Scenic Byway Visitors Center—all in historic Lincoln County. For more details, go to *www.hubbardmuseum.com.*

Anne Lockhart is an expert horsewoman who has been a champion in a variety of rodeo events. The daughter of June Lockhart of *Lassie* fame, Anne was in the 2004 TV movie *The Trail to Hope Rose*. She also portrayed Sheba in the outer space "western" *Battlestar Galactica*.

Orange Sunset Grilled Quail

4   quail
    Salt and pepper
6   tablespoons butter or margarine
¼   teaspoon orange peel
    Honey
4   slices bacon

Split the quail in half down their backs, and rinse thoroughly. Lay them out flat on a plate. Salt and pepper to taste. In a saucepan, melt the butter or margarine over medium heat. Add the orange peel, and reduce the heat to low for another 1 to 2 minutes. Remove from the heat, and brush the mixture liberally on the quail. Drizzle the quail with the honey. Place a piece of bacon on top of each bird, and secure with a toothpick. Place the quail on the perimeter of the grill so they will cook slowly. Turn frequently, and baste with butter with each rotation. Drizzle the honey as often as you feel necessary.
    Makes 2 servings.

Anne Lockhart, actress

Lee's Smoked Quail

12 whole quail, dressed
2   tablespoons olive oil
2   tablespoons Bronze Legend Rub
6   strips thick bacon

Wash the quail inside and out with cold water, and dry with paper towels. Brush the birds with olive oil, and lightly dust with the rub. Go easy with the rub or it will burn. Cut the bacon slices in half. Place the quail breast side up, and drape a half slice of bacon over each breast. Smoke on a water smoker at 250° for about 2 hours, or until the bacon is crisp and the legs move easily in the joint.
    Makes 2 servings.

*Lee Henry, Rockin' L-H Chuck Wagon
Eufaula, Oklahoma*

MAIN DISHES FOR THE GRILL, BARBECUE PIT, AND SMOKER

Grilled Dove Breast Shish Kebabs Kanaly

I have been a sport hunter for most of my life, and I especially enjoy "wing shooting" upland and migratory game birds. Several years ago this recipe was shared with me while on a dove hunting trip in Argentina. The recipe is not complicated and can be assembled many hours ahead of time if desired. We've got plenty of doves all over America, so it's not necessary to travel all the way to Argentina, but you will need to be a good shot or have a generous friend willing to offer his day's shooting limit for this great meal. Wishing you fun and safe wing shooting and a great meal to honor the day.

20   dove breasts

Marinade:
2	tablespoons vinegar
½	cup extra virgin olive oil
1	teaspoon salt
1	teaspoon coarsely ground pepper
4	cloves garlic, finely diced
1	pound sliced bacon
6	green bell peppers
40	small mushrooms
6	yellow or white onions
40	cherry tomatoes

Clean and wash the doves. Using a sharp boning knife, remove the flesh from both sides of the breastbone, leaving you with two small fillets of dove meat. Marinate the breasts in a mixture of vinegar, olive oil, salt, pepper, and garlic in the refrigerator for several hours. You can't over-marinate. I often will keep the breasts in the marinade overnight. Cut the bacon in 2-inch strips. Cut the bell pepper in 2-inch cubes. Clean and trim the feet off the mushrooms. Peel and quarter the onions. Rinse the cherry tomatoes and remove the stems.

Steve Kanaly was a star of TV's *Dallas* as Ray Krebbs, but he also played cowboys in the films *The Life and Times of Judge Roy Bean, My Name Is Nobody,* and *Leaving the Land,* as well as in the TV movie *The Cowboy and the Movie Star.* He is an expert marksman, skilled at skeet and trap shooting.

There are many varieties of skewers that will work equally as well, but I prefer using a bamboo or wooden skewer. Be sure that you soak them in cold water before assembly. Begin by holding the skewer in your hand and piercing a tomato, followed by a pepper slice, an onion slice, a dove breast, a slice of bacon, and a mushroom. Slide all the ingredients to the bottom of the skewer, and repeat the process in the same order. Bunch the ingredients together tightly, and fill the entire skewer.

I prefer to grill the kebabs on a natural grill of mesquite wood. Because of the bacon you may want to be careful not to have the fire too hot. If you prefer, a gas grill will serve the purpose as well. The cooking time will vary depending on your grill, but the kebabs should require no more than 10 to 12 minutes total cooking time. This dish is great by itself, but I often serve it with rice and a fresh garden salad with sliced avocado. I have enjoyed preparing this dish on hunting trips and film locations for many years and have yet to meet anyone who didn't think that it was one of the best dinners he ever enjoyed—even when he thought he would never enjoy eating a wild game meal.

Makes 8 servings.

Steve Kanaly, actor

Cowboy cook Leon Helton in action.

A former member of the Sons of the Pioneers, Rusty Richards is a real cowboy as well as a singer and songwriter of western songs. He is still a member of the PRCA and competes in senior roping events. He also breeds and trains quarter horses.

Cooking for a Lot of Folks

My friend Leon Helton devised one of the most interesting ways I've ever seen for cooking for a lot of people. Leon has for many years been the man who makes it all happen in the maverick camp on the famous Rancheros Visitadores Ride in the mountains above Santa Barbara, California.

I asked Leon if he'd mind sharing how he can invite eight hundred riders, plus musicians, guests, and wranglers, and feed them all at once. I have seen him and his helpers do it year after year for many years. He graciously agreed to let me share it here.

The pictures show an almost identical copy of Leon's shed, which was built by Billy Weddington for our historic Portola Ride here in Orange County. The "VP" stands for Viaje de Portola (Trek of Portola). Billy has added an axle so that it can be transported to different parts of the ranch.

The frame is made of two-inch steel pipe and covered with corrugated sheet iron attached with self-tapping screws. The front has a swing-out boom from which the meat is hung. Inside toward the back of the shed, Leon has added some more sheet iron that is curved above the fire to send the heat shooting out the front right through the meat, which has been rubbed with Leon's seasoning recipe which consists of:

12	ounces Lawry's seasoned salt
12	ounces black pepper
12	ounces granulated garlic
6	ounces white pepper
6	ounces ground sage
1½	ounces dry mustard
1½	ounces curry powder

The boom swings from over a table where the ribs are loaded and unloaded, and back in front of the fire. Leon made the baskets, which can be seen in the pictures, but he thought you could also purchase them already made. They should be sprayed thoroughly with Pam before loading, and Leon loads them two deep with the meat side out. He cooks them about 20 minutes a side, and then turns them bone side out, which doesn't take nearly that long to finish.

To keep the ribs from drying out and to add a great flavor, they are repeatedly sprayed with a sauce that is made of:

> One-half soy sauce
> One-quarter teriyaki sauce
> One-quarter Sauterne wine

Care must be taken to keep away from the intense heat coming through the ribs. Leon said he had a moustache when he first built the shed, and the first time he used it he singed his mustache, his sideburns, and his eyebrows.

Leon makes the sauce up ahead of time in a gallon jug and transfers it into spray bottles, which he and his crew use repeatedly during the cooking.

Leon says he has cooked goats, deer, chickens, turkeys, and virtually anything else you can think of in this way, and it always turns out great.

During my many years with the Sons of the Pioneers, we got in on lots of great barbecues. People would invite us to their homes, and so on. We also played lots of big fairs, and Dale Warren and I used to love to sample all the great food between shows.

Once during a television special with Roy and Dale, which took place on a ranch, we had a wonderful choir from a Korean orphanage as guests. They sang beautifully. Roy and Dale wanted it to be a memorable experience for them, so they put on a western barbecue complete with a bucking bronc. When it came time to eat, Roy and Dale put on their aprons and served the food themselves. It was a great treat for all of us to be served by Roy Rogers and Dale Evans.

As for Leon's barbecue, I would think you could build a smaller version, but keep in mind that in Leon's version the heat comes out of the top three feet, and he cautions that you need to keep the shed tight so that all the heat comes through the meat. Have fun.

Rusty Richards, singer/songwriter

Rusty Richards's friend Leon Helton uses a unique shed that allows him to cook for eight hundred hungry cowboys and cowgirls at one time in the maverick camp on the Rancheros Visitadores Ride in the mountains above Santa Barbara, California.

Among singer/songwriter Ed Bruce's compositions are "Mamas Don't Let Your Babies Grow Up to Be Cowboys," "The Last Cowboy Song," and "Theme from Bret Maverick." As an actor, he has cowboyed in *The Chisolms* and *The Return of Frank and Jesse James.* He was costar of *Bret Maverick* as Sheriff Tom Guthrie (left), with James Garner, as seen here. He also played a curmudgeonly rancher in the film *The Outfitters.*

Best Pork Butt

3 cups apple juice
½ cup apple brandy
1 container Bare-Back Pig Rub
1 (5 to 6-pound) pork butt, trimmed
   Sliced apples and oranges (optional)

In a saucepan, mix the apple juice and apple brandy. Heat until blended, keep warm, and use to baste at 1-hour intervals while the pork is cooking. Sprinkle the rub on the pork butt. Make sure the pork is covered completely. Cover and place in the refrigerator 6 to 8 hours or overnight. If you can't wait that long, wait at least 2 hours before cooking. Let the meat sit at room temperature for at least 30 minutes before cooking. Place the pork on a smoker grill rack over a water pan. In the water pan you can add sliced apples and oranges for a nice fruity steam. Smoke the meat with the lid down over medium coals, turning every hour, for 6 to 8 hours, or until the bone wiggles easily when pushed. After 3 hours, baste with the apple juice and apple brandy mixture at 1-hour intervals when you turn meat. Let the meat sit covered for 20 to 30 minutes. Slice, pull, or chop the meat and serve.

Makes 6 to 8 servings.

Lee Henry, Rockin' L-H Chuck Wagon
Eufaula, Oklahoma

Lone Star Belt Buckles Barbecued Pork Shoulder

1 (7 to 9-pound) square-cut Boston butt pork shoulder
   Soy sauce

Dry Rub:
1 to 3 tablespoons cayenne
1 tablespoon chili powder
1 tablespoon garlic salt
1 teaspoon black pepper
1 teaspoon packed brown sugar
1 teaspoon lemon pepper
1 teaspoon dry mustard
1 teaspoon cumin
1 teaspoon ground thyme
   Pinch of cinnamon

Lightly coat the pork shoulder with the soy sauce. To make the dry rub, mix together the cayenne to taste, chili powder, garlic salt, black pepper, brown sugar, lemon pepper, dry mustard, cumin, thyme, and cinnamon for the dry rub. Sprinkle the mix on the shoulder, and rub it into the pork. Wrap the meat in plastic wrap. Refrigerate for 24 hours.

If possible, use an indirect heat source to cook. I use a 50-gallon water-heater tank converted to a barrel cooker with the fire at one end and the meat at the opposite end. Use charcoal, adding hickory chunks over time. Cook at 225° for approximately 1 hour per pound, or until the interior meat temperature is 170°.

Makes 12 to 15 servings.

Ed Bruce, singer/songwriter and actor

He was born in Beverly Hills, but he became a real-life cowboy. Richard Farnsworth worked as a stunt double for such movie stars as Gary Cooper, Roy Rogers, and Steve McQueen. He acted in such films as *The Cowboys, Red River, Arrowhead,* and *The Grey Fox.* He was an Oscar nominee for his work in *Comes a Horseman* (1978) and *The Straight Story* (1999).

The Grey Fox's Double-Spicy Pork Tenderloin

You can use either a whole pork tenderloin or thick loin chops. The spicy flavor comes from the combination of the chili powder, mustard, and honey.

¼　cup prepared mustard
¼　cup honey
¼　teaspoon salt
¼　teaspoon chili powder
1　(2½ to 3-pound) pork tenderloin or 4 to 6 loin chops, cut 1 inch thick

In a bowl, combine the mustard, honey, salt, and chili powder to make a marinade. Spoon the mixture over the pork. Cover and refrigerate for 4 hours or until the next day. Lift the meat from the marinade and drain briefly. Reserve the marinade. Place on a lightly greased grill 4 to 6 inches above a solid bed of glowing coals. Cook on either an open or covered grill. If using chops, put the thickest ones on first. Cook, turning and basting occasionally, for 45 to 60 minutes for tenderloin, or 30 to 40 minutes for chops, or until meat is no longer pink in the center when slashed. To serve, cut the meat across the grain in thin, slanting slices.

Makes 4 to 6 servings.

Richard Farnsworth, stuntman and actor

Cheryl's Barbecued Pork with Peach and Pineapple Salsa

½   cup apricot jam
½   cup jalapeño jam
2   tablespoons rice vinegar
2   tablespoons tomato paste
1   plus 1 tablespoons olive oil, plus more for grilling
1   (1½-pound) pork tenderloin, halved lengthwise and cut into 16 cubes
1   medium red onion, cut into 8 wedges (halve the onion lengthwise and peel, but leave root end intact; cut each half into 4 wedges)
2   small zucchini, ends cut off and each zucchini cut into 4 pieces (about 1 inch thick)
    Coarse salt
    Freshly ground pepper
    Red pepper flakes (optional)
    Peach and Pineapple Salsa (recipe follows)

Heat the grill to medium-high. Mix the jams, vinegar, tomato paste, and 1 tablespoon olive oil. Assemble long skewers, alternating pork cubes with 2 onion wedges and 2 zucchini slices. Brush the skewers with the remaining 1 tablespoon olive oil. Add the salt and pepper. Lightly oil the grates. Place the skewers on the grill, cover, and cook, turning occasionally, until grill marks are visible, about 6 to 8 minutes. Open the grill, baste the skewers with sauce, cover, and cook, turning the skewers and basting every couple of minutes until the pork is no longer pink in the center. The meat and vegetables should be nicely glazed in 4 to 8 minutes. Red pepper flakes can be added for additional kick. Serve with Peach and Pineapple Salsa.

Makes 4 servings.

Peach and Pineapple Salsa:
2   peaches, halved and pitted, but not peeled
1   tablespoon melted butter
3   slices cored fresh pineapple, cut into ½-inch-thick slices (canned may be used)
1   cup seeded and diced plum tomatoes
1   or 2 jalapeños, minced (seeds and ribs should be removed for less heat)
¼   cup chopped fresh cilantro
¼   cup chopped fresh basil
3   tablespoons fresh lime juice
    Coarse salt and freshly ground pepper

Brush the peaches with the melted butter. Place the peaches and pineapple slices on the grill or under a broiler until charred and softened. Peel the peaches, and dice both the peaches and the pineapple. In a medium bowl, combine the peaches, pineapple, plum tomatoes, jalapeños, cilantro, basil, and lime juice. Season with coarse salt and ground pepper to taste.

Variations: You may substitute half a mango, peeled and diced, for either the peaches or the pineapple. Red pepper flakes or 1 diced habanero chile can be added for additional kick. This salsa is also great with eggs, chicken, and fish.

Cheryl Rogers-Barnett, cowboy princess

Cheryl Rogers-Barnett is the daughter of Roy Rogers and Dale Evans and appeared in her father's film *Trail of Robin Hood.* Among her childhood pets were Trigger and Bullet. She regularly rides in the Tournament of Roses Parade and is the author of *Cowboy Princess: Life with My Parents.*

Burnette Grilled Pork Chops

They'll make you smiley.

> Pork loin chops, at least ½ inch thick
> French salad dressing
> 1 teaspoon Worcestershire sauce
> Tabasco
> 2 tablespoons peanut oil
> (or light vegetable oil)
> MSG
> Ground pepper

Build a wood fire, and when it has burned down to a nice bed of hot coals, place your grate close to the fire. In a bowl, combine the French dressing, Worcestershire sauce, Tabasco to taste, peanut oil, MSG, and ground pepper, and mix well. With a fork in one hand and a cloth or brush to paint with in the other hand, constantly turn and paint the chops as they cook, until they are a lovely red-brown tone and thoroughly done. You may enjoy using the same sauce for grilling chickens cut in half and cooked the same way. When these are done fairly well on the outside, well-browned over your open fire, do not continue to cook until dried out, but place them in a covered roaster, and finish cooking them in the oven. Smiley emphasized that he believed it a mistake to cook anything over a fire until it is completely done, because the heat draws out all the moisture. He preferred to finish the job in the oven, so all the flavor would not be on the outside of the meat.

Dallas and Smiley Burnette, actor
From The Smiley Burnettes Cookbook

Dallas and Smiley Burnette published a cookbook in 1953.

Cowboy Chops

> 1 (8-ounce) jar peach jelly
> ½ cup packed brown sugar
> 1 teaspoon Worcestershire sauce
> 5 or 6 jalapeño slices, with seeds removed and finely chopped
> 2 teaspoons honey
> 6 butterfly pork chops
> Salt and pepper

In a medium saucepan, mix the jelly, brown sugar, Worcestershire sauce, jalapeño slices, and honey, and heat to a slight boil. Remove from the heat, and stir well. Place the chops in a pan. Add the salt and pepper to taste. Spoon 1 tablespoon sauce on top of each pork chop, and spread evenly. Cover the pan with foil, and place in the refrigerator for 2 to 3 hours to marinate. Spread the remaining sauce on the chops, and you're ready to grill.

Makes 6 servings.

Donnie Gay, rodeo cowboy

Pork Chops de Vile

My handle in the Single Action Shooting Society (SASS) is "Captain Vile," hence the recipe name. As I traveled America on location as a professional stuntman for the last forty years, one of my favorite places became Santa Fe, New Mexico, with its delicious and spicy cuisine.

My recipe consists of center-cut pork chops marinated in Embasa brand green chile salsa. It permeates and thoroughly tenderizes the meat while slowly cooking the chops on the barbecue grill. I start heating up some seasoned fajita fries and S&S brand Santa Fe-Style beans and creamed corn, to complement the chops. A slice of garlic bread is my finishing touch. After the meal, a flan, a Mexican custard covered in caramel and whipped cream, is served for dessert. A meal like this always reminds me of my fond times spent in all the fabulous restaurants in Santa Fe.

Neil Summers, stuntman

Stuntman and stunt coordinator Neil Summers has worked in films for forty years. He has been a stunt double for Bruce Boxleitner, Keith Carradine, Warren Oates, and James Hampton, to name a few. Among his credits are *The Quick and the Dead, The High Chaparral, Duel at Diablo, Ulzana's Raid, Chato's Land, Young Guns, MacKenna's Gold,* and *Rio Lobo.*

THE BEVERLY AND JIM ROGERS
Museum of Lone Pine Film History

The Beverly and Jim Rogers Museum of Lone Pine Film History, which began construction in early 2005, will be a small but highly specialized museum celebrating films made in the area of Lone Pine and Inyo County, California, where hundreds of westerns and other films have been made.

The museum evolved naturally from the success of the Lone Pine Film Festival that began in 1990. Its exhibits and educational programs will highlight and document the community's partnership with Hollywood studios from early silent films through today and provide visitors with detailed information on exploring, appreciating, and preserving the local landscape.

The museum exhibits will focus on such specific areas as silver screen heroes, women of the West, the *Wells Fargo* and *Lone Ranger* TV series, Hopalong Cassidy, John Wayne, Roy Rogers and Dale Evans, Gene Autry, Randolph Scott, Audie Murphy, and Zane Grey.

Attention will also be paid to specific films and their locations, stuntmen, movie posters, cowboy collectibles, and artists who have interpreted the Lone Pine landscape. On display will be the trappings of the western stars, such as their cowboy hats, saddles, guns, and spurs.

The Beverly and Jim Rogers Museum of Lone Pine Film History is located on South Main Street in Lone Pine, California. The annual film festival runs from Friday through Sunday on the weekend of Columbus Day. For more information, go to *www.lonepinefilmhistory museum.org/museum.htm.*

Tanya Tucker is a horsewoman going back to the days of her Texas childhood. Among her many song titles are "It's a Cowboy Lovin' Night," "Texas (When I Die)," "Pecos Promenade," and "San Antonio Stroll." She had a cameo in the film *Jeremiah Johnson*.

Rodney's Backyard Party Ribs

My favorite boot maker, Rodney Ammons (Ammons Boots in Nashville, Tennessee), shared with me his trick for making the best baby-back ribs I've ever had.

6   pounds of baby back ribs
    Beer
    Barbecue Sauce (recipe follows)

Place the ribs in a disposable roaster and cover with beer. Seal with aluminum foil and put in a 375° oven until the beer boils. Remove the ribs, brush with the Barbecue Sauce, and grill. Brush the ribs with the sauce frequently while grilling.

Makes about 12 servings.

Barbecue Sauce:
All great backyard barbecue sauces are improvised. Here's an easy one:

½   cup ketchup or tomato sauce
1   medium onion, finely chopped
    Salt
    Crushed horseradish
    Garlic
    Red pepper
1   tablespoon prepared mustard
1   tablespoon (approximate) Worcestershire, A-1, soy sauce, or whatever you have in the fridge
2   tablespoons brown sugar or honey (optional)

Combine the ketchup, onion, salt and horseradish and garlic and red pepper to taste, the mustard, and Worcestershire sauce in a saucepan, and cook until the onions are tender. If you like a sweet sauce, add brown sugar or honey.

Tanya Tucker, singer

Max Terhune (left) made sixty-six western films in the 1930s and '40s, starting off as Lullaby in more than twenty films of the *Three Mesquiteers* series. He made two dozen *Range Busters* films as Alibi and rode sidekick to Johnny Mack Brown in about eight movies.

Max Terhune is also remembered for his ventriloquism work with his wooden pal Elmer Sneezewood.

Bob's Smoked Ribs

2   or 3 slabs pork ribs
    Dale's steak seasoning
    Tony Chachere's Creole seasoning

Take the pork rib slabs, marinate them for about 30 minutes with Dale's steak seasoning, and then sprinkle with Tony Chachere's Creole seasoning. Preheat the oven to 300°. Bake the ribs in the oven for 1 hour and 30 minutes. While they are in the oven, start the fire in your smoker. Smoke the ribs for 2 hours at 250°, or until you think they are right. Baste the ribs about every 30 minutes with Dale's steak seasoning. Believe me, they are great.

Max Terhune, actor

MAIN DISHES FOR THE GRILL, BARBECUE PIT, AND SMOKER

Stagecoach
Grilled Short Ribs

1   pound (approximate) short ribs per person
    (this recipe can also be used for lamb
    shanks)
    Salt and pepper
2   cups finely chopped onions (sweet onions,
    such as Maui, taste best)
¾   cup ketchup
2   tablespoons white vinegar
2   tablespoons Worcestershire sauce
2   tablespoons soy sauce
½   cup sugar
¾   cup water

Start by placing the short ribs in a shallow pan. Sprinkle lightly with salt and pepper. Cover the ribs with the onions. In a separate bowl, mix the ketchup, white vinegar, Worcestershire sauce, soy sauce, sugar, and water. Pour the mixture over the short ribs. Place the pan in the refrigerator for approximately 30 minutes. Then remove the ribs one by one from the pan, and place them on the grill. Pour any sauce remaining in the pan over the short ribs. Cook slowly over a low to medium heat until they reach your preferred degree of doneness. Enjoy.

Frances Dee and Joel McCrea, actress and actor
Submitted by grandson Wyatt McCrea

Actors Joel McCrea and Frances Dee were husband and wife for fifty-seven years. Here they are seen in Paramount's 1937 western, *Wells Fargo*. Dee made more than fifty films and starred in *Four Faces West* and *Gypsy Colt*.

Riders in the Sky carry on the western music traditions of such legendary cowboy singers as Gene Autry, Roy Rogers, and the Sons of the Pioneers. The boys include (clockwise from back) Woody Paul (King of the Cowboy Fiddlers), Too Slim ("a Righteous Tater"), Ranger Doug (Idol of American Youth), and Joey (the CowPolka King). The fellers can be heard on their Grammy-winning album *Woody's Roundup Featuring Riders in the Sky,* a companion album to the soundtrack of *Toy Story 2.*

Cowpolka King's Barbecued Ribs

(with special thanks to Abilene Anderson)

Start with a rack of lean pork spare ribs with the excess fat trimmed and the brisket area on the back side trimmed completely. One typically must do some additional trimming, since some meat shops do not get too fancy with spare ribs. Prior to cooking, season both sides of the spare ribs with salt, coarse ground pepper, and celery seed. Let the ribs sit refrigerated for several hours to allow the meat to absorb the seasonings. If some of the seasoning gets rubbed off the meat, you may have to add some additional seasoning while the meat is on the grill.

Spray your grill's grates with nonstick cooking spray, and heat the grill. Turn the grill to low heat. Place the ribs on the grill, meat side down first, and close the cover. Turn the ribs over for the first time when the juices start to appear on the back side. Cook for approximately 45 to 60 minutes, or until the ribs are a rich golden brown on both sides. Turn the racks as required during cooking. Cut a bone from one rack while on the grill to check for doneness and taste. Be careful when doing this since ribs have a tendency to flare up and can burn because of the fat content that cooks away and drips onto the coals/fire. A grill where air supply can be controlled is preferred in order to control flare-ups and achieve the desired results.

Joey the Cowpolka King, Riders in the Sky

Tongue-Slappin' Baby Back Ribs

1   container Bare-Back Pig Rub
2   to 3 pounds (more or less) baby back ribs or rib slabs
3   cups Mopping Sauce (recipe follows)

Generously sprinkle the ribs on both sides with the rub. Place the ribs in a covered pan or wrap in foil, and refrigerate overnight. Let the ribs warm to room temperature, and place in a smoker at 210° to 230° for 5 to 6 hours, turning once an hour and moistening with Mopping Sauce each time you turn them. Take the ribs off the heat, mop again, and sprinkle lightly with the rub mix. Cover tightly in foil, and let rest for 20 minutes before serving.

Note: Ribs are perfect served like this, but if your guests prefer, you can serve a favorite barbecue sauce on the side.

Makes 4 to 6 servings.

Mopping Sauce:
1   cup dry rub (the one you are using)
1   cup water
1   cup vinegar
¼   cup Worcestershire sauce
¼   cup oil or butter
    Juice of 1 lemon

Combine in a saucepan the dry rub, water, vinegar, Worcestershire sauce, oil or butter, and lemon juice. Bring to a boil, and then keep at a simmer for mopping the ribs.

Lee Henry, Rockin' L-H Chuck Wagon Eufaula, Oklahoma

Outlaws-on-the-Lam Grilled Lamb

¼   cup olive oil
1   cup red wine (Merlot or Cabernet—one you
    would drink rather than just cook with)
1   tablespoon rosemary
2   or 3 cloves garlic, mashed or slivered
    Leg of lamb (about 5 pounds), butterflied

Combine the olive oil, wine, rosemary, and garlic to make your marinade. Place the lamb in a large, flat pan, and cover with the marinade. Place in the fridge, and leave for 3 to 6 hours, turning now and then. Take the lamb from the fridge 30 minutes before cooking.

Get your grill ready, and place the lamb on the grill, fat side down first. When the juice starts running out of the top side, turn the lamb over and cook until rare or medium rare at the most—never well-done. (Dad would say, "The minute it gets well-done, you have blown the whole thing.") Check it carefully. It won't need to cook longer than about 30 minutes since it is already tenderized from marinating. To serve, slice to any desired thickness across the grain like a loaf of bread.

Guy Williams
Submitted by Guy Williams Jr.

Grilled Venison Steaks Western

Have appetite, will travel a long way for these.

Venison steaks, ¾ to 1 inch thick
Minced garlic
Olive oil
Garlic pepper

Cut 3 or 4 slits in each steak. Fill the slits with minced garlic. Place in a dish, and cover with olive oil. Marinate for 4 to 5 hours in the refrigerator. Just before placing on the grill, sprinkle with the garlic pepper. Grill on medium heat because venison has less fat than beef, and you don't want it to dry out.

Johnny Western, singer/songwriter

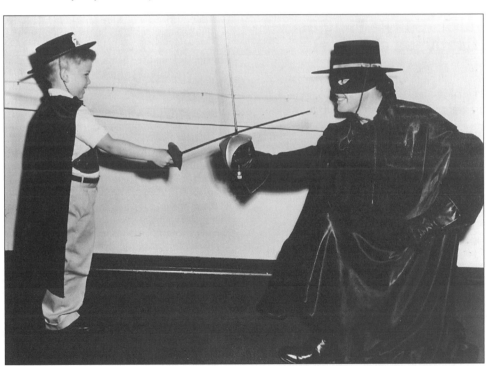

Guy Williams was beloved as TV's Zorro. Here he matches swords with his young son, Guy Williams Jr. In 1964 Williams portrayed Will Cartwright in five episodes of *Bonanza*. (Photo courtesy of Guy Williams Jr.)

The Man in Black loved cowboys. He sang the theme for TV's *The Rebel* and was a guest star in that series. He also paid a visit to *Dr. Quinn, Medicine Woman* and starred in the TV movies *Stagecoach* and *The Last Days of Frank and Jesse James.* Here, he stars opposite Kirk Douglas (right) in the 1971 film *A Gunfight.* Cash also sang the theme song to the John Wayne film *The Sons of Katie Elder.*

Johnny Cash's Barbecued Mexican-Style Fiery Goat (Cabrito en el Fuego)

This is not grilled; more like pit barbecue.

1   small-size (12 to 20 pounds) young goat, skinned and cleaned. Heart, liver, and kidneys may be used also. Suckling pig may be substituted if a goat is not available.
Salt and whole black peppercorns
5   onions
10 cloves garlic
10 jalapeño peppers, sliced
Water and beer
Vegetable oil
½   cup sugar
3   bay leaves
3   tablespoons chili powder
1   tablespoon cumin
4   habanero peppers, sliced (optional)
4   cayenne peppers, whole
Juice of three fresh lemons
Cornhusks (depending on method of preparation)
Palm leaves (depending on method of preparation)
Flour or corn tortillas

First of all, dig a pit. The pit should be three feet deep, three feet wide and four feet long, depending on the size of the goat. Build a large fire near the pit, and allow hot coals to develop. Clean the goat and rub it inside and out with salt and peppercorns. If possible, the goat should be fitted into a large and shallow iron pan. Stuff the goat with the onions, garlic, and the jalapeño peppers. Add equal parts of water and beer to the pan to cover the goat halfway. Add the oil, sugar, bay leaves, chili powder, cumin, and the habanero and cayenne peppers to the pan. Wrap the pan tightly in heavy-duty aluminum foil. Shovel red-hot coals into the bottom of the pit, at least four inches deep. Place the panned goat on top of the coals. Cover the goat with more coals till the pan is completely covered. Now shovel dirt over the coals, and pack them down tightly. Leave the goat in the ground for 12 to 16 hours. Dig the goat up, and allow it to cool slightly. Remove all the meat from the bones. Remove the garlic-onion stuffing. Save the jalapeño peppers if desired. Squeeze the fresh lemon juice over the meat. Serve the Cabrito with the stuffing and tortillas.

Note: If you use the habanero peppers, it will make this dish exceptionally hot.

My father gave me this recipe when I was

young. If an adequate pan is not available, the goat may be wrapped tightly in cornhusks, then aluminum foil, and placed directly on the coals, but make sure the foil is quite thick or it will burn.

The original method was to wrap the goat in cornhusks, then in palm leaves before placing it in the coals. If you have palm leaves, I strongly suggest this method, which eliminates the need for water or beer. Good luck!

Johnny Cash, singer, songwriter, and actor
Submitted by son John Carter Cash

Shell Creek Grilled Trout

1   rainbow or brown trout, gutted and cleaned
    Cooking oil spray
2   to 3 tablespoons diced onion
1   to 2 tablespoons diced carrots
    Butter
    Lemon juice
    Garlic powder
    Lemon pepper

Clean the trout well (you can leave the head and tail on if you prefer), and place on a piece of heavy-duty aluminum foil sprayed with cooking oil. Place the slivers of onions and carrots inside and outside of the trout, and dab the butter inside and out of the trout. Squirt some lemon juice in and out and around the trout, and then sprinkle with the garlic powder and lemon pepper. Bring the sides of foil up, and fold down toward the trout. Fold up the ends to keep juices from leaking out while cooking. Place on the grill over medium coals, and let cook slowly for about 30 to 40 minutes. Check for doneness preference and enjoy.

Makes 1 serving.

Terri "Cookie" Doty, Kedesh Ranch
Shell, Wyoming

Country music giant George Strait hails from Texas and has fifty Number One tunes to his credit. He loves rodeo and has performed in team roping. Among his hit tunes are "Amarillo by Morning," "The Cowboy Rides Away," and "Lonesome Rodeo Cowboy." He appeared as himself in the film *The Horse Whisperer.*

George's Redfish on the Half Shell

1   redfish
    Butter
    Seasoned salt
    Lime juice
    Pepper

First catch a big redfish (legal of course). Then split it down the backbone, leaving the skin on. Season each side with butter, seasoned salt, lime juice, and pepper. Lay each side skin down on the grill. Sometimes I put tinfoil on the grill to make it cleaner. Grill the fish on medium to high heat until done (approximately 10 to 15 minutes). Tasty.

George Strait, singer and roper

Janet McBride's newest two-CD collection is *Fifty Years of Yodeling with Janet McBride*. It represents the contributions she has made over the past fifty years as one of western music's top yodelers. Janet teamed with Sheets McDonald to sing "Driftwood on the River" in the Paul Newman classic *Hud*. Janet and her husband, John, still perform regularly at western events across the country.

Cowgirl's Grilled Salmon

I like really easy recipes, and this one falls into that category.

> Salmon fillets
> Butter
> Lemon slices
> Onion slices
> Salt and pepper

On a flat surface, lay out two sheets of heavy-duty foil wrap. Place the desired amount of prepared salmon onto the foil wrap. Either brush the salmon with melted butter, or place a few pats of butter on the foil alongside the salmon. On top of the salmon, place several thin slices of lemon and onion. Add salt and pepper to taste. Tightly fold the foil wrap to include the salmon and other ingredients, and secure the ends by rolling or folding. Turn the foil-wrapped salmon over so that the seam is facing down, and then tightly wrap with the second sheet of foil wrap. Place on the grill (or into the oven), and cook at medium heat for 12 to 15 minutes on each side. Your salmon will be delicious.

Janet McBride, cowgirl yodeler

Fisherman's Grilled Salmon

Denny's favorite.

> 1   large salmon fillet
> 1   teaspoon olive oil
> ½   cup white wine
>   Juice of 2 fresh lemons
>   Garlic salt
>   Salmon seasoning*
>   Paprika
>   Capers
>   Fresh parsley, chopped
>   Fresh dill
> 1   lemon, thinly sliced

Place the salmon skin side down on 2 large pieces of aluminum foil. Turn the sides up while seasoning. Sprinkle with the olive oil, white wine, and lemon juice. Season to taste with the garlic salt and salmon seasoning. Top with the paprika, capers, parsley, fresh dill, and lemon slices. Seal the foil tightly, place on the barbecue grill, and cook over medium heat 15 to 20 minutes.

Makes about 4 servings.

*I found some excellent salmon seasoning in Vancouver, British Columbia, while Denny was filming his commercial for Gorton's. Use your favorite.

Nancy and Denny Miller, actor

More than a TV cowboy, Denny Miller is seen in TV commercials as the Gorton's Fisherman. The actor also played basketball at UCLA for famed coach John Wooden, swung through the jungle as Tarzan, and had fun on *Gilligan's Island*.

Handsome leading man Glenn Ford made a wagon full of western films over the years, including *Texas, 3:10 to Yuma, Cowboy, The Desperadoes, The Man from Colorado, The Violent Men, Jubal, The Sheepman,* and *The Rounders.* He also starred in *Cade's County,* a contemporary western-police drama on CBS in the early 1970s.

Glenn Ford's Canadian Grilled Salmon

In the morning, catch and fillet a nice size salmon. The following recipe is for half of the fish.

Marinade:
½   cup salad oil
1   teaspoon sugar
1   teaspoon garlic powder
½   teaspoon salt
⅔   teaspoon coarse Lawry's pepper
¼   cup rye whiskey
3   tablespoons soy sauce

In a bowl, combine the oil, sugar, garlic powder, salt, Lawry's, rye whiskey, and soy, and refrigerate for 1 hour to blend the flavors. Marinate the salmon fillet, fresh side down, for 1 to 4 hours in the refrigerator. When you are ready to grill the salmon, remove the salmon from the marinade and discard the marinade. Place the salmon fillet, skin side down, on the grill over glowing (not flaming) coals. When you are ready to turn the fish, separate it from the skin by running a spatula between the skin and the fish. Turn the fish, and using the skin as a cooking surface, place the uncooked side on the skin. Cook until the salmon meat flakes, about 20 to 25 minutes.

Note: It may be necessary to cut the fillet into 3 or 4 pieces (taking care not to cut through the skin) to facilitate turning it. The cooking time will be less.

Glenn Ford, actor

In the touring car are Sons of the Pioneers (left to right) Tim Spencer, Karl Farr, Bob Nolan, Pat Brady, Lloyd Perryman, and Hugh Farr. Western singer and songwriter Tim Spencer was a founding member of the Sons of the Pioneers with Bob Nolan and Roy Rogers. As a tunesmith, he wrote such classics as "The Everlasting Hills of Oklahoma," "Room Full of Roses," "Timber Trail," "Cowboy Camp Meeting," "Blue Prairie" (cowritten with Bob Nolan), and "Cigareetes, Whusky and Wild, Wild Women."

Cowboy Camp Salmon Fillets

1   fresh salmon, halved
2   cubes melted butter or margarine
5   to 10 garlic cloves, chopped
1   cup Parmesan cheese

After catching and then cleaning the salmon, take off the head and tail, and then fillet the bones from the salmon, leaving the skin on. Lay each half of the salmon on a sheet of aluminum foil with the skin side down. Place on the grill, cover, and cook until the salmon is almost done, about 15 minutes. Meanwhile, combine the melted butter and garlic. Pierce the salmon fillets with a fork, and then pour the butter and garlic mixture over the fillets. Cover and cook until the salmon is about done. Then sprinkle the Parmesan cheese on the fillets, cover, and cook for about 5 more minutes. You can now take a spatula to lift the cooked salmon off of the salmon skin and serve. Cleanup is easy since all you need to do is lift up the aluminum foil and the salmon skin and throw them away.

Makes 2 servings.

Tim Spencer, Sons of the Pioneers

More than a Beverly Hillbilly, Buddy Ebsen was Rex Allen's saddle pal in several Republic films. He partnered with Fess Parker as friend George Russell in the Disney *Davy Crockett* miniseries, played the sheriff on *The Mickey Mouse Club*'s serial *Corky and White Shadow*, and starred in the TV western movie *The Daughters of Joshua Cabe*.

Sunset Salmon with Sautéed Vegetables over Pad Thai Noodles

This is a marinated salmon, grilled with corn on the cob and vegetables and served over pad thai rice noodles.

1 whole side of salmon without bones, with skin on one side (approximately 2 pounds)
½ cup firmly packed brown sugar
1 (20-ounce) bottle soy marinade (Kikkoman or other)
½ cup virgin olive oil
1 extra-large, zipper-lock storage bag
7 sweet white or yellow ears of corn (you can use frozen if not in season)
1 stick real butter (cowboys didn't use margarine)
1 (4-ounce) container Jane's Krazy Mixed-Up Salt
1 roll of genuinely heavy-duty aluminum foil or large aluminum cooking bags
1 (10-ounce) bag frozen mixed vegetables or frozen broccoli
1 (16-ounce) bag pad thai rice noodles
1 (7-ounce) jar Thai Kitchen Original pad thai sauce or pad thai noodles and sauce in a box

Fish Prep:

Wash the salmon in water to remove any scales from the meat side. Throw the sugar, soy marinade, olive oil, and salmon into the zipper bag and seal it. Squish it around for about a minute to mix. (Salmon can marinate overnight in the fridge or just for an hour.)

Vegetable Prep:

Peel the ears of corn, and wrap each of them in aluminum foil with ⅛ stick of butter and five good shakes of Mixed-Up Salt. Wrap the corn tightly to prevent anything from leaking out. Do not use cheap aluminum foil because it will burn and ruin the food. Reynolds or thick aluminum grilling bags are good. If you use the cooking bags, use about 3 cobs per bag. In a flat, heavy pan-cake pan, sauté the frozen veggies in a mixture of ⅛ stick butter and 2 dashes of virgin olive oil. Add shakes of Mixed-Up Salt, and cook on medium heat until slightly brown. Do not clean the pan. Cowboys don't like washing dishes, so let's reuse this one later on. Fill a big saucepan about halfway with water, and bring it to a boil. Throw in the noodles, but do not let them cook for very long. You want only to blanch them until you can squeeze them in two with your fingers. Drain the water and let stand.

Grilling:

Light the gas or charcoal grill, or the wood under the cow-branding station. Make sure the grill is good and hot and the coals are evenly distributed. Make a tray out of aluminum foil, and double it so that it is strong. Turn up the edges so that no liquid can spill out. With tongs, lift the salmon out of the marinade and onto the tray, skin side down. Add ¼ stick of butter on top, and carefully rest the salmon on the grill. Any remaining marinade can be poured over the salmon while it grills. Throw the corn on the grill around the salmon. Turn the corn every 5 minutes. Remove the corn after 15 to 20 minutes, depending on how hot the grill is. Corn can have slight browning on the sides. Salmon can cook without turning until dark brown and firm to touch. Do not be afraid to let salmon burn around the edges a little. Cowboys kinda' like it that way.

Finish Noodles:

When all grilling is done, put the rice noodles into the same vegetable pan used for sautéing the vegetables. Add ⅛ stick of butter and 3 tablespoons pad thai sauce, and pan-fry on medium heat. Fold the sauce into the noodles until completely mixed. Never leave the noodles alone. Continue to fold and fry until some of the edges are singed, about 1 to 2 minutes.

Plate and Present:

Find a big flat ceramic plate, and remove the salmon from the foil by gently peeling it from its skin, which will now be glued to the foil. Unwrap the corn and put it around the salmon like a frame. In an oval or pasta-type serving bowl, put the noodles and then the sautéed vegetables on top. Bang the triangle for the outlaws.

Feeds about 7 dirty, cattle-worn, and hungry cow folk.

Buddy Ebsen, actor

Johnny Ringo's Grilled Salmon

¼ cup light soy sauce
¼ cup oil (canola, vegetable, or peanut)
2 level teaspoons ground ginger
1 level teaspoon packed brown sugar
1 level teaspoon Dijon mustard
2 to 3 drops sesame oil
2 to 3 drops liquid smoke (if you have it)
 Juice of ½ lemon
 Salt and pepper
½ whole salmon fillet

In a mixing bowl, combine the soy, oil, ginger, sugar, mustard, sesame oil, liquid smoke, lemon juice, and salt and pepper to taste. Mix thoroughly to make a marinade. Remove any rib bones or small bones from the salmon by using tweezers. Cut the salmon into 3 or 4 large pieces. Place the salmon skin down (if not skinned) in a flat baking dish, and pour the marinade over the fillets. Cover with Saran Wrap, and place in the refrigerator for at least 1 hour. Heat the grill to medium, and place the salmon skin side down on the grill for 5 minutes. Brush on the marinade, and turn for no more than 5 minutes (if you turn it for longer, it will be dry). The total cooking time should be 10 minutes: 5 minutes per side. You can remove the skin after the fish has been turned, if you wish. Keep marinating and then lift and serve immediately with the remaining marinade drizzled on top. Yum-yum!

Note: To bake in the oven, preheat the oven to 325° and bake for a maximum of 18 to 20 minutes. Serve immediately with the remaining marinade drizzled on top.

Makes 4 servings.

Don Durant, actor

Don Durant played the title role in the TV series *Johnny Ringo,* which ran from 1959 to 1960; he portrayed a gunfighter—"the fastest gun in all the West"—who decided to take the side of the law. Durant composed the music and lyrics, and performed the show's theme song.

MAIN DISHES FOR THE GRILL, BARBECUE PIT, AND SMOKER

Rio Rancho Salmon Fillet with Capers and Dill

1   large salmon fillet
      Light soy sauce
2   tablespoons capers, drained
⅓   cup finely chopped red bell pepper
¼   cup finely chopped dill weed
2   tablespoons lemon juice

Place the salmon on a large piece of lightly greased, heavy-duty aluminum foil. Sprinkle with the soy sauce and capers. Top with the red pepper, dill weed, and lemon juice. Wrap aluminum foil securely around the fish to form a packet. Preheat the grill to medium heat. Cook for 15 to 20 minutes, or until the fish is tender and flakes with a fork.

Makes 2 servings.

Gail and Earl Bellamy, director

Jamaican Cowboy Salmon

I experienced this dish doing a film in Jamaica. I was riding a horse through the mountains and stopped to see some locals grilling up a local fish (I can't remember what it was). I was so impressed that I asked for the recipe, which I have changed slightly to my tastes, substituting my favorite fish and making a few other adjustments in the ingredients.

Salsa:
1   ripe mango, peeled and diced
4   green onions, chopped
2   garlic cloves
1   tablespoon sesame oil
¼   teaspoon dry ginger
1   tablespoon light soy sauce
2   tablespoons chopped fresh cilantro
1   fresh banana pepper
      Juice of 1 fresh lime
      Sea salt and black pepper
1   fresh red chile pepper, chopped and seeds removed
½   red bell pepper, chopped

Salmon Rub:
1   small onion, finely chopped
2   garlic cloves, chopped
1½   tablespoons chopped fresh thyme
1   tablespoon paprika
1   teaspoon ground cumin
½   teaspoon cayenne
      Sea salt and black pepper
1   tablespoon packed brown sugar
1   large salmon fillet

For the salsa, mix together the mango, onions, garlic, oil, ginger, soy, cilantro, banana pepper, lime juice, sea salt and black pepper to taste, chile pepper, and red bell pepper. Chill for 30 minutes, and the salsa's ready to serve. For the rub, combine the onion, garlic, thyme, paprika, cumin, cayenne, sea salt and black pepper to taste, and brown sugar, and mix well.

Wash the salmon under cold water. Pat dry with a paper towel. Rub the salmon rub over the salmon, and place it in the refrigerator for 2 hours. When ready to cook, place the salmon on the grill, preferably charcoal with wood chips to provide some flavoring. I prefer button, hickory, cherry, and mesquite woods, which I always get through *www.kalamazoogrill.com,* where I also purchased my grill. Grill for approximately 20 minutes. The cooking time varies according to the thickness of the fish. Test by taking a fork to the thinnest side. If it flakes, the salmon is either done or very close to done, depending on how you like it. Remember, as with all fish and meats—and especially salmon—it will continue to cook even after you've removed it from the grill. So if you like your fish "rare," keep that in mind. Great hot or, on the next day, cold. Enjoy!

Makes 4 servings.

Stuart Whitman, actor

"I never drew first on
a man in my life.
That's the only way to
stay clean. You play
it by the rules.
Without the rules,
you're nothing."

—Burt Lancaster
in *Lawman* (1971)

Ray "Crash" Corrigan was a bodybuilder who made more than forty westerns, mainly playing two characters: Tucson Smith in the *Three Mesquiteers* films, and himself in the *Range Busters* series. He later built Corriganville, a western town that was used for filming western movies and TV shows.

Crash Corrigan's Crash-Course Grilled Salmon

Salmon steak (boneless) or fillet
Soy sauce
Black pepper
Butter or margarine, melted

Take your salmon steak or fillet, rub with soy sauce, and sprinkle with black pepper. Coat both sides with butter or margarine, place on the grill, and cook for 15 minutes. Turn one time and cook another 15 minutes.

Ray "Crash" Corrigan, actor
Submitted by son Tom Corrigan

Bacon-Wrapped Albacore Fillets

4   (12-ounce) albacore tuna fillets (or yellowfin or bluefin tuna)
½   pound thickly sliced ranch-style bacon
⅓   stick butter (do not use margarine)
½   cup soy sauce
2   tablespoons lemon juice
2   tablespoons orange juice
2   tablespoons grated fresh ginger
1   teaspoon minced garlic
2   tablespoons packed brown sugar
    Dash of Tabasco (optional)
    Freshly ground pepper

Rinse and dry the fillets. Cook to about two-thirds done. Wrap each fillet with the bacon and secure with toothpicks. Place the fish in a noncorrosive container. Mix the butter, soy, lemon juice, orange juice, ginger, garlic, brown sugar, Tabasco if using, and pepper in a small saucepan, and bring to a slow boil. Simmer for 1 minute. Cool to room temperature. Pour about half of the mixture over the fish, and marinate for 1 hour in the refrigerator. Place the fish on a hot, greased grill for approximately 7 minutes. Mop with the remaining marinade, turn, and cook 5 minutes or so. Do not overcook.

Feeds 4 hungry cowboys.

Cliff Emmich, actor

Character actor Cliff Emmich has been a guest on the TV series *Little House on the Prairie, Bret Maverick,* and *Walker, Texas Ranger.* He played the bartender in the 1976 TV western series *The Macahans.*

Tuck's Smoked Fish

Brine:
- 1 cup salt
- 2 cups packed brown sugar
- 15 bay leaves
- 3 tablespoons whole black peppercorns
- 15 cups water
- 5 pounds fish of choice (fresh tuna, halibut, or marlin suggested)

Marinade:
- 4 cups pure maple syrup
- 2 cups packed brown sugar
- 1 cup sweet molasses
- 1 cup honey
- ¼ cup soy sauce
- 1 tablespoon ground ginger

For the brine, mix together the salt, brown sugar, bay leaves, peppercorns, and water in a large pot. Place the fish in the brine, and refrigerate for 10 hours. Remove the fish, rinse, and pat dry. For the marinade, mix the syrup, brown sugar, molasses, honey, soy, and ginger. Place the fish in the marinade, and refrigerate for 6 hours. Smoke the fish in a smoker for 2 to 4 hours, depending on the thickness of the fish. Brush on the marinade every half hour.

Note: Use maple, apple, and alder smoking chips in smoker.

Makes 8 to 10 servings.

Forrest Tucker, actor

Doc's Dockside Grilled Tuna

- Albacore or yellowfin tuna, cut into 8 medallions
- ¼ cup olive oil
- Juice of 1 lemon
- 3 garlic cloves, split
- Salt and pepper
- Chopped tomatoes
- Cilantro

In a bowl, mix the olive oil, lemon juice, garlic, and salt and pepper to taste. Place the fish in the marinade for 2 hours in the refrigerator. To cook, grill the fish for 3 minutes per side over medium heat. Prior to serving, sprinkle the fish with some chopped tomatoes and cilantro. Bon appetit!

Makes 4 servings.

Howard McNear, actor
Submitted by son Kit and Sue McNear

Howard McNear (left) looks on as Fred MacMurray gets pinned in the 1959 film *Good Day for a Hanging.* As the former Doc on radio's *Gunsmoke* and the future Floyd the barber of Mayberry, it's not clear whether McNear might be evaluating MacMurray's general health or simply assessing his haircut in this scene.

TEXAS RANGER
HALL OF FAME AND MUSEUM

Few law enforcement agencies are as steeped in history and romance as the Texas Rangers. Since 1823, when Texas founder Stephen F. Austin authorized two companies of rangers "for the common defense," the Rangers have battled threats to the peace and tranquility of the Lone Star State.

The Texas Ranger Hall of Fame and Museum was founded in 1968 to honor and preserve the memory and traditions of the Rangers, and the current facility is a mandatory stopover for tourists and historians alike.

The Hall of Fame pays homage to Rangers who have died in the line of duty, and the museum itself contains thousands of artifacts, including original field equipment, badges, and firearms.

Among the weapons on display are several Colt revolvers and some of the guns involved in the pursuit of the notorious outlaws Bonnie and Clyde. The museum also includes a Research Center that serves as an official library and archives.

Recently the museum partnered with Wrangler Western Wear to offer a line of official Texas Ranger clothing. A special program allows children to become "Junior Texas Rangers." For a twenty-five-dollar contribution, kids get a signed Honorary Appointment certificate that is suitable for framing, two toy badges, and their names included on the Junior Hall of Fame Honor Roll.

The Texas Ranger Museum and Hall of Fame is located at 100 Texas Ranger Trail in Waco, Texas. For more details, go to *www.texasrange.org*.

Texas Ranger's Gulf Coast Shrimp

1½ pounds shrimp
1   cup clam juice
½   cup butter
6   cloves garlic, minced
4   scallions, minced
1   to 2 tablespoons Tabasco
1   tablespoon Worcestershire sauce
2   bay leaves
1   to 2 teaspoons cayenne
2   teaspoons paprika
2   teaspoons dried thyme
2   teaspoons dried oregano
1½ teaspoons salt
1   teaspoon coarsely ground black pepper
½   cup dark corn syrup
¼   cup molasses

Shell the shrimp, reserving the shells. In a pot, combine the shells and the clam juice. Bring to a boil, and then let simmer, uncovered, for 15 minutes. Strain this broth and combine it in a large pot with the butter, garlic, scallions, Tabasco, Worcestershire sauce, bay leaves, cayenne, paprika, thyme, oregano, salt, pepper, corn syrup, and molasses. Bring the mixture to a boil, and cook, uncovered, until thick, about 10 minutes. Cool to room temperature, and add the shrimp. Refrigerate

for 2 to 4 hours. When you're ready to cook the shrimp, place them on a hot grill, and brush with the marinade. Grill the shrimp until desired doneness. Boil the remaining marinade to reduce a bit, and serve with the shrimp.

Makes 4 servings.

William Smith, actor

Rough-and-tumble William Smith was a guest on many TV westerns before becoming one of the stars of *Laredo* as Ranger Joe Riley from 1965 to 1967. He put up his dukes with Clint Eastwood in a great fistfight in *Any Which Way You Can.*

MAIN DISHES FOR THE GRILL, BARBECUE PIT, AND SMOKER

Steve Stevens (center) was a talent agent for some of Hollywood's top cowboy actors. Among his many clients were Chuck Connors (left), Johnny Crawford (right), Jack Palance, Claude Akins, and Slim Pickens.

Steve Stevens went West himself as a young man in episodes of TV's *The Roy Rogers Show, Zorro,* and *Gunsmoke.*

Cowboy Agent's Grilled Shrimp Soft Tacos

1   green onion, chopped
1   sweet Texas onion, chopped
1   bunch cilantro, finely chopped
     Few dashes of green Tabasco (medium hot)
2   tomatoes, finely chopped
     Juice of ½ lemon
1   pound shelled large shrimp
1   dozen small flour tortillas
     Mayonnaise
     Ketchup

In a bowl, mix the green onion, Texas onion, cilantro, Tabasco, tomatoes, and lemon juice to make a salsa. Soak the shrimp in water for an hour, and then cook them on the grill. Chop the shrimp. Put the tortillas on the grill until hot. Spread the mayonnaise and ketchup on the tortillas, and add the shrimp and salsa.
   Makes 12 tacos.

Steve Stevens Sr., agent

One of Hollywood's greatest stuntmen, Jock Mahoney doubled such stars as Errol Flynn, Randolph Scott, Gregory Peck, and Charles Starrett.

Sea Ranch Scallops

1 pound premium apple-cured, hickory-smoked bacon
2 pounds fresh scallops
2 tablespoons mayonnaise
2 tablespoons sweet relish
Juice of 4 lemons

Cut the bacon into 1- to 2-inch strips. Place the scallops on skewers alternately with the bacon strips. Grill the scallops until the bacon is cooked and the scallops are slightly browned on the edges. Mix the mayonnaise, relish, and lemon juice, and use for a dipping sauce. Yippee yi-eee, matey!

Makes 4 to 6 servings.

Jock Mahoney, stuntman and actor

Grilled Portobello Pizzas

6 large portobello mushrooms, stemmed, and gills removed
Extra virgin olive oil (for brushing)
Kosher salt
Garlic pepper
1 cup store-bought pesto sauce
1 cup store-bought roasted garlic salsa
½ cup goat cheese, crumbled
¼ cup Parmigiano-Reggiano, grated
1 cup queso fresco or Monterey Jack cheese

Preheat the grill to high heat. Brush both sides of the mushrooms with olive oil, and sprinkle the inside of each with salt and garlic pepper. Place the mushrooms on the grill bottom side up. Grill for 2 to 3 minutes on each side, rotating halfway through to achieve grill marks. Remove from the grill, placing the mushrooms bottom side up. Fill with your choice of the assorted sauces, and top with your choice of cheese. Return the mushrooms to the top rack or shelf of your barbecue, close the lid, reduce the heat to medium-high, and cook for 5 minutes or until the cheese is melted. Remove the mushrooms, place on a cutting board, and cut into triangles like a pizza. Serve immediately.

Makes 6 servings.

Apache and Jack Ging, actor

"Well, a man doesn't ask for thirds just to be polite. He may take seconds for that reason but when he takes thirds, it's because he likes them."

—Jock Mahoney in *Money, Women and Guns* (1958)

MAIN DISHES FOR THE GRILL, BARBECUE PIT, AND SMOKER

MAVERICK MEALS

Rodeo Ring Bacon-Wrapped Fillet with Mushroom and Onion Glaze

2   plus 2 tablespoons sweet butter
4   (8-ounce) beef tenderloin fillets
4   slices smoked bacon
     Bob Tallman's Steak Dust
1   large sweet yellow onion
12 ounces sliced mushrooms
½   cup Bob Tallman's Ranch Rub

In a heavy skillet, melt 2 tablespoons butter over medium heat. Wrap each fillet with a strip of the smoked bacon, and secure with a toothpick (2 if necessary). Season both sides of the fillets generously with Bob Tallman's Steak Dust. Place the fillets in the skillet, and cook until each side has slightly browned, approximately 3 minutes per side.

Preheat the oven to 400°. Remove the wrapped fillets from the skillet, and place the partially cooked fillets on a plate. Cut the onion into quarters, and then into ¼-inch slices, and put the slices into the skillet that held the fillets. Over medium heat, cook the onions for about 5 minutes, and then add the sliced mushrooms. Continue cooking for 5 more minutes. Place the fillets in the oven on a 12 x 8-inch cookie sheet, and cook for 5 minutes at 400° for medium rare, 7 minutes for medium to medium-well. Add the remaining 2 tablespoons butter to the onions and mushrooms, and lower the heat to medium-low. Add Bob Tallman's Ranch Rub to the mushroom and onion mixture, and continue cooking over medium-low heat. Remove the fillets from the oven, and put them on plates. Spoon the mushroom and onion sauce generously over the fillets and serve.

Makes 4 servings.

Bob Tallman, rodeo announcer

Bob Tallman is known as "the Voice of Professional Rodeo" by more than sixty million rodeo fans across the United States and Canada each year. A six-time recipient of the Pro Rodeo Cowboys Association (PRCA) announcer of the year award, he is the founder of Bob Tallman's Texas Style Fixin's brand cooking spices.

Brothers Jack (middle) and Joe Hannah (right) and Joe's son Lon (left) make up the Sons of the San Joaquin, famous for their cowboy family harmony. The California trio kicked off their career in 1987 and has been likened to the classic sounds of the Sons of the Pioneers. Among their record albums are *A Cowboy Has to Sing, Songs of the Silver Screen, From Whence the Cowboys Came, Gospel Train,* and *Horses, Cattle & Coyotes.*

Barbecued Chuck Roast Without the Barbecue Pit

1   (4 to 7-pound) chuck roast (boneless preferred)

Sauce:
1   cup red wine or red wine vinegar
1   cup water
½   cup ketchup
¼   cup packed brown sugar
     Several drops liquid smoke (important)
2   tablespoons Worcestershire sauce
1   teaspoon salt or garlic salt
1   teaspoon pepper
1   teaspoon garlic powder (fresh garlic can be used)
1   tablespoon chili powder
1   onion, chopped

Place the meat in a large baking dish. For the sauce, combine the red wine, water, ketchup, brown sugar, liquid smoke, Worcestershire sauce, salt, pepper, garlic powder, chili powder, and onion, and simmer for 20 minutes. Preheat the oven to 325°. Pour the sauce over the meat and cover. Bake covered for 4 to 5 hours. Serve in chunks.

Note: To cook in a slow cooker, cut the sauce recipe in half and cook on low for 8 to 10 hours.

Makes 8 to 12 servings.

Jack Hannah, Sons of the San Joaquin

Patrick Wayne worked on TV's *Branded* in 1965 and played Howdy Lewis in *The Rounders* series in 1966. He also appeared in the films *Rio Grande, The Searchers, The Alamo, McLintock!, Cheyenne Autumn, Big Jake, Young Guns,* and *Rustler's Rhapsody*.

Big Jake's Braised Beef Short Ribs

1	bottle red wine
½	cup chopped carrots
⅔	cup chopped leeks (white part)
½	cup chopped onions
3	garlic cloves, mashed
10	sprigs Italian parsley
2	sprigs thyme
1	bay leaf
8	bone-in short ribs (about ½ pound each)
	Oil
	Salt and pepper
	All-purpose flour
2	to 3 cups veal stock
2	to 3 cups chicken stock

In a wide pot, bring the wine, carrots, leeks, onions, garlic, parsley, thyme, and bay leaf to a boil. Tilt the pot away from the burner, and carefully ignite the mixture with a match. Allow any of the alcohol to burn off, and then ignite the mixture again. If there are no flames, then the alcohol is completely cooked away. Allow the marinade to cool.

In a plastic bag with a zipper seal, pour the marinade over the short ribs, seal, and refrigerate for 8 to 24 hours. Remove the meat from the marinade, and strain the marinade into a saucepan, reserving the vegetables. Bring the marinade to a simmer, and skim off any impuri-ties that rise to the top. Remove from the heat. In a large skillet, heat the oil to about ⅛-inch depth over high heat. Season both sides of each piece of meat with salt and pepper, and then dust with the flour. Place the meat in the hot oil, and cook until well browned on all sides (about 2 minutes per side), adjusting the heat to keep the meat from burning. Remove the meat to a heavy pot or casserole dish big enough to hold all of the meat snugly in one layer. Pour off the excess oil from the skillet, return the skillet to the heat, and cook the reserved vegetables until they begin to caramelize, about 3 to 4 minutes. Spread the vegetables over the meat in an even layer. Add the marinade and 2 cups each of veal stock and chicken stock. The meat should be covered with liquid. If not, add more stock as necessary.

Preheat the oven to 275°. Bring the liquid to a simmer on the stove. Press a parchment paper snugly over the meat. Place the dish in the oven, and bake until the meat is tender, about 3 to 4 hours. Remove the meat from the pot, and strain the liquid. Discard the vegetables. Skim the fat from the braising liquid, and reserve about one-third of the liquid for reheating the ribs. Transfer the remaining liquid to a saucepan, and reduce to a sauce consistency. Serve the meat covered with the sauce. Enjoy!

Makes 8 servings.

Patrick Wayne, actor

Ina Autry's
Veal Chops California

1½ cups uncooked prunes
½   cup fat or salad oil
1   cup coarsely chopped onion
½   pound mushrooms, sliced
1   cup tomato sauce
4   large veal chops
    Salt
    Few grains of pepper
2   plus 2 cups water

Cook the prunes for 10 minutes in about ½ cup water. Remove the pits. Cut the prunes into medium-size pieces. Heat the fat or salad oil in a frying pan. Sauté the onion and mushrooms for 5 minutes. Add the tomato sauce, and cook 5 minutes longer. Add the prunes, chops, salt, pepper, and 2 cups of the water. Cover and simmer for 1 hour. Add the remaining 2 cups water as needed.

Makes 4 servings.

Gene Autry, singer and actor

Gene Autry was the quintessential singing cowboy. A singer and songwriter, he was a star of practically every entertainment medium from radio and film to rodeo and TV. Autry made ninety-five feature films from the 1930s into the 1950s before starring in his own TV series.

Museum of the American West

Nestled in Los Angeles's famous Griffith Park is the Museum of the American West. Legendary singing cowboy Gene Autry founded the institution as the Autry Museum of Western Heritage in 1988; it merged with the Women of the West Museum in 2002 and switched to its current name in 2004.

The museum collection numbers nearly eighty thousand items and focuses on preserving and interpreting the history and culture of the American West. Among the highlights of the seven galleries are an authentic Osage wedding dress, Sitting Bull's pipe bag, a map of Tombstone from 1881 (the year of the famous gunfight at the O.K. Corral), an autographed photo of Annie Oakley, and a restored stagecoach from the 1850s. Western art is in abundance, including original works by such distinguished artists as Thomas Moran and Frederic Remington.

Of particular interest to western movie fans is the Imagination Gallery, which focuses on images of the American West in popular culture. One of William "Hopalong Cassidy" Boyd's hats is on display, as are original posters from classic westerns.

The jewel of the collection might just be Gene Autry's Martin D-45 guitar, which was made specifically for Autry—one of only ninety produced. Or maybe it's one of the beautiful, ornate saddles or the impressive collection of law-enforcement badges. There's truly a western gem awaiting at every turn in this museum.

The Museum of the American West is located at 4700 Western Heritage Way in Los Angeles. For more information, go to *www.autry-museum.org*.

The Texas Trailhands have been blazing a trail across the West with their brand of Texas swing, which has garnered them numerous awards for their sound from the Western Music Association. Band members are (clockwise from bottom right) Miss Devon, Rodeo Kate, guitarist and harmonica player Chuck Wagon Chuck, bunkhouse bassist Hoot Al, and "last of the cowboy drummers" Roncho Ron. Among their mighty fine albums are *Lone Star Swing* and *In the Moo*.

Miss Devon's Never-Fail Technique for Succulent Rib-Eye Steaks

Virgin olive oil
Several cloves garlic, crushed
Rib-eye steaks
Your favorite meat seasoning
1 Texas Ruby Red grapefruit

When grilling meats indoors on my hot cast iron griddle, I warm olive oil with crushed fresh garlic. Add the steaks that have been coated with your favorite meat seasoning. Now, let 'em sear a few minutes. Just as the steaks are crusted and sorta' sticking to the griddle, squeeze half of a huge Texas Ruby Red grapefruit all over the searing meat. When the steaks begin to soften and loosen, and the juice is well reduced, turn the steaks over, and repeat the process using the other half of the grapefruit. As the second side of the steaks becomes well seared and crusted, and the second half of the grapefruit is well reduced, turn off the heat, squeeze out the last livin' drop from both halves of the grapefruit, cover with a heavy cast-iron lid, and let it continue to cook as the temp cools and the meat juices moisten the steaks to a medium doneness. The trick is to time the juice squeeze/turnover process to achieve your preference of doneness without overcooking.

Note: Miss Devon loves grapefruit and highly recommends eating fine chocolate between bites of grapefruit. It helps intensify the taste of the chocolate. Yummm!

Miss Devon, Texas Trailhands

Miss Devon warbles pretty as a bluebird and swings rhythm guitar for the Texas Trailhands. She was once the voice of Jessie the Yodeling Cowgirl with the Riders in the Sky.

Matinée Man's Favorite Meat Loaf

Following the cowboy code, I will not tell a lie. I can't cook to save my life. I certainly appreciate good cooking, however, and my longtime housekeeper, Elena Ingles, whips up a wonderful meat loaf. She was kind enough to share her recipe with all of you.

1	envelope Lipton's onion and mushroom soup mix
1½	ounces water
3	ounces ketchup, plus some for topping
2	ounces Heinz 57 sauce, plus some for topping
2	eggs
1	large fresh onion, chopped
12	ounces fresh mushrooms
2	pounds extra-lean ground beef
¾	cup bread crumbs
	Dash of onion powder
	Dash of garlic powder
	Dash of parsley

In large bowl, combine the onion and mushroom soup mix with the water, 3 ounces ketchup, 2 ounces 57 sauce, and the eggs. In a small skillet, sauté the onion and mushrooms. Add the ground beef, bread crumbs, sautéed onion and mushrooms, onion powder, garlic powder, and parsley to the soup mix and eggs in the large bowl. Mix well.

Preheat the oven to 325°. Place the mixture in a 9½ x 5½-inch meat loaf pan. Mix some 57 sauce with ketchup, and spread evenly over the top of the loaf. Cook, uncovered, for 40 minutes. Then cover with tin foil, and cook for 2 hours, or until the meat is cooked completely. Put a knife in the center to see if it's done. If the knife comes out clean, it's done.

Makes 4 to 6 servings, and sometimes just 3.

Leonard Maltin, film critic

FIVE UNSUNG WESTERN FILMS

Leonard Maltin

Even among western fans, there are specialists—those who love the Saturday matinée B movies of yore, those who prefer the spaghetti westerns of the 1960s and '70s, and still others who like antiheroes more than white-hats.

I have a fairly broad taste for this genre, but even so, I'm surprised when some friends who share my appetite for westerns tell me they haven't seen some films I'm especially fond of.

Here are five prime examples:

1. ***Hell's Hinges*** (1916). This to me is the quintessential William S. Hart movie, in which he plays his signature character, a bad man who turns out to have a conscience after all. Despite its age, I think this still plays extremely well, with something substantial at stake for all the major characters. I love Hart, and wish he were better known today.

2. ***Law and Order*** (1932). Long before westerns became dark of tone and bleak of spirit, Universal made this spare, tough-as-nails variation on the Wyatt Earp/Doc Holliday saga. The great Walter Huston stars; his son John cowrote the script. The cast also features a pair of western icons, Harry Carey and Raymond Hatton, and two young, barely known actors who would step into their shoes in years to come, Walter Brennan and Andy Devine.

3. ***The Last Outlaw*** (1936). Harry Carey plays a notorious bandit who's released from prison after twenty-five years, only to discover that the "Old West" he knew so well has pretty much disappeared. (Shades of *The Grey Fox*!) John Ford cowrote this amusing story, which costars Hoot Gibson, Henry B. Walthall, and Tom Tyler.

4. ***Seven Men from Now*** (1956). This Randolph Scott vehicle, produced by John Wayne's Batjac Company, was unseen for more than forty years. Now restored (by the UCLA Film and Television Archive), it takes its place among those wonderful, unpretentious 1950s westerns that provide stimulating entertainment even today. Burt Kennedy's script, Budd Boetticher's direction, and a knockout supporting performance by Lee Marvin are among the reasons it's so good—and it's just seventy-nine minutes long.

5. ***Quigley Down Under*** (1990). Tom Selleck has proved to be the western's best friend in recent years, starring in a series of well-made, extremely popular, cable TV films. This theatrical release was considered a box-office failure, but it's one of his best—a tried-and-true story about a hired gun who turns on his crooked boss, and a set not in the Old West but in the western-like terrain of Australia. Laura San Giacomo and Alan Rickman costar, with Simon Wincer (*Lonesome Dove*) behind the camera.

Leonard Maltin is best known for his long run on television's *Entertainment Tonight,* and his even longer run as editor of the annual paperback reference *Leonard Maltin's Movie Guide.* He has written a number of other books and appears as both host and expert on a number of DVD releases of classic movies. He also teaches at the University of Southern California; publishes a newsletter for old-movie buffs, *Leonard Maltin's Movie Crazy;* and maintains a Web site, *www.leonardmaltin.com.*

The American cowboy of film, John Wayne starred in 150 movies, most of them westerns. From *The Big Trail* to *Singing Sandy* and from *Stagecoach* to *True Grit,* Duke is the silver screen cowboy. Period.

Glamorous Meat Loaf

1½   pounds ground beef
½   cup chopped onion
2   eggs
1   cup tomato sauce
1   cup bread crumbs
1   ripe banana
     Mashed potatoes (4 servings)

Preheat the oven to 325°. Mix together the beef, onion, eggs, tomato sauce, bread crumbs, and banana. Bake for 1 hour. After your meat loaf is done, transfer onto a platter, and let all the juices run out. Discard the juices. In a pastry bag with a No. 6 star tip, swirl the potatoes evenly over the entire meat loaf. Put it under the broiler until the potato stars on the top turn golden brown.

   Makes about 6 servings.

Pilar and John Wayne,
actress/artist and actor

Grandma's Meatballs

"Grandma" was Josephine Giacona-Corrao.

1	pound ground beef
1	pound ground pork
4	large eggs
5	ounces freshly shredded Romano cheese
5	ounces freshly shredded Parmesan cheese
1½	cups chopped purple onion
4	to 5 cloves garlic, chopped
2	tablespoons chopped parsley
1	tablespoon chopped basil
½	tablespoon chopped oregano
	Salt and pepper
3	or 4 slices sourdough bread

In a large mixing bowl, combine the ground beef, ground pork, eggs, both cheeses, onion, garlic, parsley, basil, oregano, and salt and pepper. Take the slices of sourdough bread, wet them with water, and then wring out the excess water. Add the wet bread to the other ingredients, and mix everything together with your hands until all the ingredients are combined. Roll into your desired meatball size, place the meatballs on an ungreased cookie sheet, and put them in the oven. Broil the meatballs, turning until cooked all the way through. Remove the meatballs from the oven. Place them into your favorite spaghetti sauce to soak up the juices. They will truly melt in your mouth at mealtime. Bon appetito!

Makes about 2 dozen good-size meatballs.

Clay O'Brien Cooper,
actor and rodeo cowboy
Submitted by wife Alisa Cooper

Rodeo cowboy Clay O'Brien Cooper has been roping all of his life. With partner Jake Barnes, they won seven world team-roping championships. But the man behind the gold belt buckle can also act.

Cooper was one of John Wayne's young trailhands when he was eleven years old and made *The Cowboys* and also starred opposite Roy Rogers in *MacKintosh and T.J.* He also played young Weedy in the TV series version of *The Cowboys*.

Singer/songwriter Marty Robbins crooned hits in many fields, from country and western to pop. One of his top albums was *Gunfighter Ballads & Trail Songs,* for which he wrote and recorded the classic "El Paso." Also the singer of "Big Iron" and "The Hanging Tree," Robbins made five western films, including *Guns of a Stranger* (as seen here), *Ballad of a Gunfighter,* and *The Badge of Marshal Brennan.*

El Paso City Skillet Casserole

1   pound ground beef
1   onion, chopped
2   teaspoons cumin
1   to 3 teaspoons ground red pepper (optional)
2   teaspoons oregano
    Vegetable oil (optional)
2   potatoes, grated
6   eggs, beaten
    Salt and pepper

In a large skillet, brown the meat, onion, cumin, red pepper, and oregano on the stovetop or campfire. Add oil if needed. Add the potatoes to the meat, and stir to prevent sticking. (Add a little vegetable oil, if needed.) When the potatoes are browned, add the eggs. Continue to stir until the eggs are done. Add salt and pepper to taste.

Makes 4 servings.

Marty Robbins, singer

Joe's Special

1   pound sliced bacon, cut into 2-inch pieces
1   pound ground beef
3   onions, finely chopped
13   cups (4 26-ounce cans) spinach
    Salt and pepper

In a large frying pan or skillet (not non-stick), fry the bacon and ground beef until both are beginning to brown. Drain off a little bit of the grease, but leave ample for cooking the onions and spinach. Stir in the onions. Drain the spinach and add to the skillet. Chop the spinach in the skillet with a knife or the edge of a metal spatula. Add salt and pepper to taste. Continue to fry the skillet contents until the meats are cooked through and all ingredients are hot and well mixed. It looks awful but tastes great.

Makes 8 to 10 servings.

Mike Buckner, U2 Chuck Wagon
Vale, Oregon

Chef Smiley Burnette has the beverages ready, while Gene Autry's got soup and salad for starters. The lovable sidekick, Smiley Burnette, who was often known on film as Frog Millhouse, made more than 130 films in the 1930s, '40s, and '50s. He wrote more than three hundred western songs.

Five-in-One Meal

2   pounds ground beef
1   pound sausage
6   to 8 potatoes
3   onions, finely chopped
13   cups (4 26-ounce cans) corn
1   (26-ounce) can Campbell's tomato soup
     (don't add water)

In a skillet, fry the ground beef and sausage until just browning. Do not drain. In a large Dutch oven, layer in first the potatoes, then the onions, corn, meat, and the tomato soup. Cook in the Dutch oven until the spuds are done, about 45 minutes to 1 hour.
    Makes 12 to 16 servings.

Mike Buckner, U2 Chuck Wagon
Vale, Oregon

Devilburgers

1   pound lean ground beef
1   tomato, crushed into paste (we use a blender)
1   tablespoon French's yellow mustard
1   tablespoon Worcestershire sauce
     Salt and pepper
     MSG
     Day-old bread, sliced
     Thin slices of two or three varieties of cheese

In a bowl, mix the ground beef, fresh tomato paste, mustard, Worcestershire sauce, salt, pepper, and MSG. It's best to knead the mixture by hand for thoroughness. Spread it ¼ inch thick on the slices of day-old bread, making sure that the meat entirely covers the bread to its very edges or else the bread will burn. Cook under a broiler, and when the meat is done, top it with small narrow slices of two or three varieties of cheese, which will melt nicely when you slip it back under the broiler. When the meat shows little brown crusty places and the cheese has melted, serve with sweet pickles, olives, and a cold drink, or your black coffee, if you prefer. You can eat these with a fork, or cut them in half and eat with your fingers like a sandwich.

Dallas and Smiley Burnette, actor
From The Smiley Burnettes Cookbook

Lloyd and Buddy's Tamale Pie

Tamale Piecrust:
1   cup Quaker masa harina
1   tablespoon vegetable oil
½   teaspoon salt
1   cup water

Tamale Pie Filling:
2   tablespoons butter
½   cup chopped onion
⅓   cup chopped green bell pepper
1   clove garlic
1   pound ground beef
1   (10-ounce) can tomatoes, drained
1   (4-ounce) can chopped green chiles
1   (7-ounce) can whole-kernel corn, drained
½   cup chopped ripe olives
1   (7-ounce) can whole olives
2   teaspoons chili powder (can add more to taste)
1   teaspoon salt
2   tablespoons all-purpose flour
½   teaspoon cumin
½   cup grated Monterey Jack cheese

To make the piecrust, combine the masa harina, oil, salt, and water in a bowl and mix. Grease a 9 or 10-inch pie plate. Press the mixture into the pie plate. Preheat the oven to 400°. To make the filling, melt the butter in a large saucepan. Sauté the onion, pepper, and garlic until tender. Add the ground beef and brown. Drain. Add the tomatoes, chiles, corn, olives, chili powder, salt, flour, and cumin. Pour into the crust. Bake for 20 to 25 minutes. Sprinkle with the cheese. Return to the oven until the cheese is melted (about 5 minutes). Let stand for 5 minutes before serving.

Makes 6 to 8 servings.

Lloyd Perryman, Sons of the Pioneers

The Sons of the Pioneers are (left to right) Pat Brady, Hugh Farr, Karl Farr, Bob Nolan, Tim Spencer, and Lloyd Perryman.

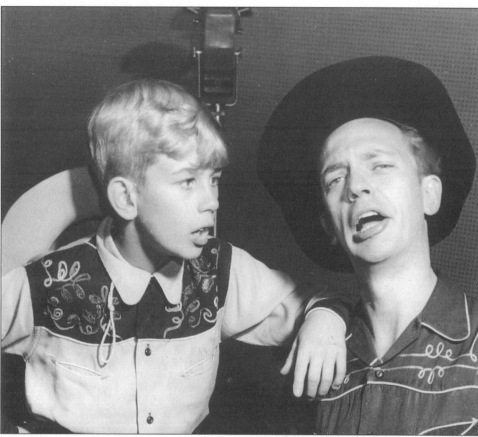

Partnering with Clive Rice on radio's *Bobby Benson and the B-Bar-B Riders* was a wiry young cowpoke named Don Knotts, who furnished the voice of the old geezer Windy Wales.

Bobby Benson's Mom's Cottage Pie

5	medium potatoes (about 1½ pounds)
2	medium onions, chopped (about 1½ cups)
1	clove garlic, finely chopped
¼	cup extra virgin olive oil
1	pound lean ground beef
1	(15-ounce) can green peas
1	(4-ounce) can sliced mushrooms
3	large carrots, sliced and cooked
2	tablespoons Worcestershire sauce
1	tablespoon browning sauce (such as Kitchen Bouquet)
	Salt and pepper
1	cup milk
1	tablespoon butter
	Grated Parmesan cheese

In a large pot, boil the potatoes in water. In a large frying pan, cook the onions and garlic in olive oil until the onions are translucent. Add the ground beef, stirring to crumble and to mix with the onion and garlic. Cook until the meat is well-done. Do not drain. Add the peas and mushrooms with liquids from their cans. Drain the carrots and add to the mixture along with the Worcestershire sauce, browning sauce, and salt and pepper to taste. There should be enough liquid for easy stirring, but not splashy. Add a bit of water if necessary, and place all in a 2-quart baking dish.

Preheat the oven to 375°. Mash the potatoes. Add the milk, butter, and salt to taste. Add more milk if necessary to make the potatoes soft enough to easily cover the mixture in the baking dish. Be sure to spread the potatoes completely to the sides of the dish, and make an air hole in the center of the potatoes to release the steam. Sprinkle the Parmesan cheese generously over the top, and bake for 30 minutes, or until the potatoes brown slightly. Let stand a few minutes and serve. This is a one-dish meal and is complemented with a tossed salad.

Makes 4 servings.

Clive Rice, radio cowboy

"Walkin' Talkin'" Charley Aldridge has worked with a posse of cowboys in music and movies since the 1950s. He produced western stage shows for many top TV cowboy stars at the Corriganville Ranch; opened his own western town, Fort Aldridge, for a short time near Nashville; wrote and scored the music for the Marty Robbins western *Guns of a Stranger;* and coproduced Robbins's film *Ballad of a Gunfighter.*

Washita River Tamale Pie

On the stock farm where I was raised in Oklahoma, this was a real fav'rite of mine. Our hired hands also liked it, so I seldom got seconds.

1½   pounds lean roast beef
½   pound ground beef
     Vegetable oil
2   medium-size onions, chopped
3   bell peppers, chopped
1   (15-ounce) can creamed corn
1   (28-ounce) can stewed tomatoes, chopped
1   cup chili (no beans)
1   cup yellow cornmeal
1   (6-ounce) can pitted black olives
¾   cup shredded Cheddar cheese
     Sour cream and/or guacamole as garnish
     (optional)

In a roasting pan, cook the roast beef until tender, and then shred it. In a skillet, brown the ground beef, and drain off the excess grease. In a separate skillet, heat a little oil, and cook the onions and peppers over medium heat until tender. Preheat the oven to 350°. In a large pot, heat the corn, tomatoes, and chili. Add the onions and peppers. Add the meats and heat until the mixture bubbles. Slowly add the cornmeal to thicken the mixture. Toss in the olives and put the mixture in a casserole dish. Bake for 30 to 45 minutes. Top with the shredded cheese for the last 5 minutes of baking time. Garnish with sour cream or guacamole, if desired.

Makes 8 servings for ordinary folks or 2 hungry cowboys.

Charley Aldridge and kin, musician, writer, and actor

High Noon Creamed Dried Beef

3   tablespoons butter
3   tablespoons all-purpose flour
2   cups milk
¾   teaspoon salt
¼   teaspoon pepper
1   jar thinly sliced dried beef

In a saucepan over medium heat, melt the butter and stir in the flour until smooth. Add the milk slowly while stirring constantly. Cook until thick. Stir in the salt and pepper. Add the dried beef. Serve over toast.

Makes 2 servings.

Dorothy and Tex Ritter, singer and actor

The chef is Tex Ritter (center) as he stands with son Tom Ritter (left) and a friend at his Nashville barbecue pit preparing barbecue for his restaurant, Tex Ritter's Chuck Wagon, in the spring of 1972. Cowboy singer and actor Ritter made dozens of western films and was the voice behind the classic theme from *High Noon* that begins with the piercing lament, "Do not forsake me, oh my darling." (Photo by Les Leverett)

TEX RITTER MUSEUM

The Tex Ritter Museum in Carthage, Texas, pays honor to the town's native son, cowboy actor and singer of *High Noon,* Tex Ritter. (Carthage is also proud to claim country music's Jim Reeves.)

The Tex Ritter Museum opened in 1993 in an old, two-story house off the downtown square. Located upstairs, the three-thousand-square-foot museum is filled with memorabilia from the singing cowboy's career. This includes Ritter's custom-made Nudie suits, his cowboy hats and boots, and five of his guitars.

There are Ritter record albums and autographed items and letters, as well as the original posters and lobby cards from his many films. Visitors will find a Gibson guitar made especially for Ritter, his piano, handwritten sheet music of his original songs, and even furniture from the den of his home in Nashville. Also on display are many photos, the law books from Ritter's student days at the University of Texas, and one of the microphones from his radio show.

In 2002 Carthage also became home to the Texas Country Music Hall of Fame. "We had such success with the Tex Ritter Museum that we decided to honor some of the Texans who had made contributions to country music," said Tommie Ritter Smith, a cousin of Tex's who works for the Carthage Chamber of Commerce. "We have inducted twenty-five native Texans linked to country music. People come because they love Ernest Tubb, Dale Evans, Tex Ritter, and Jim Reeves."

Most recently, a Jim Reeves exhibit has opened. It features many items from his singing career as well as the baseball uniform he wore for the St. Louis Cardinals.

Other memorabilia represented in the Texas Country Music Hall of Fame include tennis shoes, a leather jacket, and a Ping putter from Willie Nelson; a saddle that belonged to Bob Wills; party dresses from Cindy Walker; a suit and hat from Ernest Tubb; and a Golden Boot award and Army Ranger uniform from Kris Kristofferson.

The Tex Ritter Museum is located at 310 West Panola Street in Carthage, Texas. For more information, go to *www.carthagetexas.com.*

Pistol-Packin' Piroshki

Piroshki was a favorite of actor/artist George Montgomery. While filming in Moscow in 1984, he ordered piroshki, which he said were tough and did not compare to those melt-in-your-mouth meat pies his mother made at the family homestead on the "Big Sky" plains of Montana. This handed-down, Letz family recipe for piroshki comes from George's sister Frasinia Rose (Letz) Dolack.

Dough:
- 1 quart milk
- 2 tablespoons sugar
- 1 scant tablespoon salt
- 2 tablespoons oil
- 2 ounces butter
- 2 cakes dry yeast
- ½ cup warm water
- 2 eggs, beaten
- 3 sifters all-purpose flour (about 12 cups total; high-quality unbleached flour will do)

Filling:
- 2 ounces butter
- 5 medium-large onions, finely chopped
- 1 pound ground beef liver
- 2 pounds ground round
- 5 hard-cooked eggs, chopped
  Salt and pepper
- 1 gallon cooking oil for frying

To make the dough, in a large stainless steel pot, mix and warm the milk, sugar, salt, oil, and butter. Dilute the yeast cakes in the water, and add to the milk mixture. Then add the beaten eggs to the milk mixture. Sift the flour into the mixture to make a dough. Work the dough for 15 minutes or so. Cover, wrap towels around the container, and set in a warm place. When the dough rises, press it down, cover, and let it rise again.

For the filling, heat the butter in a skillet, and cook the onions until golden. Then add the ground liver and ground round until browned and juicy. Add the chopped eggs, and season to taste with the salt and pepper. Roll a portion of the dough into a long cylinder (about 2 inches in diameter) with the palms of your hands. Slice off a piece of the roll about 1½ inches thick. On a lightly floured board, place the circle of dough, cutside down. Work outward lightly with your fingertips, stretching the dough until it is about 3½ inches in diameter. Place a tea-spoon of the filling into the center of the circle. Take opposite sides of the dough and bring them together at the top to gently cover the meat filling. Press the edges together, starting at the center top and working down each side of the little meat pie until it makes a completely sealed semicircle. Cover with a clean dishtowel, and let the piroshki sit in a warm place until ready to fry in deep, hot fat. They'll rise again, and when they cook, they'll expand even more. Fry in the cooking oil until golden brown—crisp on the outside and juicy inside. Place the fried piroshki onto a platter covered with a paper towel to absorb any excess cooking oil. Serve with a bowl of sour cream.

Makes about 60 piroshki, 10 to 12 servings.

George Montgomery,
actor and western artist
Submitted by George Montgomery
Foundation of the Arts

George Montgomery starred as Matthew Rockford and was also narrator of TV's *Cimarron City* from 1958 to 1960. The former boxer and stuntman was a leading man in many films. Among his movies were *The Cisco Kid and the Lady*, *The Texas Rangers*, *Black Patch*, and *Fort Ti*. He was also famous for his furniture making and sculpting.

Leo's Perfect Oven Chicken

This is the way Dad cooked chicken. He seasoned it, and shoved it in a very hot oven. It always tasted great. Always.

—Tara Gordon

1   roasting chicken
    Salt
    Pepper
    Garlic powder

Preheat the oven to 400°. Sprinkle the salt, pepper, and garlic powder liberally all over the chicken and inside the cavity. Place the chicken, leg side down, in a broiling pan, and bake uncovered for 20 minutes. Then turn the chicken over (leg side up), and cook for another 40 to 60 minutes until cooked through. The chicken comes out crispy and garlicky on the outside, and juicy on the inside. It's always perfect.

Leo Gordon, actor

Leo Gordon was one of the great tough guys of western films and television. He showed up in the TV series *Bonanza, Gunsmoke, Cheyenne, The Rifleman, Rawhide,* and *Laredo.* He was generally menacing in the films *Hondo, Black Patch, Kitten with a Whip, My Name Is Nobody, The Jayhawkers,* and *Night of the Grizzly.*

HOPALONG CASSIDY'S CREED
FOR AMERICAN BOYS AND GIRLS

The highest badge of honor a person can wear is honesty. Be truthful at all times.

Your parents are the best friends you have. Listen to them and obey their instructions.

If you want to be respected, you must respect others. Show good manners in every way.

Only through hard work and study can you succeed. Don't be lazy.

Your good deeds always come to light. So don't boast or be a show-off.

If you waste time or money today, you will regret it tomorrow. Practice thrift in all ways.

Many animals are good and loyal companions. Be friendly and kind to them.

A strong, healthy body is a precious gift. Be neat and clean.

Our country's laws are made for your protection. Observe them carefully.

Children in many foreign lands are less fortunate than you. Be glad and proud you are an American.

Hoppy's Fried Chicken

⅓   cup all-purpose flour
1   teaspoon paprika
1   teaspoon salt
½   teaspoon powdered ginger
¼   teaspoon ground pepper
1   (2½ to 3-pound) broiler-fryer chicken, cut up
    Shortening or butter for frying

Combine the flour, paprika, salt, ginger, and pepper in a plastic bag. Add 2 or 3 pieces chicken. Shake to coat the pieces. Repeat for the rest of the chicken pieces. In a large skillet, heat the shortening or butter until a drop of water sizzles. Brown the meaty pieces first, then the remaining pieces. Brown one side, and then turn when lightly browned, after about 15 or 20 minutes. Reduce the heat, cover tightly, and cook 30 or 40 minutes, or until tender. Cook uncovered for the last 10 minutes. Use the pot drippings for gravy.

Note: If you like a crusty coating, add bread crumbs to the flour mixture.

Makes 4 to 6 servings.

Hopalong Cassidy
Submitted by Grace Bradley Boyd ("Mrs. Hopalong Cassidy")

Marcy's Cold Summer Fried Chicken

A summertime favorite, this dish will go very well with both the 1997 Pinot Blanc and the 1997 Mélanges du Rhone.

- 6 chicken breasts
    Worcestershire sauce
- 3 (12-ounce) cans evaporated milk
    Tabasco
    Cornmeal
    All-purpose flour
    Salt
    Mazola, grape seed, or olive oil

I don't have exact measurements for this recipe anymore. I suggest working with your own tastes and style. Split, bone, and clean the chicken breasts to get 12 halves. Skinless breasts are optional; however, the flour mixture will not adhere well. In a bowl, blend 10 to 12 "big" shakes of Worcestershire sauce, the evaporated milk, and a "touch" of Tabasco. You want more of the Worcestershire flavor than the Tabasco. Pour the mixture over the chicken halves. Place in an ovenproof baking dish, cover with plastic wrap, and refrigerate for 12 to 24 hours. Remove the chicken breasts from the refrigerator and drain. Fill a paper bag with cornmeal approximately three-fourths full. Add the flour to the remaining one-fourth of the bag, and add a touch of salt. Shake one chicken breast half at a time in the mixture. Add oil to a wok heated to high. Add one chicken breast half to the hot oil, and cook on one side for 5 minutes. Turn and cook until done. Remove the chicken, and use a paper towel to blot any excess oil. Refrigerate the chicken again for a minimum of 12 hours. You want the chicken pieces to be as cold as you can get them.

Note: I like to serve this dish with a fresh cold corn salad of sautéed corn, ground cumin, garlic, and diced red bell peppers. In addition, serve with cornbread with green chile peppers. Enjoy!

Makes 12 servings.

Fess Parker, actor

Fess Parker was king of two wild frontiers: he was Walt Disney's Davy Crockett in the 1950s and NBC's Daniel Boone in the 1960s.

Duke's Favorite Chicken Marsala

2	cloves garlic, finely chopped
3	tablespoons olive oil
	Dash of salt
12	pieces chicken (cuts of your choice)
2	cups stewed tomatoes
	Dash of paprika
¼	teaspoon basil
¼	teaspoon oregano
¼	teaspoon rosemary
½	cup Marsala dry wine
	Salt and pepper

In a large skillet or sauté pan, heat the garlic with the oil and a dash of salt. Sauté the chicken until golden brown. Discard the oil. Add the tomatoes, paprika, basil, oregano, rosemary, Marsala, and salt and pepper. Cover and simmer for about an hour. Serve with white rice.

Makes 6 servings.

Pilar and John Wayne,
actress/artist and actor

Just like on TV's *Gunsmoke*, there really was a Long Branch Saloon in Dodge City, Kansas. It was named after the town of Long Branch, New Jersey.

Skillet Chicken Parmesan

4 plus 2 tablespoons grated Parmesan cheese
1½ cups marinara sauce
6 boneless chicken breast halves, about 1½ pounds
1½ cups shredded mozzarella cheese

Stir 4 tablespoons of the Parmesan cheese into the marinara sauce. Spray a skillet with cooking spray and heat 1 minute. Add the chicken pieces to the skillet, and cook until browned. Drain. Pour the marinara sauce over the chicken. Turn the breasts over to coat both sides with sauce. Cover and cook over medium heat for 10 minutes or until done. Top with the mozzarella cheese and the remaining 2 tablespoons of the Parmesan cheese. Let stand for 5 minutes or until the cheese is melted.

Makes 6 servings.

Tim Holt, actor
Submitted by son and daughter-in-law Jay and Sandie Holt

Tim Holt was known as one of the fastest draws among the Hollywood cowboys, as he could clear his revolver from his holster in about a sixth of a second. A favorite cowboy of the 1940s, he made more than sixty films, including *My Darling Clementine, Stagecoach, Law West of Tombstone,* and *Under the Tonto Rim.* He also starred in *Treasure of the Sierra Madre* and *The Magnificent Ambersons.*

Nicknamed "Two Gun Bill," William S. Hart was one of the first great western stars of the silver screen. He made more than fifty silent-movie westerns between 1914 and 1925. He even wrote and directed many of them himself. Among his titles were *The Tollgate, The Man from Nowhere, Grit,* and *Tumbleweeds.* (Photo courtesy of Friends of Hart Park & Museum)

Hart-of-the-Southwest Chicken Casserole

Corn tortillas
Cooked and boned chicken
Shredded mozzarella cheese
Olive oil
1 onion, finely chopped
Flour
Milk, warmed
Green onions, chopped
Canned green chiles, chopped

Tear enough of the corn tortillas to cover the bottom of a 13 x 9-inch casserole dish. Add a layer of chicken and a layer of cheese. Repeat the layers. Preheat the oven to 350°. In a medium pan, heat a little olive oil, and sauté the onions until translucent. Add more oil and some flour to make a roux. When the roux is slightly browned, add warm milk to make a white sauce. Add some chopped green onions and chopped canned chiles. Pour this over the chicken and cheese, and bake in the oven for approximately 45 minutes. Add more cheese to the top before serving.

Makes 6 to 8 servings.

William S. Hart
Submitted by Donna Chipperfield,
President/CEO, Friends of Hart Park and
Museum

WILLIAM S. HART RANCH AND MUSEUM

When cowboy star William S. Hart (1864–1946) passed away, he bestowed an enduring gift on the citizens of Los Angeles. He willed his 265-acre ranch and its twenty-two room mansion to the city for the establishment of a public park and museum.

One of the first bona fide movie stars in history, Hart was a Shakespearean actor whose travels in the American West made him something of an expert on the subject. Disappointed by the crudity and inaccuracy of western movies, Hart got into pictures partially to ensure a more realistic depiction of the Old West.

The actor spent his spare time amassing a tremendous collection of western artifacts and movie memorabilia, almost all of which is on display or in storage at the museum. Visitors view original paintings by Frederic Remington and paintings and sculptures by Charles Russell, who was a close friend of the actor. Hart amassed a substantial collection of Indian beadwork and more than fifty Navajo rugs.

The institution displays some of Hart's original costumes, his makeup kit, and vintage movie posters. The park surrounding the Spanish Colonial Revival mansion includes an original ranchhouse where visitors can see the gambling equipment from *The Cold Deck* (1917), one of Hart's westerns.

The park also features natural trails, picnic areas, and live animals, including a small herd of American bison presented to the park by Walt Disney. And best of all, admission to the museum and park is free—just as Hart decreed in his will.

Hart Park and Museum is located at 24151 San Fernando Road in Newhall, California. For more details, go to *www.hartmuseum.org*.

Penny's Henny
Salad Casserole

4   cups cooked, bite-size chicken pieces
2   cups cooked brown rice*
2   cups cooked wild rice*
2   cups diced celery
½   cup chopped green bell pepper
½   cup chopped red bell pepper
2   (8-ounce) cans water chestnuts, diced
2   cups mayonnaise
½   cup chopped parsley

Preheat the oven to 350°. Combine the chicken, brown and wild rice, celery, bell peppers, water chestnuts, mayonnaise, and parsley in a large casserole, and bake in the oven about 45 minutes.

Makes 6 to 8 servings.

*1 cup raw rice equals 3½ cups cooked.

Gloria Winters Vernon, actress

San Cobra Chicken

½   cup all-purpose flour
½   cup bacon grease or lard
2   teaspoons onion salt
    Dash of black pepper
1   teaspoon cayenne
2   teaspoons paprika
1   teaspoon ground cumin
1   (approximately 3-pound) chicken, cut into serving pieces

Barbecue Sauce:
¾   cup water
¾   cup ketchup
2   tablespoons grated onion
1   clove garlic, minced
1   tablespoon chopped parsley

In a bowl, blend the flour, bacon grease or lard, onion salt, black pepper, cayenne, paprika, and ground cumin. In a baking dish, spread this coating over the chicken pieces. In a saucepan, make the barbecue sauce: combine the water, ketchup, onion, garlic, and parsley. Heat the sauce to boiling, and pour over the chicken. Bake at 325° for about 1 hour, or until tender. Or, soak the chicken in the sauce for three hours and then grill.

Makes 4 to 6 servings.

Kirby Jonas, writer

Easy, Pleasin' Chicken
Noodle Casserole

1   package wide egg noodles
    Butter for noodles plus ½ cup butter
1   cup cut-up cooked chicken
1   (10¾-ounce) can cream of chicken soup, undiluted
½   cup mayonnaise
1   tablespoon lemon juice
    Salt and pepper
2   cups shredded Cheddar cheese
3   to 4 cups cornflakes or Special K cereal

In a large pot of water, cook the noodles, and then drain and lightly butter them. Spray a 12 x 9-inch pan with cooking oil (or grease with butter). Spread the noodles in the pan. (You may have some left over to put in the refrigerator.) Preheat the oven to 350°. In a bowl, mix together the chicken, soup, mayonnaise, and lemon juice, and lightly add the salt and pepper. Spread the mixture over the noodles, and sprinkle with the Cheddar cheese. Melt the ½ cup butter, and mix with the cereal. Spread the cereal mixture on top of the cheese. Loosely cover with foil. Cook for 35 minutes.

Makes 6 to 8 servings.

Bob Eubanks, rodeo cowboy

Famed as *The Newlywed Game* host, Bob Eubanks really is a cowboy. KTLA's man in the booth for the Pasadena Tournament of Roses Parade is a team roper and raises quarter horses on his ranch in the Santa Ynez area of California.

Liberty Chicken and Broccoli Casserole

6   chicken thighs
3   chicken breasts
2   or 3 ribs celery
1   large onion, cut
3   (10-ounce) packages frozen broccoli
     Salt and pepper
2   (10¾-ounce) cans cream of chicken soup
     (do not dilute)
1   cup mayonnaise
1   cup sour cream
1   plus 2 cups grated mild Cheddar cheese
2   cups crumbled cornflakes
     Butter

In a large pot, cover the chicken, celery, onion, and broccoli with water, and simmer for at least 1 hour. Cool and discard the water, celery, and onion (I save it and make chicken vegetable soup later). Discard the chicken skin, and bone the chicken. Cut into bite-size pieces. Next, lightly grease an 11 x 7 x 2-inch baking dish. Add a layer of the cooked broccoli, cut into bite-size pieces, and then a layer of the chicken. Add salt and pepper to taste. Preheat the oven to 350°. In a bowl, combine the soup, mayonnaise, sour cream, and 1 cup Cheddar cheese. Mix well. Spread this mixture over the chicken and broccoli. Top with the remaining 2 cups Cheddar cheese and the cornflake crumbs. Dot with the butter, and bake for 20 minutes or until hot. Eat and enjoy.

Makes 6 to 8 servings.

Montie Montana,
trick roper, actor, and rodeo cowboy

Montie Montana made about a dozen westerns spanning the 1930s to the 1960s and was famed for his expertise as a trick roper and rider. He once roped President Dwight Eisenhower. He rode in more than sixty Rose Bowl Parades, entertained in rodeos for more than seventy years, and was in such films as *The Kid From Texas, Hud,* and *The Man Who Shot Liberty Valance.*

"America's Number One Cowboy's Sweetheart," Patsy Montana poses with her own little sweetheart, daughter Beverly, in this 1939 photograph. The Cowgirl Hall of Fame inductee sold a million copies of her self-penned "I Want to Be a Cowboy's Sweetheart" in 1935. (Photo courtesy of Beverly Losey)

Patsy's Arkansas Chicken and Dumplings

1 large, fat hen, cut into sections
   Green onions
   Celery
   Garlic
1 or 2 cans biscuits
   All-purpose flour

Place the hen sections in a large stew pot. Cover with water. Bring to a boil. Put on low, and cook for 1 hour or until the meat is falling off the bones. With a slotted spoon remove the chicken. Place on a cookie sheet to cool. When sufficiently cooled, pull the meat from the bones. (Country cooking hint: Bones can be covered with water again in a saucepan with a little salt and apple cider vinegar and stewed again for another hour for more delicious broth for future recipes. The salt and vinegar leaches the rest of the minerals from the bones.) Start bringing the broth slowly back to a boil. Chop some green onions, celery, and garlic, and sauté slightly in a skillet. Add them to the broth.

Take 1 or 2 cans of biscuits (depending on how many folks have dropped in), or if you're a stickler for authenticity, prepare your own favorite biscuit recipe using broth instead of milk. Roll each biscuit on a well-floured board to about the thickness of a lasagna noodle. Cut in 2-inch strips. When all the strips are cut, drop a few at a time in the boiling broth, being careful not to let the boil die down. When all of the strips are in the pot, add the boned chicken, stirring slightly. Lower the heat, cover, and cook for about 20 minutes more or until the dumplings are done. Add salt and pepper to taste.

Serve with wilted salad greens straight from the garden. To wilt greens, fry a couple of slices of bacon. Pour the hot bacon grease over the greens. Crumble the bacon over the salad. Guaranteed not to have any leftovers.

Makes 4 to 6 servings.

Patsy Montana, singer/songwriter

R. W. Hampton is a true cowboy who hails from Sedan, New Mexico. He possesses a voice that makes you think of trail drives and the open range. A top-selling singer and songwriter of western music, his current albums are *The Last Cowboy: His Journey, Born to Be a Cowboy, The One That I Never Could Ride,* and *Then Sings My Soul.* Hampton has made ten movies, including *Wild Horses, The Tracker,* and *The Gambler III.*

Big Red's Wild Fowl or Chicken with Sourdough Dumplin's

Winner of Pawnee Bill's Chuck Wagon Cook-Off, 2000.

- 1   **stewing chicken, wild fowl, or 6 quail (no buzzards or chicken hawks)**
- ½   **teaspoon salt**
- 1   **teaspoon black pepper**
      Ingredients for Perfect Sourdough Biscuits (see recipe on page 182)
- 1   **cup plus 6 tablespoon all-purpose flour**
- 2   **hard-cooked eggs, chopped**

Place the meat, ½ teaspoon salt, and 1 teaspoon black pepper in an 8-quart pot. Cover liberally with water (approximately 3 quarts). Bring to a boil, and then boil gently for 1 hour, adding water occasionally to keep the water level near 3 quarts. Approximately 20 minutes before the meat has finished cooking, mix up a batch of Perfect Sourdough Biscuits. Flour the work surface, and just before you turn the sourdough out of the mixing bowl, add 1 more cup of flour to stiffen the dough. Handle the dough as little as possible to produce tender biscuits or dumplin's. Turn the dough onto a floured work surface, and press out flat until approximately ¼ inch thick. Lightly dust the top of the dough with flour. Let the dough rest while you remove the meat from the pot and place it in a flat loaf pan. Set aside to cool. Remove 2 cups of the broth to cool, leaving the remaining broth in the pot at a simmer.

With a floured shot glass, start cutting round dumplin's, and gently drop them into the simmering broth. Stir each time after dropping approximately 15 dumplin's. This will keep them from sticking together. When all the dumplin's are in the pot, stir to dampen. Cover and let simmer for about 15 minutes, stirring occasionally to keep the foam down. Leave the dumplin's slightly simmering while you bone the cooled meat. Chop the meat into 1-inch squares. (This process needs to be done quickly.) Mix 6 tablespoons flour into the 2 cups of broth that was set aside earlier to cool. Stir until smooth. Remove the lid on the dumplin's, and pour this mixture into the broth. Stir until mixed well. The mixture will thicken. Season to taste with salt and pepper. Add the diced meat and chopped eggs to the dumplin' mixture. Cover tightly, lower the flame, and simmer for 15 minutes. Cover must not be removed while dumplin's are cooking. If steam escapes, the dumplin's will not be light. This is a favorite in cold weather.

Lee Henry, Rockin' L-H Chuck Wagon
Eufaula, Oklahoma

Clearview Ranch Enchilada Dinner

1 tablespoon cooking oil
2 to 3 pounds chicken meat, cubed into bite-size pieces
1 (8-ounce) package cream cheese, softened
1 (4-ounce) can diced green chiles
12 medium-size flour tortillas
2 (10-ounce) cans green enchilada sauce (mild is better)
2 cups grated Cheddar or mozzarella cheese, or both

Grease a 12 x 9-inch pan (or larger if making extra). In a large pan, heat the oil and cook the chicken over medium heat until done. In a separate bowl, mix together the cream cheese and green chiles, and then add the mixture to the chicken. Cook over low heat, stirring to mix, until the cheese is melted. Remove the pan from the heat. Place spoonfuls of the mixture on the tortillas and roll up. Lay the rolls, side by side, in the prepared pan. (The pan should be crowded when done.) Pour the enchilada sauce over the tortillas. Sprinkle the grated cheese on top of the sauce.

If storing overnight or freezing, cover with plastic wrap and then aluminum foil. To bake, preheat the oven to 350°, and then place the uncovered and thawed pan in the oven for about 20 minutes, or until the cheese is melted and lightly browned. Serve with a fresh green salad, crisp tortilla chips, a good salsa, and guacamole.

Makes 6 to 8 servings.

Lisa and R. W. Hampton,
cowboy singer/songwriter

Closing Time Chimichangas

60 ounces chicken or beef
1 egg
1 tablespoon water
10 (12-inch) tortillas
30 ounces shredded Cheddar or Monterey Jack cheese
    Choice of toppings (salsa, guacamole, sour cream, lettuce, and tomatoes)

Cook the meat. Shred the meat. Preheat the oven to 425°. In a bowl, mix the egg and water. Coat both sides of a tortilla with the egg mixture. Place 6 ounces meat and 3 ounces cheese in the tortilla. Roll the tortilla like a burrito. Place the chimichanga folded side down on a greased baking sheet. Repeat the procedure for the remaining nine tortillas. Spray the tortillas lightly with cooking spray. Bake for 8 minutes. Turn the chimichangas over with a spatula, and bake for 5 minutes more.

Makes 10 servings.

Mickey Gilley, singer

Country music star Mickey Gilley opened Gilley's Club in Pasadena, Texas, in 1971. The world-famous honky-tonk was the inspiration and the backdrop for the film *Urban Cowboy.* He portrayed himself in the 1980 box-office champion. He also was a guest on *Fantasy Island,* where he did a bit of line dancing with Herve Villechaize (left). Today, Gilley performs at his club in Branson, Missouri.

Stuntman Jesse Wayne is a veteran of dozens of western films and TV series, such as *Bonanza, Gunsmoke, The Virginian,* and *Wagon Train,* and he played one of the Scully brothers on *Nichols.* Here, he pulls a revolver on Rex Bell Jr. in the 1964 film *Young Fury.*

Cowboy Curried Chicken Salad Sandwich

Dressing:
- 2   cups mayonnaise
- ½   cup commercial chutney
- 3   tablespoons mild curry powder

Salad:
- 6   bone-in chicken breasts
      Kosher salt and freshly ground black pepper
- ½   cup coarsely chopped walnuts
- ½   cup dark raisins
- ¾   cup finely chopped celery
- 4   croissants

To make the dressing, combine the mayonnaise with the chutney and the curry powder in a small bowl. Mix well. To prepare the salad, season the chicken breasts with salt and pepper, and put them in a large skillet. Add water to cover. Put a lid on the skillet, and simmer the chicken until it is cooked through, about 20 minutes. Remove the chicken from the poaching liquid, and refrigerate for at least 1 hour. When the chicken is chilled, remove the skin and cut the meat from the bones. Dice the meat, and place it in a large bowl. Add the walnuts, raisins, and celery, and mix well. Moisten the salad with the curry dressing. Cut the croissants in half. Fill each with the chicken salad and serve.

Makes 4 servings.

Jesse Wayne, stuntman

Rio Grande Chicken Enchilada Pie

¼ cup butter
1 medium onion, chopped
1½ cups cubed cooked chicken
1 (10¾-ounce) can cream of chicken soup
4 ounces chopped green chiles
1 medium bag taco-flavored tortilla chips
10 ounces grated sharp Cheddar cheese

In a skillet, melt the butter. Sauté the onion in the butter until the onion is translucent. Add the chicken, soup, ¾ of the soup can of water, and the chiles. Mix and simmer for 30 minutes. Preheat the oven to 350°. In an 8-inch pan, layer the tortilla chips, then half the chicken sauce, and then half the cheese. Repeat the layers. Bake in the oven for 30 minutes (or microwave 10 minutes on roast).
    Makes 4 to 5 servings.

Gail and Earl Bellamy, director

Saddle-Up Stuffed Turkey Breast

1 boneless turkey breast, pounded until thin
    Special Seasoning (recipe follows)
1 (5-ounce) bag baby spinach
6 to 8 slices provolone cheese
6 to 8 slices smoked ham (optional)
    Melted butter

Preheat the oven to 350°. Sprinkle the turkey breast with Special Seasoning. Spread a layer of spinach over the seasoned breast, and then add layers of provolone and then ham, if using. Roll up the turkey in jelly-roll style, and secure with kitchen string. Place the breast on an oiled rack in a roasting pan. Baste with the melted butter, and sprinkle with the Special Seasoning. Roast until the internal temperature is 180°, about 1½ to 2½ hours, depending on the size of the breast. Remove from the oven, and let rest for 15 minutes before slicing (be sure to remove all the string before slicing). Make a pan of gravy out of the drippings.

Special Seasoning:
1 cup Lawry's seasoned salt
1 cup lemon pepper
1 cup mesquite seasoning
½ cup onion salt
½ cup garlic salt

Mix the Lawry's, lemon pepper, mesquite seasoning, onion salt, and garlic salt. Use as needed. Store in a container in a cool, dry place.

Jane Woods, Laughing Water Ranch Fortine, Montana

Tumbleweed Turkey Meatballs

1 pound ground turkey breast
    Bread crumbs
2 large carrots, grated
1 onion, chopped
    Dried sage
    Chopped parsley
2 eggs
1 tablespoon milk
    Vegetable oil

In a bowl, place the minced turkey, a couple of generous handfuls of bread crumbs, the carrots, onion, and a little sage and parsley for seasoning. Beat the eggs and milk together, and pour over the turkey mixture. Mix together well with your hands, and then form the minced mixture into balls (about the size of golf balls). In a nonstick pan with a little vegetable oil over medium heat, fry the meatballs until they are sufficiently browned. Serve with mashed potatoes and grilled tomatoes.
    Makes about 36 meatballs.

Sir Roger Moore, actor

Long before he was The Saint and 007, Sir Roger Moore was a cowboy. He starred in the 1959 TV series *The Alaskans* and was British cousin to James Garner as Beau Maverick in *Maverick* in 1960. He also starred with Clint Walker in the film *Gold of the Seven Saints*.

Fess Parker dropped his buckskins for more western-styled duds in *The Jayhawkers!* Among his other western films are *Old Yeller, The Great Locomotive Chase, The Light in the Forest,* and *Smoky.*

Spanish Pork Roast

This is a tried and true recipe I have had for years. The marinade is a bit sassy and is a perfect partner with Fess Parker Merlot. Serve with wild rice and mushrooms, baby carrots, and an organic, mixed green salad garnished with avocado and grapefruit slices.

5   cloves garlic, crushed
2   pinches of oregano
½   teaspoon cumin powder
    Dash of cayenne
½   cup red vinegar
    Salt and pepper
1   (2 to 3-pound) pork roast

Combine the garlic, oregano, cumin, cayenne, vinegar, and salt and pepper in a small bowl. Pour the mixture over the pork roast, and let marinate for two hours in the refrigerator, basting intermittently (the roast can even marinate overnight). When you're ready to cook, preheat the oven to 300°. Place the roast in a roasting pan, and bake for 2½ to 3 hours or until done. Enjoy.

Makes 4 servings.

Marcy and Fess Parker, actor

Frost-on-the-Pumpkin Pork Chops

1   cup canned pumpkin
1   (8-ounce) jar medium-hot salsa
1   chipotle chile
⅓   cup grated Parmesan cheese
½   teaspoon ground nutmeg
2   tablespoons packed brown sugar
¼   teaspoon ground cinnamon
1   teaspoon ground cumin
1   teaspoon chili powder
½   teaspoon salt
½   teaspoon black pepper
1   teaspoon olive oil
4   boneless pork chops, cut 1 inch thick

In a medium saucepan, combine the pumpkin, salsa, chipotle, cheese, and nutmeg. Cook over medium heat, stirring occasionally, until the mixture is about to boil. Reduce the heat to low, and simmer for 10 minutes, stirring occasionally. In a medium bowl, combine the brown sugar, cinnamon, cumin, chili powder, salt, and pepper. Sprinkle the mixture over the pork chops. In a nonstick skillet, heat the olive oil over medium-high heat. Add the pork chops, and cook for 8 to 10 minutes, or until browned on both sides. Serve the pork chops on top of or beside a generous dollop of the pumpkin mixture.

Makes 4 servings.

Terry Frost, actor

Writer and actor Terry Frost was in dozens of episodic TV westerns and made more than 120 films from the early 1940s to the early 1970s, including such titles as *Waco, Barbed Wire,* and *Outlaws of Texas.*

"America's Western Sweetheart," Belinda Gail has been the Western Music Association's female performer of the year four times and was selected for the same honor in 2004 by the Academy of Western Artists. She often performs with Curly Musgrave, with whom she recorded the album *When Trails Meet*.

America's Western Sweetheart Pork Chops and Onions

4   to 6 pork chops
    Soy sauce
¼   cup olive oil
    Lemon pepper
    Granulated garlic
2   large red or yellow onions, sliced
1   cup all-purpose flour seasoned with lemon
    pepper and granulated garlic
¼   cup wine (your choice of type; optional)

Sprinkle the pork chops with the soy sauce on both sides, spreading it lightly with your fingers, and set aside to allow to marinate while you prepare the skillet and onions. In a large skillet over medium-high heat pour in the olive oil, and sprinkle it lightly with lemon pepper and granulated garlic. Add the onions, and sauté lightly, just until the onions begin to look translucent around the edges. Remove the onions from the skillet. Dredge the pork chops in the seasoned flour, and brown them on both sides in the skillet that you just used to sweat the onions. Remove the pork chops, and add a thin layer of the cooked onions back to the skillet. Place the browned pork chops on the thin layer of onions, and add the remaining onions on top of the pork chops. At this point you may add the wine. Cover the skillet, and reduce to a simmer for 30 minutes.

Makes 4 to 6 servings.

Belinda Gail, singer

Movie cowboy Ben Cooper is not only good-looking but also quick on the draw. He flashed his smile and his six-gun in such films as *Johnny Guitar, Gunfight at Comanche Creek, Arizona Raiders, The Fastest Guitar Alive, Support Your Local Gunfighter*, and *Lightning Jack*. He is a favored emcee on the western movie festival circuit.

Quick-Draw Pork Chops

2   to 4 pork chops, about 1 inch thick
    Garlic pepper
    Butter-flavored cooking spray
    Ginger-Sesame Marinade, either Lawry's or your favorite brand
½   ounce red wine plus more for sauce
    Dr. Pepper (not Diet)

Rub the chops with garlic pepper. Using a nonstick pan coated with butter-flavored spray, sear the chops. Sear one side for 2½ minutes over medium-high heat. Turn the chops over. While searing the second side, apply the marinade to the top side. After 2½ minutes, turn the chops and marinate the other side. Cook for 1 minute. Pour the red wine over the chops. Cover and lower the heat. As the liquid starts to coagulate and bubble, add 3 to 5 tablespoons of Dr. Pepper and cover. Cook for another minute or two or until desired doneness. Remove the chops from the pan, and cover them to keep them warm. Add more wine, marinade, and Dr. Pepper to the pan, and gently simmer to make a sauce. Drizzle the sauce over the chops and enjoy.

Makes 2 to 4 servings.

Ben Cooper, actor

Grizzly Pork Chop Potato Casserole

2 to 4 pork chops
  Flour
  Seasonings
  Vegetable oil for browning
1 box Betty Crocker scalloped potatoes

Preheat the oven to 375°. Coat the pork chops with flour and season as desired. In a frying pan, brown the pork chops in the oil. In a Dutch oven, mix the scalloped potato mix as directed on the box. Place the pork chops on top of the potatoes, and bake for about 40 minutes.

Makes 2 to 4 servings.

Gregg Palmer, actor

Robert Loggia played cowboys as a guest on such series as *Wagon Train, Rawhide, Gunsmoke, The High Chaparral,* and *The Big Valley.* His most colorful western character was Elfego Baca—based on the real-life Mexican American, a lawman and a lawyer who knew Billy the Kid and Pancho Villa—in the 1958 Disney series *The Nine Lives of Elfego Baca.*

Slow Cooker Spare Ribs Loggia

2 pounds pork spare ribs
1 (10¾-ounce) can tomato soup
1 onion, chopped
2 cloves garlic, minced
2 tablespoons packed brown sugar
2 tablespoons Worcestershire sauce
1 tablespoon soy sauce

Put the spare ribs in a large pot, and cover with water. Bring to a boil, and cook for 15 minutes. In a large mixing bowl, mix together the soup, onion, garlic, brown sugar, Worcestershire sauce, and soy sauce. Move the ribs from the pot of water to a slow cooker. Pour the sauce over the ribs. Put the lid on the slow cooker, and cook on low for 6 to 8 hours, or until the ribs are tender and the sauce is the desired thickness.

Makes 4 servings.

Robert Loggia, actor

Gregg Palmer played a cowboy in episodes of practically every classic TV western. He also worked in some of the top western films, such as *The Shootist, Shenandoah, The Rare Breed, Chisum, Big Jake,* and *True Grit.*

Adrian's
Stuffed Leg of Lamb

Filling:
- 1 cup cooked wild rice
- 1 medium onion, chopped
- 8 canned apricot halves, cut up
  Salt
  Lemon pepper
- ¼ teaspoon curry powder
- 1 large leg of lamb (have your butcher make a pocket in the leg by removing the large bone at the top of the leg)
  Lemon juice
  Garlic salt
  Salt
  Lemon pepper
  Crushed oregano leaves

For the filling, mix together in a bowl the rice, onion, apricots, salt and lemon pepper to taste, and the curry powder. Stuff the lamb pocket with the rice mixture. Close with toothpicks. Preheat the oven to 350°. Line a roaster with a sheet of heavy-duty aluminum foil. Place the lamb fat side down on the aluminum foil. Sprinkle generously with the lemon juice, garlic salt, salt and lemon pepper to taste, and oregano leaves. Turn the lamb and repeat the process. Cover the lamb with foil. Cook for 1 hour. Reduce the heat to 250°, and continue to cook slowly until done. We often serve this dish with Brussels sprouts.

Makes 10 to 12 servings.

Adrian Booth Brian and David Brian, actors

Adrian Booth, a.k.a. Lorna Gray, was the star of numerous serial cliffhangers and B-westerns, working opposite such cowboys as John Wayne, Bob Livingston, Monte Hale, Wild Bill Elliott, and Rod Cameron. Among her more than sixty film credits are *Red River Range, Deadwood Dick,* and *Home on the Range.*

Quick-draw expert Arvo Ojala designed many of the leather holsters and gun belts used by Hollywood's movie and TV cowboys, and that's him you see being gunned down by Marshal Dillon at the beginning of many episodes of *Gunsmoke*.

Dodge City Venison-Cabbage Rolls

1 **large white cabbage**
 Water
1 **teaspoon salt**

Filling:
1 **onion, finely chopped**
1 **cup ground deer or elk**
½ **cup minced hot sausage**
 Cabbage cooking liquid (use in topping as well)
2 **cups chopped cabbage**
2 **cups boiled rice**
1 **teaspoon salt**
¼ **teaspoon white pepper**
1 **teaspoon marjoram**

Topping:
1 **to 2 tablespoons corn syrup**
 Butter or fat
 Cabbage cooking water for basting

Gravy:
3 **cups pan juice**
2 **tablespoons all-purpose flour**
 A little cream

Cut the base off the cabbage, and cook the cabbage in salted water until the leaves are soft. You can carefully loosen the outer leaves as they soften. Lift the cooked cabbage onto a large plate to drain. Reserve the cooking water. Loosen the leaves one by one, and chop the small inner leaves for the filling.

To make the filling, in a skillet, heat a small amount of oil, add the onions, and cook until the onions are translucent but not brown. In a pot, combine the meat, 1 cup of the cabbage cooking water, chopped cabbage, rice, salt, white pepper, and marjoram. Cook over medium heat, and stir into a smooth mixture. If the mixture is too thick, add some more of the cabbage cooking water. Flatten the cabbage leaves. Lift a good tablespoonful of filling onto the leaf, and roll it up, tucking the edges round the mixture. Place the rolls side by side in a 13 x 9-inch baking dish, and for the topping, pour the corn syrup and a little butter or fat over them. Bake the rolls for 1 hour at 350°. Halfway through the baking, turn the rolls over, and baste them every now and then with cabbage water.

To make the gravy, strain the juices from the pan into a saucepan over medium heat. In a separate bowl, mix the flour and water together, and then slowly stir the flour mixture into the saucepan. Add a little cream to the mixture, and stir until heated through and smooth. Serve the cabbage rolls with boiled potatoes.

Makes 6 to 8 servings.

Arvo Ojala, quick-draw expert, and gun-belt and holster innovator

Sons of the Pioneers cofounder Bob Nolan sports a smile for the camera in 1945.

Bob's Pioneering Technique for Smoked Oven Trout

After cleaning your trout, pat it with coarse salt both inside and out. Wrap the trout in aluminum foil, and put it in the refrigerator for 1 hour per pound. Remove the trout from the refrigerator, and wash thoroughly, both inside and out. Preheat the oven to 225°. Line a pan with foil. Sprinkle the trout very lightly inside and out with liquid smoke. Prop the fish belly side down by pulling flesh out on each side for support. Create a "tent" of foil over the fish, and bake for 1 hour per pound. When done, the trout will separate into flakes. Remove to a plate and serve.

Note: Bob used liquid smoke in the recipe to get the smoked flavor. His main meal of the day up at Big Bear Lake was the single trout he would catch off the dock at Gray's Landing almost every evening. He probably had a number of ways to prepare it, but the smoked recipe was one of his favorites. Bob said it was also delicious served on crackers with white wine. Bob emphasized the low temperature—definitely somewhere between 200° and 250°. Dixie tried this recipe on at least five occasions in the past with very satisfactory results each time. She got the same results, a thoroughly cooked but moist fish.

Bob Nolan, Sons of the Pioneers
Submitted by Dick and Dixie Goodman

Bob Nolan crosses paths with Charles Starrett (left) and Irish Meredith in the 1939 film *Spoilers of the Range.*

John Fletcher hosts *The Record Roundup*, playing everything from western tunes to punk rock, on radio station KFJC in the San Francisco Bay area. His hero is Gene Autry.

Rough and Ready Spaghetti

In a pan, fry a pound of top choice ground burger.
Add some sliced sausage to flavor it further.
Salt and pepper to taste will make it quite nice.
Throw in some oregano; this is the main spice.
Add two cans of diced tomatoes; simmer while boiling the spaghetti.
The next part is why this spaghetti is called rough and ready.
Mix it together for tomorrow or now.
But finish by frying until crispy brown.
Top it with plenty of Parmesan cheese.
When you're asking for seconds, remember to say "Please."
This recipe is in rhyme for a very good reason.
I try to be like my hero, Cindy Walker, no matter the season.

John Fletcher, deejay at KFJC, San Francisco

A Cord Pasta

Here is a pasta dish from Texas. It'll make a native Italian wish he came from somewhere "deep in the heart . . ."

2   pounds farfalle (bowtie) pasta
     Olive oil—a lot
6   to 8 cloves garlic, or more if you like
     Rosemary
     Basil
     Savory
     Oregano, fresh or dried
     Salt
     Black pepper
6   to 8 chicken breasts, cut into strips
2   bunches broccoli, cut up (peel the stems and use them, too)
½   (7-ounce) can black olives, preferably kalamata
5   ounces sun-dried tomatoes (from a jar)
     Hot red pepper flakes

Put a large pot of water on to boil for the farfalle. In a large skillet or wok (my preference), combine the olive oil, garlic, some rosemary, basil, savory, oregano, salt, pepper, and the chicken. Brown the chicken. Remove all from the wok, and add more oil, garlic, and herbs to the wok. Add the broccoli, olives, sun-dried tomatoes, and hot pepper flakes to taste. Cook until the broccoli is done, stirring frequently. If you want the broccoli more steamed than stir-fried, put a lid on the wok for part of the time. When it's done, add the cooked chicken back to the wok, and mix it into the broccoli. Strain the cooked farfalle without shaking out all the water, and add to the wok. Mix it all together and serve. Then stand back and be satisfied by the pleasure you've given to those who partake.

Makes about 16 servings.

Alex Cord, actor

Alex Cord was a rodeo cowboy who went on to become a movie star cowboy in the 1966 remake of the classic *Stagecoach*. Cord also starred in *Grayeagle* and *A Minute to Pray, A Second to Die* and was a guest on the TV series *Gunsmoke, Branded,* and *The Virginian.*

Texan Johnny Lee made a big mark in country music with his giant hit "Looking for Love" from the film *Urban Cowboy*. The country singer has numerous hits under his belt, including "Cherokee Cowboy" and "Yellow Rose of Texas."

Urban Cowboy's Brown Spaghetti

   Butter
   Minced garlic
1 onion, chopped
1 green bell pepper, chopped
3 ribs celery, chopped
   Chicken parts
1 package boneless pork steaks
1 package link sausage
   Salt and pepper
1 small bundle green onion tops
½ bottle Kitchen Bouquet
1 package spaghetti noodles

In a large, hot skillet, melt a little butter. Sauté garlic to taste, onion, bell pepper, and celery. In a large pot, add the chicken pieces—whatever parts you like. Add the pork steaks and link sausage. Add salt and pepper to taste. Add the veggies from the skillet to the pot. In another pot, boil three quarts of water. Take off heat and add all the meat and veggies and the green onion tops. Add the Kitchen Bouquet. Bring to a boil and then add the package of spaghetti. When it starts to boil again, reduce the heat to a simmer. Put a lid on, and let the mixture simmer until done, about 45 minutes. Strain and serve.

Makes about 8 servings.

Johnny Lee, singer

Dante's Pasta Salsiccia

Extra virgin olive oil
6 **cloves garlic, finely chopped**
2 **(16-ounce) cans whole peeled tomatoes with basil**
Fresh parsley, chopped
Salt and pepper
2 **links hot Italian sausage, removed from casings**
2 **links sweet Italian sausage, removed from casings**

In a medium pot, heat enough olive oil to sauté the garlic until it is almost tan in color, being careful not to let it burn. Chop the tomatoes in a blender, and then add them to the pot with the garlic. Add some parsley and salt and pepper to taste. In a frying pan, brown the sausage links. Do not cook them through. Add the sausage to the sauce, and then bring the sauce to a boil for 20 minutes. Lower the heat and simmer for 1 hour and 30 minutes. Serve the sauce over the pasta of your choice.

Note: This sauce will taste better if you allow it to cool off and then refrigerate it overnight. Heat it up and serve it the next day. The flavor is much better.

Makes 4 to 5 servings.

Michael Dante, actor

Actor and athlete Michael Dante made more than thirty motion pictures, including *Winterhawk, Arizona Raiders, Fort Dobbs,* and *Apache Rifles*. His TV western credits include *Cheyenne, Maverick, Bonanza,* and *Custer*. He is host of the Southern California radio program *The Michael Dante Celebrity Talk Show*.

Known as "the Arizona Cowboy" and "the Voice of the West," Rex Allen was the last of the silver screen singing cowboys. He made about twenty western films from 1950 into the early 1960s. Here, Rex Allen Sr. and Jr. enjoy a day at the ranch.

Almost Fat-Free Lasagna

12   lasagna noodles, about 12 ounces
2   cups grated fat-free mozzarella cheese
¼   cup grated Parmesan cheese

Lasagna Sauce:
1   large white onion, chopped
½   teaspoon salt
2   large cloves garlic, crushed
1   (24-ounce) can whole tomatoes
2   tablespoons parsley flakes
1   teaspoon granulated sugar
3   (8-ounce) cans tomato sauce
1   teaspoon dried basil leaves

Cheese Mixture:
1   (24-ounce) carton fat-free ricotta cheese
2   tablespoons parsley flakes
¼   cup grated Parmesan cheese
2   large cloves garlic
1½   teaspoons dried oregano

For the sauce, cook the onion, salt, garlic, tomatoes, parsley, sugar, tomato sauce, and basil in a 12-inch skillet. Heat to boiling, stirring occasionally. Reduce the heat, and simmer until slightly thickened, about 45 minutes. For the cheese mixture, combine the ricotta cheese, parsley, ¼ cup grated Parmesan cheese, garlic, and oregano, and mix well.

To make the lasagna, while the sauce is cooking, boil and cook the noodles according to directions on the package. Preheat the oven to 350°. Spread approximately 1 cup of the sauce in the bottom of an ungreased 13 x 9 x 2-inch baking dish. Top with 4 lasagna noodles. Spread approximately 1 cup of the cheese mixture over the noodles. Top the cheese mixture with approximately 1 cup of sauce. Sprinkle the sauce with ⅔ cup of the fat-free mozzarella cheese. Repeat with 4 noodles, cheese mixture, sauce mixture, and ⅔ cup mozzarella. Top with the remaining 4 noodles and sauce mix; sprinkle with the remaining mozzarella and the remaining ¼ cup Parmesan cheese. Bake uncovered in the oven for 45 minutes. Let stand for 15 minutes before cutting.

Makes 6 to 8 servings.

Rex Allen and Rex Allen Jr.,
actors and singers

Rex Allen Jr. carries on the tradition of his late, great singing cowboy dad as he performs concerts around the country today. Among his album titles is *The Singing Cowboys,* which he recorded with his dad in 1995. He recorded the single "Last of the Silver Screen Cowboys" with his dad and Roy Rogers.

Wild West Spaghetti Sauce

1	to 1½ pounds hamburger meat
½	pound Italian sausage
1	onion, chopped
1	green onion, chopped
1	green bell pepper, chopped
4	or 5 garlic cloves, finely chopped
½	to ¾ cup chopped fresh parsley or
1½	tablespoons dried parsley
1	tablespoon oregano
½	teaspoon cayenne
1	tablespoon salt
1	(7-ounce) can mushrooms
1	(2-ounce) jar pimientos
1	(29-ounce) can tomato sauce
1	(6-ounce) can tomato paste
1	(10-ounce) can Ro-tel original diced tomatoes and green chiles
1	cup white wine

In a large skillet, brown the hamburger meat and sausage with the onion. Add the green onion, green pepper, garlic, parsley, oregano, cayenne, salt, mushrooms, pimientos, tomato sauce, tomato paste, Ro-tel tomatoes, and wine. Simmer 2 hours or so, stirring occasionally.

Dale Robertson, actor

REX ALLEN
MUSEUM

The Rex Allen Museum features artifacts from the life and times of Rex Allen, who was born and raised just a few blocks away from the museum site.

Dozens of photographs tell the story of the life and career of the last of the silver screen's singing cowboys—"the Arizona Cowboy." The posters from all of Allen's films are on display. His movies are shown at various times during the day.

His silver-inlay saddle and many of his fancy outfits from performances as a cowboy showman are on display. The exhibit includes some of his shirts, pants, boots, and a double holster set with his six-guns.

The museum houses his first gold record for "Crying in the Chapel," a series of the Rex Allen comic books, two of his fiddles, his very first guitar (a six-dollar Sears & Roebuck model), shoes that Koko "the Wonder Horse" wore on stage, and the buggy from Allen's TV series *Frontier Doctor.*

Across the street from the museum is a bronze statue of Rex Allen with his guitar. Koko was buried in front of the statue, and Allen's ashes were spread next to the memorial.

The Rex Allen Museum is located at 150 N. Railroad Avenue in Willcox, Arizona. For more details, go to *www.pinkbanana.com/rex.*

With more than forty hits on the music charts, country music's Kenny Rogers found a gold mine in his hit tune "The Gambler" and turned the song into five popular TV movies. He also was a cowboy in the TV movies *Wild Horses* and *Rio Diablo*.

Gambler's Bolognese Sauce

A sure bet.

2 pounds lean ground beef or turkey
3 portobello mushrooms, chopped
1 large red bell pepper, seeded and chopped
1 yellow onion, finely chopped
1 clove garlic, minced
2 fresh tomatoes, diced
1 (4-pound) jar Ragu sauce
1 (6-ounce) can tomato paste
½ cup water
Granulated sugar
Salt and pepper

In a large skillet, cook the meat until browned, and then drain off the excess fat and liquid. In a large saucepan, sauté the mushrooms, pepper, onion, garlic, and tomatoes until tender. Add the meat, Ragu, tomato paste, and water. Stir in the sugar and salt and pepper to taste. Simmer, stirring occasionally. Serve over your favorite pasta.

Makes about 1 gallon.

Wanda and Kenny Rogers, singer and actor

Wayne Family Spaghetti Sauce alla Milanese

2½ pounds ground beef
5 tablespoons olive oil
2 large white onions, chopped
1 (6-ounce) can tomato paste
4 tablespoons all-purpose flour
Salt and pepper
1 (16-ounce) can peeled tomatoes
2 cups chicken broth
1 (8-ounce) can mushroom pieces, drained
1½ cups Burgundy or Bordeaux wine
5 cloves garlic, mashed
2 medium tomatoes, diced
2 tablespoons finely chopped celery
¼ teaspoon basil*
¼ teaspoon sage*
¼ teaspoon thyme*
¼ teaspoon oregano*
¼ teaspoon curry powder
1 bay leaf

In a skillet, sauté the meat until brown. Remove from the heat and drain. In a large pot, heat the olive oil. Add the onions, and cook until translucent and golden. Add the meat to the pot, and then add the tomato paste, flour, and salt and pepper to taste. Mix well. Reduce the heat. Mash the peeled tomatoes, and add to the meat mixture along with any tomato juice that remains in the can. Add the chicken broth, mushrooms, wine, garlic, fresh tomatoes, celery, herbs, and bay leaf. Cover and simmer for at least 1 hour and 30 minutes, stirring occasionally.

Note: I always freeze this sauce. It keeps very nicely.

Makes about 4 quarts.

*2 tablespoons Italian herb mix can be used instead of individual herbs.

Pilar and John Wayne, actress/artist and actor

CAMPFIRE KETTLES

Throw Yer Loop Fer Potato Soup

Three cups of water
Let come to a boil
Then, one peeled potato
Half an onion . . . that's all
Sprinkle Mrs. Dash
One cube of bouillon
Half a teaspoon of salt
Eat all until gone!
Love ya!

Cindy Walker, songwriter

Jim Hardie's Corn Chowder

6 slices bacon
1 stick butter
¾ cup chopped celery
1 medium onion, sliced
1 cup all-purpose flour
1 (30-ounce) bag hash browns
8 cups chicken broth
1 cup Mexican-style corn
1 cup niblets corn
1 cup creamed corn
  Salt and pepper
2 pints half-and-half

In a saucepan, cook the bacon, butter, celery, onion, and flour over medium heat for 3 to 5 minutes, or until the onion is translucent. Add the hash browns, broth, three corns, and salt and pepper to taste. Simmer for 1 hour. Add the half-and-half right before serving.
    Makes 12 to 16 servings.

Dale Robertson, actor

Texan Cindy Walker, seen here with Gene Autry's Champion, may be the greatest female country and western songwriter of all time. A member of the Country Music Hall of Fame, she has composed such tunes as "Lone Star Trail," "Cherokee Maiden," "Blue Canadian Rockies," "You're from Texas," "Distant Drums," "You Don't Know Me," and "Dream Baby." Bing Crosby, Gene Autry, Ernest Tubb, Eddy Arnold, and Jim Reeves have recorded her songs. She wrote thirty-nine songs for Bob Wills to use in his eight western films.

Vivacious Sue Ane Langdon has appeared in a corral-full of TV westerns from *Gunsmoke* and *Bonanza* to *The Outlaws* and *Tales of Wells Fargo*. Her western films include *The Rounders, The Cheyenne Social Club, Frankie and Johnny*, and *Hawken's Breed*.

Galloping Gazpacho

Gazpacho is a cold soup that originated in Spain. I've had it there. I've also had it in the United States—New York City, Houston, Scottsdale (had it there with the wonderful cowboy, Ben Johnson), Denver, a couple of restaurants in Los Angeles, at a barbecue at a ranch in Santa Inez, California, and, of course, I make it here at home at our little rancho in the San Fernando Valley. Every time I've had it (including when I've made it), it was a little different. If there was a different addition that I liked, I added it to my basic recipe. One of the biggest differences is that sometimes everything is thrown into a blender, making it a thick liquid. Maybe you would like it that way. I prefer a crunchy version (using no blender), and it all starts with these basic ingredients all added to a large bowl, since this makes approximately 10 cups.

6   large, fresh, ripe, red tomatoes, chopped [I've done this, and they're good, but 3 (16-ounce) cans of already diced tomatoes are also good and a lot less work.]
2   cups peeled, seeded, and chopped cucumbers
½   cup chopped fresh red bell peppers
½   cup chopped fresh green bell peppers
½   cup chopped white or yellow onions
¼   cup olive oil
½   cup freshly squeezed lemon juice
3   tablespoons pressed fresh garlic (I'm a garlic freak.)
½   cup apple cider vinegar
1   or 2 teaspoons Better Than Bouillon (beef)
½   cup hot waterr
1½ cups frozen corn kernels
½   cup white Chablis wine
1   (4-ounce) can sliced black olives with juice
2   cups tomato juice

In a large bowl, combine the tomatoes, cucumbers, peppers, onions, olive oil, lemon juice, garlic, and vinegar. In a separate medium bowl, dissolve the Better Than Bouillon in the hot water. Add the corn kernels to the bouillon mixture and stir. Add the corn mixture to the large bowl of ingredients, and then add the wine, black olives with juice, and tomato juice. Stir gently and chill, chill, chill. This must be served cold—even to the point of putting an ice cube in each individual serving bowl.

Note: So much of a gazpacho is according to taste. More, or less, or none of the above ingredients (except for the tomatoes, cucumbers, onions, and peppers; those are pretty much necessary) can be used or not used. Some more additions/garnishes are chopped fresh parsley, cilantro, pimiento, capers, Tabasco, V-8 juice, croutons, salt, and pepper. Be creative. This should be a good, cool accompaniment to that hot, spicy barbecue, cowboy!

Makes about 12 servings.

Sue Ane Langdon, actress

Range Rider's Chicken Chile Lemon Soup

1 chicken fryer, cut up
  Vegetable oil
5 yellow onions, chopped
1 tablespoon salt
1 jalapeño pepper, diced
1 tablespoon dried, crushed red chile
4 garlic cloves
  Juice of 7 lemons
4 chicken bouillon cubes
1 cup Sauvignon Blanc
½ cup chopped cilantro

Brown the chicken pieces in a small amount of oil in a stockpot. Add water to cover the chicken (approximately 8 cups). Add the onions and salt. Bring to a boil, and simmer until the chicken is tender and falling off the bone. Let cool and skim off the fat. Strain the stock, and remove the meat from the bones. Return the meat to the stock, and add the jalapeño, crushed red chile, garlic, lemon juice, bouillon cubes, Sauvignon Blanc, and cilantro. Bring to a boil, and simmer for 20 minutes. Serve with a sliced sourdough baguette.

Jock Mahoney, stuntman and actor

Jock Mahoney acted in the western flicks *The Doolins of Oklahoma, Pecos River, Joe Dakota, Slim Carter,* and *Bandolero!* He starred in two TV western series, *Range Rider* and *Yancy Derringer* (as seen here in 1959), in which he played an ex-Confederate soldier turned card sharp who kept a derringer in his hat.

The 1976 world champion bareback rider, singer/songwriter Chris LeDoux writes and sings about the lifestyle of the westerner, especially the rodeo cowboy. He has recorded more than thirty-five albums and has roped in sales of more than six million records. This cowboy knows what he's singing about.

Wells Fargo Chicken Lentil Soup

One of Dale's favorite recipes.

4   boneless chicken breasts
½   cup lentils
¼   cup olive oil
4   (14-ounce) cans chicken stock
2   (15-ounce) cans whole tomatoes, drained, juice reserved
2   cups grated cabbage
2   cups chopped celery
2   cups diced zucchini
2   cups chopped onions or leeks
2   tablespoons lemon juice
¼   cup cooking sherry
     Tabasco, curry, salt, pepper, and herbs for seasoning

In a medium saucepan, slowly cook the chicken breasts in boiling water for 45 minutes. In a separate, large saucepan, cook the lentils in the olive oil, chicken stock, and the juice from the canned tomatoes for 30 minutes. In a bowl, combine the tomatoes, cabbage, celery, zucchini, and onions. When the lentils are done, add the vegetables from the bowl. Cut the chicken into bite-size pieces, and add the chicken to the pan along with the lemon juice, sherry, and Tabasco, curry powder, salt, and pepper to taste. Cook until the vegetables are tender.
Makes 12 to 16 servings.

Mr. and Mrs. Dale Robertson, actor

Call-of-the-Wild Gumbo

This isn't as good as the real Louisiana gumbos I've eaten in Cajun country, but it's pretty good when you haven't been able to get a fix of the real stuff in a while.

4   tablespoons butter
2   tablespoons all-purpose flour
2   cloves garlic
½   cup chopped onion
½   cup chopped green pepper
½   cup chopped tomatoes
1   (6-ounce) can tomato paste
1   bay leaf
2   tablespoons Worcestershire
⅛   teaspoon ground cloves
⅛   teaspoon ground basil
1   (15-ounce) can okra
2   beef bouillon cubes
2   cups crabmeat or shrimp or crawdad tails (crawfish)
¼   cup parsley flakes
1   teaspoon chili powder
     Pepper
2   cups water
2   cups uncooked rice
     Louisiana hot sauce

In a big pot, melt the butter, add the flour, and mix well. Cook on low heat for 15 minutes, or until light brown. Add the garlic, onion, and green pepper. Cook until tender. Add the tomatoes, tomato paste, bay leaf, Worcestershire, cloves, basil, okra, and bouillon, and cook for 30 minutes. Add the fish, parsley flakes, chili powder, pepper to taste, and the water. Cook the rice in a separate pot. After the rice is done and the gumbo has cooked about 45 minutes to 1 hour, put it on the table and dig in.

Directions for eating: Put a couple of scoops of rice on your plate and a couple of scoops of gumbo on it. Add Louisiana hot sauce to your desired taste. Cheddar cheese and crackers are good as a side dish. Bon appetit. Fill up and bust!
Makes about 4 servings.

*Chris LeDoux,
rodeo cowboy and singer/songwriter*

Macho Chili-Tamale Soup

This recipe is very easy and flexible. It's great for parties—makes a lot, or makes a little. Remove or add items as desired.

- 2 (14-ounce) cans chili, with or without beans
- 1 (14-ounce) can corn
- 1 (14-ounce) can diced tomatoes (seasoned tomatoes add to the flavor)
- 1 cup frozen potatoes O'Brien (scalloped potatoes with peppers)
- 1 (14-ounce can) tamales, cut into 1-inch chunks (get rid of the fat they are packed in, but try to save the gravy)

Place the chili, corn, and tomatoes into a large soup pot. Add a couple of cans of water to get the consistency desired. Heat to a boil over an open grill for the best flavor. Add the potatoes O'Brien, and simmer to suit your personal taste. Just prior to serving, add the tamales. Serve with a crusty bread such as sourdough.

Makes 8 to 10 servings.

Cathy Lee Crosby, actress

Cathy Lee Crosby not only played Wonder Woman, but she also worked on the western-themed film *Roughneck* and the miniseries *Heaven & Hell: North & South, Book III*. Her mother, Linda Hayes, was Roy Rogers's leading lady in several films during the early 1940s.

Warm Up Your Yodel Chili

2 pounds coarse ground beef (not too lean)
1 large white onion, chopped
1 clove garlic, minced
½ teaspoon or more salt
1 tablespoon parsley flakes
½ teaspoon ground black pepper
1 teaspoon MSG
½ teaspoon Season All
½ teaspoon (or big pinch) crushed basil leaves
½ teaspoon oregano leaves
½ teaspoon cayenne
2 tablespoons chili powder
1 (14-ounce) can beef bouillon
1 (15-ounce) can kidney beans

Put the ground beef, onion, and garlic in a large, cast iron pan over medium heat. When lightly browned, add the salt, parsley, pepper, MSG, Season All, basil, oregano, cayenne, chili powder, and bouillon. Simmer for 30 minutes, and then skim off the fat. Add the kidney beans, including the juice. Simmer for 30 more minutes. I like to serve mine with chopped fresh tomato on top of each serving. Warm up the leftovers the next day, and serve with corn tortillas.

Makes about 4 servings.

Carolina Cotton, singer and actress

Robert Mitchum's first film was *Hoppy Serves a Writ* in 1943. The motion-picture star made numerous westerns, including *Blood on the Moon, The Lusty Men, El Dorado, 5 Card Stud,* and *The Good Guys and the Bad Guys.* He was also the narrator for *Tombstone.*

Chris Mitchum worked in the western films *Chisum, Rio Lobo, Big Jake, The Last of the Hard Men,* and *Tombstone.*

Chili Mitchum

Both my father and I were lifetime members of the International Chili Society, which, in its heyday, held the International World Championship at the Tropico Gold Mine, three miles from Rosemond, California, in the Mojave Desert.

Carroll Shelby (former World Champion), C. V. Woods (a.k.a. Woody), and others ran it. Dad and I were judges. When they lost the site, and with the passing of Woody, the event shifted from its big "celebrity bash" status and moved to Reno, where it is claimed to be the world's biggest food contest.

When he didn't have the time to make the chili recipe below, my dad's favorite was a bag of Shelby's Texas Chili. Just follow the directions. It should be noted that real "chili-heads" do not add beans.

You will see a wide variety of ingredients in today's chili recipes. This one, with a little variance, sticks to what you'd find on a cattle drive—a rough cut of beef, to start. What you won't find here are pork, Tabasco sauce, sausage, chicken, and so on.

—Chris Mitchum

Stew meat (I usually allow at least ½ pound per person)
Olive oil
Garlic
Onion
Bell pepper (red, green, and/or yellow; 1 of each is fun)
Cumin
Oregano
Cayenne
Cracked red pepper
1 (16-ounce) can Contadina stewed tomatoes
2 (16-ounce) cans tomato sauce
Beer
Paprika
New Mexican red chile powder
Salt and pepper
Masa harina (corn) flour

Let's make this for 10 people. Start with 5 pounds of stew meat cut into ½-inch squares. In a really large frying pan (or, in its absence, you may have to brown this in 2 or 3 batches), pour enough olive oil to thinly cover the bottom of the pan. (As the meat cooks down, a lot of moisture comes out of it.) Let's say we can get 2½ pounds in the pan at one time. Put in 5 cloves garlic minced, ½ onion chopped (more, if you like onion), and ½ bell pepper chopped (more if you like; it's fun to mix colored bells to make the chili more appealing to the eye). Add the meat.

Turn the heat on at medium-low to medium. When the meat starts to sizzle (brown), turn the heat down a notch, and add 5 rounded teaspoons cumin and 2½ rounded teaspoons oregano. (I usually use cumin at a ratio of 2 to 1 over oregano. I see oregano more as an Italian spaghetti spice and not right to dominate chili.) Next add 1 teaspoon cayenne and 1 teaspoon cracked red pepper (I find it cooks down with a little different flavor from cayenne). In a large pot, put in the can of Contadina stewed tomatoes (it's my favorite brand, but you can use your own favorite), two cans tomato sauce, and two bottles of beer. Lone Star or Coors are my favorites, but a light (as opposed to dark) beer is necessary. Heat to a simmer. When the meat is browned, some people like to pour off the liquid. I think it adds flavor, so I dump the whole thing into the pot. (Repeat the meat process if you are doing this in shifts.) Cover the pot, and bring to a slow simmer. Loosen the top so steam can escape, and a low heat should do it. Throughout the day, as the chili cooks down, add more beer, cumin, oregano (at a 2-to-1 ratio), and cayenne to taste. Put in 2 teaspoons paprika. (This is mainly for that nice red color.) Add 5 teaspoons New Mexico red chile powder. This is actually a red chile, also called the California or Perfecto chile. It is not a "chili powder" mix. We just made that with the cumin, oregano, and cayenne.

I will start in the morning and render it down all day—adding beer, cumin, and oregano, and cayenne to taste. Turn it off at night and cover. In the morning, fire it up, again, and repeat the rendering/adding process. About 30 minutes before serving, add salt and pepper to taste. When ready, the chili should stand a wooden spoon straight up. That's called "tight" chili. I usually like a little moisture in mine.

If you do not like the fat in the chili, the morning of the second day use a spoon to take it off. It will be jelled on top. Again, I like the added taste. When ready to serve, if the chili is too dry, add more beer. If it is too wet, take some masa harina corn flour (it gives it a south-of-the-boarder flavor), and put a heaping tablespoon in a bowl. Add some broth from the chili (you don't want to add it in cold), and mix it until it's a soupy "cream of rice" texture. Add it into the chili while stirring. Repeat until the desired texture is reached.

I like salad and garlic French bread with this. Serve it up and enjoy!

Robert and Chris Mitchum, actors

Singing cowboy and guitar player Monte Hale starred in thirty westerns in the 1940s and 1950s, including *Home on the Range, The Man from Rainbow Valley, Under Colorado Skies,* and *Giant*—in which he taught James Dean a fine little rope trick.

Quick-Draw Chili Beans

For those who don't have all day.

- 1½ pounds lean ground beef
- 1 onion, chopped
- 1 package Lawry's chili flavoring
- 2 (15-ounce) cans red kidney beans
- 2 (15-ounce) cans pinquitas (small pink beans)
- 3 (15-ounce) cans chili beans

Brown the ground beef in a skillet over medium heat. Add the onion, and cook until tender. Stir in the chili flavoring and the red kidney, pinquita, and chili beans (do not drain). Simmer for at least 30 minutes.

Serving Variation: If you're not cooking for a crowd, use 1 can of each kind of the three beans and 1 pound ground beef.

Makes 10 to 12 servings.

Jack Hannah, Sons of the San Joaquin

Hale and Hearty Chili

Monte makes fabulous chicken and dumplings, fried chicken, and so on, but his chili is everyone's favorite.

—Joanne Hale

- 3 pounds club beef, coarse-ground
- 1 pound ground lean pork
  Oil for browning
- 3 garlic cloves, chopped
- 3 cups chopped onion
- 3 to 4 tablespoons chili powder
- 2 teaspoons salt
- 1 teaspoon pepper
- 4 cups diced tomatoes
- 2 cups tomato sauce (or more)

In a skillet, brown the meat in an oil of your choice. Drain off the excess fat and juice. Stir in the garlic, onions (reserving a few for topping), chili powder, salt, and pepper. Add the tomatoes and tomato sauce. Simmer, uncovered, over low heat for 1½ to 2 hours. Serve with the reserved chopped onions.

Makes 8 to 10 servings.

Monte Hale, actor

Hazel Family Easy Chili

This chili is delicious, but is not spicy hot. For those who like their chili without jalapeños and red-hot chile sauces, it is one that serves well. It should be served with plenty of liquid, not too thick. The Hazels have been making it for forty years.

3   slices bacon
1   flank steak (the bigger the better)
1   yellow onion, chopped
1   (28-ounce) can red chili sauce (I use Las Palmas brand)
1   (28-ounce) can Italian-style stewed tomatoes
3   (28-ounce) cans pinto beans (I use Las Palmas brand)
     Salt and pepper
     Garlic powder (optional)

Use a large, deep, covered pot to make the chili. Cut the bacon into small pieces, and cook in the pot. Cut the flank steak into bite-size pieces, and add to the pot. Cook in the bacon grease until the meat is well-done. Add the onion and red chili sauce, and cook for 30 to 40 minutes on slow simmer, stirring frequently. Add the tomatoes, and cook until the tomatoes have cooked down, about 30 minutes to an hour. Drain the juice from the pinto beans, and then add the beans to the pot. Reserve the sauce from the beans to add liquid as needed. Cook until the beans are just beginning to soften. Serve in bowls with crackers or cornbread. Some grated cheese and chopped onions go well on top. Salt and pepper to taste. A little bit of garlic powder adds to the flavor.

Makes 6 to 8 servings.

Bill Hazel, Frontierland cowboy

Bill Hazel leads a burro pack train through Ghost Town at Knott's Berry Farm in 1960. He cooked over an open fire, brewed coffee, and made Dutch-oven biscuits while palavering with visitors and posing for photographs. He was also a gunfighter and stuntman in the early 1960s at Frontierland in Disneyland.

Wild Side Wild-Game Chili

- 2 pounds game (deer, elk, antelope, etc.)
- 1 pound pork
- 4 heaping tablespoons chili powder or chili blend (my favorite is Reno Red; other good brands are Morton, Williams, and Gephardt)
- 1 (16-ounce) can stewed tomatoes
- 1 (12-ounce) can Ro-tel chiles
- 8 ounces puréed red chiles
- ¼ pound butter
- 1 medium onion, chopped
  Juice of ½ lemon
- 1 large rib celery, chopped
- 1 heaping tablespoon fresh garlic, chopped
  Worcestershire sauce
  Meat tenderizer
  Salt and pepper

Cut the game and pork into ½-inch cubes, and trim the fat, bone, and gristle away. This is the tedious part, so recruit some help. In a pot of water, boil the chili powder, tomatoes, Ro-tel chiles, and red chiles for 15 to 20 minutes until tender. Pour the mix into a blender with enough of the water to make a purée. Set aside. (In the Southwest, a ristra, or package of red chiles, is easy to find. In other parts of the country, you may have to go to a specialty or gourmet shop. Be sure to break them open to inspect for mold or bad spots and remove most of the seeds. The more seeds the hotter.)

In a large skillet, thoroughly mix the game, pork, butter, onion, lemon, celery, and garlic. Sprinkle them liberally with the Worcestershire sauce and tenderizer. Add the salt and pepper to taste. Lightly brown the mixture, and then transfer it to a large pot for cooking. (If your skillet is small, it may be easier to do the browning in two batches instead of one.) Add the tomato-chile purée to the pot, and cook for a couple of hours on a low enough fire to prevent scorching. (If desired, add a heaping tablespoon of ground cumin and enough red pepper to suit your hotness, and cook for another 30 minutes.) For more flavor, let it stand overnight in the refrigerator. Enjoy with some flour or corn tortillas. Happy eating!

Makes 10 to 12 servings.

Hank Thompson, singer

Western swing man Hank Thompson has been going strong since the 1940s with his Brazos Valley Boys (who were voted the Number One Country Western Band for fourteen consecutive years during the 1950s and '60s). Thompson has sold more than sixty million records and among his hits are "The Wild Side of Life," "Humpty Dumpty Heart," "Oklahoma Hills," and "Six Pack to Go."

While many fans remember him as *Petticoat Junction's* Uncle Joe, Edgar Buchanan rode with the best of the West in the films *Ride the High Country, Rawhide, Shane, Coroner's Creek,* and *Cave of Outlaws.* On TV he starred in *Judge Roy Bean* in 1956, was saddle pal Red Connors to Hopalong Cassidy and partnered with Glenn Ford in *Cade's County.*

Road-Kill Chili

2   pounds fresh road-kill (ground beef, bear, elk, or venison)
1   pound ground Italian sausage
½   pound Mexican chorizo sausage
1   (16-ounce) can tomato sauce
1   (16-ounce) can crushed tomatoes
2   bottles beer
1   teaspoon oregano
2   jalapeño peppers, diced
1   tablespoon cumin powder
3   tablespoons chili powder
1   tablespoon salt
1   teaspoon black pepper
4   cloves garlic, chopped
1   large yellow onion, diced
1   medium green bell pepper, diced
1   bunch cilantro, chopped
1   cup cooked pinto beans
1   cup cooked kidney beans
1   cup cooked white beans

Put the road-kill and sausages in a large pot over medium heat and brown, stirring occasionally. Add the tomato sauce, crushed tomatoes, beer, oregano, jalapeños, cumin powder, chili powder, salt, black pepper, garlic, onion, green pepper, and cilantro. Stir in the three kinds of beans, and cook over medium heat for 30 minutes, stirring occasionally. Reduce the heat to low and cover. Cook, covered, for 1½ hours, stirring occasionally. Serve in bowls with diced onions, shredded Cheddar cheese, chopped cilantro, and/or hot sauce for an extra kick.

Makes 8 to 10 servings.

Edgar Buchanan, actor
Submitted by son Buck Buchanan

Morgan Woodward (center) is surrounded by an all-star band of outlaws in the 1968 film *Firecreek*. James Best and Jack Elam flank Woodward at left, and Gary Lockwood and Henry Fonda are looking wily on the right. Despite the "Eats" sign visible in the background to the left of Woodward, it's doubtful that food is foremost on the minds of these bad hombres. They're hungry for a fight. But when they stir up trouble with local good guy James Stewart, they may have bitten off more than they can chew.

You must have seen this face a hundred times. Actor Morgan Woodward was a guest on *Gunsmoke* for a record nineteen episodes, including one of his favorites, "Lobo," in which he played a mountain man and wolf hunter. Woodward was topnotch as a heavy in dozens of TV and movie westerns. He played Shotgun Gibbs in *The Life and Legend of Wyatt Earp* and was in the feature films *The Great Locomotive Chase*, *Firecreek,* and *Death of a Gunfighter*, to name a few. Many also recollect him as the cool prison guard in reflective sunglasses in the film *Cool Hand Luke.*

Bad Guy Stew

This bad guy is really good.

- 1 (3 to 4-pound) chicken
- 2 (15-ounce) cans crushed tomatoes
- 3 very large potatoes, cubed
- 2 large onions, chopped
- 1 pod red pepper
- 1 scant tablespoon chili powder
- 1 or 2 (15-ounce) cans cream-style corn
   Seasoning

Cover the chicken with water in a 6 to 8-quart pot. Simmer until well-done. Bone and chop the chicken into fairly large pieces. Reserve the chicken stock. Return the chicken to the chicken stock, and add the tomatoes, potatoes, onions, pepper pod, and chili powder. Simmer at least 2 hours. Remove the pepper pod. Thirty minutes before serving, add the corn. Cook, stirring occasionally. Season to taste. This should be a thick stew.

Makes 10 to 12 servings.

Morgan Woodward, actor

Oregon Trail
Beef and Bean Stew

A real stew art.

2   tablespoons oil
3   pounds beef stew meat
1   onion, chopped
1   carrot, chopped
1   rib celery, chopped
4   cloves garlic, minced
1   tablespoon dried rosemary leaves
½   cup white wine
2   cups chicken stock
1   (16-ounce) can plum tomatoes
1   teaspoon salt
1   teaspoon pepper
2   (10-ounce) packages frozen lima beans

In a Dutch oven, heat the oil, and brown the beef on all sides. Remove the beef, and drain all but 1 tablespoon of the fat. Add the onion, carrot, and celery. Cover and cook over medium-low heat until the vegetables soften, about 5 minutes. Add the garlic and rosemary, and cook for 1 minute. Add the wine and chicken stock, and simmer for 2 minutes, scraping the brown bits from the bottom of the pot. Add the beef, any accumulated juices, the tomatoes, salt, and pepper, and simmer partially covered until the beef is tender, about 1 hour and 30 minutes. Add the lima beans to the pot, and cook until tender, 10 to 15 minutes. Skim the fat, and adjust the seasonings to taste.

Makes 8 servings.

Peggy Stewart, actress

Expert horsewoman Peggy Stewart was featured in sixty western films from the late 1930s into the early 1950s, including four serials. Her film credits include *Wells Fargo, Cheyenne Wildcat, The Black Lash, Stagecoach to Denver,* and *Oregon Trail,* as seen here with Sunset Carson in 1945.

Character actor Gene Evans was all over the West on TV and in films. Besides ten appearances on *Gunsmoke* and other TV series such as *The Lone Ranger, Rawhide,* and *Bonanza,* he appeared in the feature films *Nevada Smith, The War Wagon, Support Your Local Sheriff, The Ballad of Cable Hogue,* and *Pat Garrett and Billy the Kid.*

South Texas Beef Stew

What would a cattle drive be without a chuck wagon meal of traditional beef stew? While many variations exist for this all-time favorite, you just can't go wrong with this simple recipe. Add dumplings (see the recipe for South Texas Dumplings on page 181), and you have created a winner.

2   pounds beef stew meat, cubed
1   large onion, chopped
6   carrots, peeled and sliced
1   (15-ounce) can crushed tomatoes
3   ribs celery, chopped
3   potatoes, peeled and cubed
1   tablespoon chili powder
    Salt and pepper

In a large stew pot, cook the meat in water until nearly done. Add the onion, carrots, tomatoes, celery, potatoes, chili powder, and salt and pepper, and cook on a low fire for approximately 1 hour. Serve hot from the fire.
    Makes 8 to 10 servings.

Barbara and Lonnie Tegeler,
Rocking T Chuck Wagon
Chappell Hill, Texas

Slum Stew

I have searched for Gene's favorite recipes in our mother's card files. His undisputed best was corn fritters, but I haven't found that card box. When Gene came home from the war, he asked Mom to fix that "cheap stew" that she used to make that he thought was so good. He said it was not like the army stew that he had been throwing up for the last three years.

Well, I found it, and my guess is that the name Mom called it was Slum Stew. The recipe card has it as "Panola Hawaiian Cowboy Stew." Our mother had written: "Gene's favorite, but don't tell him the name." Keep in mind that this thing is about fifty years old and our mother was a butcher. True!
                                —Bud Evans

2   pounds Swiss steak (today that's a 1-inch London broil bottom round), cut into 1-inch cubes
½   cup soy sauce
4   cups boiling water
1   teaspoon Worcestershire sauce (or A-1, but the taste will be different)
1   teaspoon chopped garlic (can substitute garlic powder)
½   cup chopped fresh onions
2   teaspoons salt
¼   teaspoon black pepper
1   teaspoon packed brown sugar
4   potatoes, peeled
6   carrots, sliced ¼ inch thick
1   handful cut green beans, or 1 (9-ounce) package frozen cut green beans
6   small white onions (about 1 inch in diameter), or canned
2   tablespoons all-purpose flour
¼   cup cold water

Marinate the beef cubes in the soy sauce for 1 hour, turning once. Place in a Dutch oven. Brown the cubes well in their fat. Add water, Worcestershire sauce, garlic, chopped onions, salt, pepper, and brown sugar. Cover and simmer for 1 hour and 30 minutes, stirring occasionally. Cut the potatoes into 1-inch cubes, and add the potatoes, carrots, green beans, and white onions to the stew. Cook until the vegetables are tender, maybe 15 minutes. Thicken with a mixture made from the flour and cold water. Most importantly, taste before serving. If additional seasoning is necessary, add it.
    Makes 6 to 8 servings.

Gene Evans, actor
Submitted by brother Bud Evans

BRONCO BUSTERS

Red River Barbecue Sauce

½   cup vegetable oil
¼   cup lemon juice or lime juice
⅛   cup red wine vinegar
⅛   cup Worcestershire sauce or soy sauce

Combine the oil, lemon juice, wine vinegar, and Worcestershire sauce. Brush on the meats periodically as needed. This is especially good for basting beef or chicken.

*Pilar and John Wayne,
actress/artist and actor*

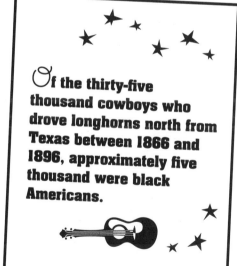

*O*f the thirty-five thousand cowboys who drove longhorns north from Texas between 1866 and 1896, approximately five thousand were black Americans.

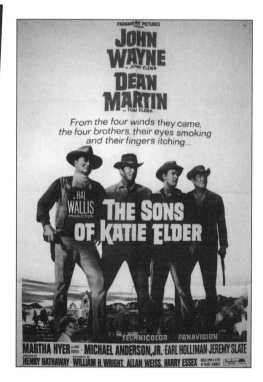

Fort Apache
Barbecue Sauce

A friend I work with (Ken) worked this out through trial and error.

18	ounces C Masterpiece barbecue sauce
6	ounces La Choy sweet-and-sour sauce
2	ounces Tiger sauce (original)
4	tablespoons honey teriyaki sauce
3	tablespoons packed brown sugar
1	teaspoon garlic powder
½	teaspoon sweet basil
½	teaspoon sage
¼	teaspoon ground cayenne

To make the sauce, mix together the barbecue sauce, sweet-and-sour sauce, Tiger sauce, teriyaki sauce, brown sugar, garlic powder, basil, sage and cayenne. This is best served on pork loin ribs, frog legs, crawdads, dove, quail, pheasant, duck, goose, rabbit, elk, and rattlesnake.

Lee Aaker, actor

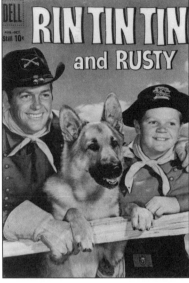

This Dell comic book from yesteryear features James Brown as Lieutenant Rip Masters, Rin Tin Tin as Rinty, and Lee Aaker as Rusty. Yo ho, Rinty!

Lee Aaker starred as Rusty, the best friend of canine hero Rin Tin Tin, in the 1950s TV series *The Adventures of Rin Tin Tin,* set at Fort Apache, Arizona. Aaker was also in the western films *Hondo* and *Destry.*

Cisco Kid's Barbecue Sauce

It's great. Would we kid you?

- 1 cup olive oil
- 1 cup chili sauce
- 3 cloves garlic, squeezed
- 1 onion, finely chopped
- 2 tablespoons Gulden's mustard
- 4 to 6 tablespoons honey
  Salt (at least 1 teaspoon)
- 1 teaspoon coarse ground black pepper
- ½ teaspoon crushed dried oregano
- 1 teaspoon basil leaves
- ⅓ cup chopped cilantro, or parsley if not available
- ⅔ cup chopped parsley

Mix together the olive oil, chili sauce, garlic, onion, mustard, honey, salt to taste, black pepper, oregano, basil, cilantro, and parsley. Shake well. I usually assemble the ingredients in a large canning jar, and mix everything as I add each item. I add the chopped parsley at the end.

Duncan Renaldo, actor

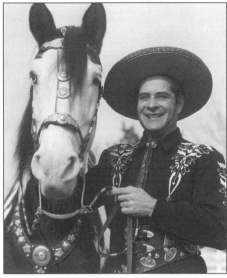

Duncan Renaldo rode his horse Diablo on the TV range from 1950 to 1956 as the Cisco Kid, "the Robin Hood of the West," a character created by O. Henry. Cisco's partner was Pancho, played on TV by Leo Carrillo. (Photo courtesy of Richard Renaldo)

Duncan Renaldo (the Cisco Kid) has steak hot off the grill ready for his hungry hombres, his children (left to right) Stephanie, Jeremy, and Richard. Renaldo made several cliffhangers in the 1930s and was in more than seventy films, including *Heroes of the Saddle, Gauchos of El Dorado,* and *The San Antonio Kid.* (Photo courtesy of Richard Renaldo)

Gordon "Wild Bill" Elliott made more than two hundred films and more than seventy-five westerns. The name change came after he starred in the 1938 serial *The Great Adventures of Wild Bill Hickok.* He played that character in more than a dozen films, as well as characters named Wild Bill Saunders and Wild Bill Elliott, before becoming Red Ryder for more than a dozen films in the mid-1940s.

Grapevine Canyon Barbecue Sauce

Great on chicken, beef, and pork.

13 cups (106 ounces) ketchup
1   (12-ounce) can tomato paste
3   cups Worcestershire sauce
4   cups molasses
1   cup honey
4   tablespoons liquid smoke (optional)
3   cups packed brown sugar
1   tablespoon dry mustard
4   tablespoons garlic powder
1   tablespoon cumin
1   teaspoon crushed red pepper
2   teaspoons cayenne
2   tablespoons chili powder
1   tablespoon coriander

In a large pan, mix together the ketchup, tomato paste, Worcestershire sauce, molasses, honey, liquid smoke if using, brown sugar, dry mustard, garlic powder, cumin, red pepper, cayenne, chili powder, and coriander. Simmer for 20 minutes.

Makes about 2 gallons.

*Grapevine Canyon Ranch
Pearce, Arizona*

Wild Bill Elliott's Barbecue Sauce for Ribs

1   (18-ounce) bottle hickory-flavored
    barbecue sauce
½   cup ketchup
    Dash of Worcestershire sauce
¼   cup soy sauce
    Garlic salt
2   tablespoons molasses or ½ cup packed
    brown sugar
1   tablespoon granulated sugar
⅓   cup vinegar
1   heaping teaspoon ground cinnamon
½   teaspoon oregano
¼   teaspoon thyme
¼   teaspoon sweet basil
    Chili powder

Mix together the barbecue sauce, ketchup, Worcestershire sauce, soy, garlic salt to taste, molasses, sugar, vinegar, cinnamon, oregano, thyme, basil, and chili powder to taste. Cover the ribs to be barbecued with the sauce, and bake for 2 hours at 275° and then 1 hour at 325°.

*Wild Bill Elliott
Submitted by niece Diane Braga*

BARBECUE SAUCES, MARINADES, AND RELISHES

Lusty Barbecue Sauce

Just right for pork.

½ green bell pepper, diced
1 rib celery, diced
¼ pound butter or margarine
1 clove garlic, minced
1 (10¾-ounce) can chicken gumbo soup
2 (12-ounce) bottles ketchup
1 (10¾-ounce) can condensed onion soup
½ cup water
¼ cup wine vinegar
½ teaspoon Tabasco
    Salt and pepper
1 cup Sauterne wine

In a saucepan, cook the green pepper and celery in the butter or margarine until soft. Combine with the garlic, gumbo, ketchup, onion soup, water, vinegar, Tabasco, and salt and pepper to taste. Simmer about 30 minutes. Remove from the heat, cool slightly, and add the wine. Meat should be "dipped" into the sauce, then grilled over a charcoal fire. Repeat as desired. Serve the sauce over the barbecue. Pass extra sauce in a tureen. They'll come back for more.

Dirk London, actor

That Wind Blown Look

Regular timetables seldom work outdoors. The heat of the fire, thickness of the meat, and even the unpredictability of the wind are variables that affect timing. Start the fire early. To reach the glowing-coal stage takes at least an hour. Start cooking only when the fire dies down to glowing coals. Don't be a slowpoke: Never poke a charcoal fire because that will slow down the process.

—Dirk London

Dressed in black, he was known as "the King of the Bullwhip." Lash LaRue's weapon of choice? A whip, of course. He starred in such titles *as Law of the Lash, Return of the Lash,* and *The Black Lash.*

Lash's Lariat Coffee and Apricot Barbecue Sauce

2 tablespoons olive oil
1 medium onion, chopped
¾ cup brewed coffee
½ cup apricot preserves
1½ cups ketchup
¼ cup cider vinegar
1 tablespoon Worcestershire sauce
1 cup packed brown sugar
4 tablespoons molasses
1 teaspoon crushed garlic
1 tablespoon mustard powder
1 tablespoon ground cumin seed
1 tablespoon chili powder
2 teaspoons salt
1 teaspoon black pepper
½ teaspoon ground cayenne

In a large saucepan, heat the olive oil, and cook the onions until translucent. Add the coffee, preserves, ketchup, vinegar, Worcestershire sauce, brown sugar, molasses, garlic, mustard powder, cumin, chili powder, salt, pepper, and cayenne. Bring to a gentle boil, and then gently simmer on low heat for 15 to 20 minutes, stirring occasionally. Remove the sauce from the heat, and allow to cool for about 15 minutes. Pour the mixture into a food processor or blender, and purée until smooth. It tastes great as a sauce for beef, chicken, or pork.

Makes about 6 cups.

Lash LaRue, actor

Johnny Bond appeared in nearly thirty western films, usually singing with the Jimmy Wakely Trio. Bond wrote the classic western tune "Cimarron" and hundreds of other songs, which earned him entry into the Country Music Hall of Fame. Johnny Bond and the Cimarron Boys were regulars on Gene Autry's radio show, *The Melody Ranch*. He also wrote an autobiography of his song-publishing partner Tex Ritter. He pals around here with Smiley Burnette (right).

Johnny's Bonded Steak Sauce

No one outside the family has this recipe (until now).

Until he passed away in 1978, Johnny Bond lived in a Spanish-style, one-story house in Burbank, California, which he bought when he moved to California to audition for Gene Autry in 1940. Every Sunday he would grill steaks for his family, rain or shine. (It never rains in California.) Any friends who just happened to drop by were always welcome to join in. Frequent guests were Jimmy Wakely, Tex Ritter, Merle Travis, Joe Maphis, and Wesley Tuttle.

Johnny's backyard was a beautiful courtyard with a brick wall surrounding the property. Plum, pomegranate, lemon, and grapefruit trees graced the landscaping. Johnny would put the fruit in the front yard with a sign, "Please help yourself." His friends would gather in the private courtyard while Johnny seared Porterhouse steaks on a charcoal grill—no gas or electricity allowed. When the coals were too hot to keep his hand over the grill, on went the steaks. The higher the flames surrounding the steaks, the better. They

quickly burned to a crisp on the outside, leaving them rare on the inside. If any guests preferred medium or well-done, they never mentioned it. Pass more steak sauce, please.

Johnny cooked up a bunch of Porterhouse steaks, accompanied by baked potatoes and wife Dorothy's fresh green beans. He always made sure there were leftovers for Monday, to be eaten with homemade black-eyed peas and cornbread.

Ketchup
Steak drippings
Worcestershire sauce
Tabasco
Freshly ground pepper

Fill a small bowl about three-quarters full with ketchup. Drain the drippings from freshly grilled steaks into the bowl. Top off with just enough Worcestershire sauce to cover the ketchup. Add a few drops of Tabasco to taste (Johnny's was not too hot). Add the pepper to taste (Johnny put just a bit of pepper). Stir it all up and enjoy.

Johnny Bond, singer/songwriter
Submitted by daughter Sherry Bond

Smoke's Secret Spice Rub

Rory Calhoun—"Smoke" to friends and family—used this rub on all his signature dishes. If you're feeling lazy, just use Lawry's seasoned salt.

- ¼ cup kosher salt
- 1 teaspoon dry mustard
- 1 teaspoon paprika
- 1 teaspoon turmeric
- 1 tablespoon granulated sugar
- ½ teaspoon dried onion
- ½ teaspoon garlic powder

Mix together the salt, mustard, paprika, turmeric, sugar, onion, and garlic powder. Rub on meats or add as a seasoning to any dish. The amounts indicated should be enough for 6 (16-ounce) steaks or 3 whole chickens.

Rory Calhoun, actor

The Texan's Garlic Oil Marinade

A key ingredient in many Calhoun concoctions.

- 1 bottle corn or vegetable oil (about 1½ quarts)
- 1 head garlic, chopped (enough to fill 1 or 2 inches in the bottom of the bottle)
- 2 tablespoons dry mustard (or more to taste)
- 2 tablespoons Smoke's Secret Spice Rub (see recipe above) or seasoned salt (or more to taste)
  A couple of dashes of Worcestershire sauce

Mix together the oil, garlic, dry mustard, Smoke's Secret Spice Rub, and Worcestershire sauce. The oil marinade should age for at least 2 days before using. Aging for 2 weeks is even better. Refrigerate. Shake before using.

Rory Calhoun, actor

Robert Horton starred in two western TV series. He was trail scout Flint McCullough on *Wagon Train* from 1957 to 1962. He starred as an amnesiac cowboy trying to track his past on *A Man Called Shenandoah* from 1965 to 1966.

Flint's Flank-Steak Marinade

- ¼ cup vegetable oil
- 2 tablespoons soy sauce
- 2 tablespoons lemon juice
- 1 teaspoon celery salt
- 1 clove garlic, minced, chopped, or squeezed
- 2 tablespoons chopped green onions
- 1 tablespoon cracked black pepper

Mix together the oil, soy sauce, lemon juice, celery salt, garlic, green onions, and black pepper. Marinate your steak for 4 to 6 hours in the refrigerator.

Makes enough for 2 small or 1 normal flank steak. For anything more than that, double the recipe.

Robert Horton, actor

Johnny Ringo's Green Sauce

½ cup raw spinach (dry)
2 tablespoons finely chopped parsley
2 tablespoons finely chopped chives
2 tablespoons chopped dill
1½ cups mayonnaise
½ cup sour cream
   Juice of ½ lemon

Purée the spinach in a food blender or processor. In a bowl, combine the parsley, chives, dill, mayonnaise, sour cream, and lemon juice with the spinach, and purée until totally blended. Cover and let the mixture sit overnight in the refrigerator in order to give the flavors time to blend together. This is especially good with poached salmon or most other fish that have been "plainly" cooked.

Makes about 2 cups.

Don Durant, actor

Varvel's Marvelous Grease Gravy

This is Dale's mother's recipe.

1 pound spicy patty sausage
¼ cup all-purpose flour
4 cups whole milk
   Lots of pepper
   Salt

In a skillet, fry the sausage until crisp, and drain on paper towels. Pour the flour into the skillet with the hot grease, and blend well. Pour in the milk all at once, and stir to amalgamate. Add more milk if desired. Gravy should be thin. Add lots of pepper. Add salt to taste. Serve with biscuits. When placing biscuits in a baking dish, be sure to be very generous with extra oil. Pour the gravy over the hot biscuits.

Dale Robertson, actor

Circle-the-Wagons Jalapeño Relish

12 jalapeño peppers
1 medium onion
⅓ cup yellow mustard

Remove the seeds from the jalapeños, and chop the peppers into ⅛-inch pieces. Chop the onion into pieces the same size as the chopped peppers. Mix the pepper and onions together, and add the mustard. Let stand for about 1 hour before serving over steaks or pork. This relish is also great for hot dogs or other sandwiches.

Makes about 2 cups.

Donna and Dennis Williams,
Circle Double D Chuck Wagon
Neosho, Missouri

"Never sell that, kid. Sitting in another man's leather is like wearing another man's boots. Never sell your saddle."

—Kirk Douglas in *Man Without a Star* (1955)

ROLLIN', ROLLIN', ROLLIN'

Martha's Refrigerator Rolls

1 quart milk
1 cup salad oil
1 cup sugar
1 teaspoon salt
2 packages active dry yeast
½ cup warm water
1 teaspoon baking soda
1 teaspoon baking powder
9 cups all-purpose flour
   Melted butter

In a saucepan, combine the milk, salad oil, sugar, and salt. Bring to a boil. Let cool. Soften the yeast in the water. Sift together the baking soda, baking powder, and flour. Add them and the yeast mixture to the milk mixture and mix well. Cover and let rise at room temperature until doubled in bulk. Punch down and refrigerate 3 hours to 10 days (covered tightly). To use, preheat the oven to 400°. Roll out the dough to ¼-inch thickness, and cut with a 2½-inch biscuit cutter. Dip the dough in melted butter, and crease the roll with a dull knife to make Parkerhouse rolls. Let rise until they look light and airy. Bake for 10 to 15 minutes. The rolls can be frozen after baking.

Makes about 12 dozen rolls.

Lazy Hills Guest Ranch
Ingram, Texas

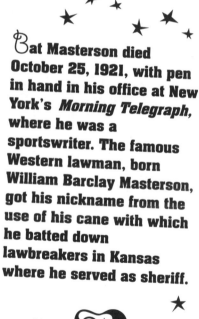

Bat Masterson died October 25, 1921, with pen in hand in his office at New York's *Morning Telegraph*, where he was a sportswriter. The famous Western lawman, born William Barclay Masterson, got his nickname from the use of his cane with which he batted down lawbreakers in Kansas where he served as sheriff.

Donald Kay "Little Brown Jug" Reynolds made thirteen westerns from 1944 to 1951 as sidekick to Gene, Roy, and the Durango Kid and was the last of the Little Beavers with Jim Bannon as Red Ryder.

Little Brown Jug's Breakfast Rolls

1   cup chopped pecans
1   package frozen dough for dinner rolls (Parkerhouse or other)
1   stick butter, melted
1   small (approximately 3-ounces) package butterscotch pudding (not instant)
1   tablespoon milk
1   cup firmly packed brown sugar

The night before serving, grease a Bundt pan. Sprinkle the pecans on the bottom of the pan. Cover the bottom of the pan with a single layer of frozen rolls that barely touch each other. In a saucepan, combine the butter, pudding mix, milk, and brown sugar. Heat until well blended and just about to boil. Remove the mixture from the heat, and pour evenly over the dough. Loosely cover the top of the container with waxed paper. Let rise 6 to 8 hours or overnight at room temperature. When ready to bake, preheat the oven to 350°. Bake uncovered for about 20 minutes, or until golden brown. Quickly invert the rolls onto a serving plate and serve.

Variations: Try vanilla pudding and 1 tablespoon of ground cinnamon instead of butterscotch pudding. You can also use a frozen bread dough that is not in roll form. Let the dough thaw. Pull and roll the thawed dough into golf ball-size pieces. Place in the bottom of the pan, and proceed as described above. This recipe will also work using a Dutch oven instead of a Bundt pan.

Makes about 8 servings.

Don Kay Reynolds, actor

South Texas Dumplings

While beef stew was a favorite of the cowboys, the cook was always looking for a way to change it up. One of the most popular and easiest ways was to add dumplings.

6   eggs
6   tablespoons water
1   plus ½ teaspoon salt
3   to 4 cups all-purpose flour

In a mixing bowl, whip the eggs. Add the water and 1 teaspoon salt. Gradually add the flour until thick. Bring a pot of water and ½ teaspoon salt to a boil. Drop the egg mixture by full teaspoons into the boiling water. Cook for approximately 5 minutes, and remove from the water. Add the dumplings to soup or stew.

Makes 8 to 10 dozen dumplings.

Barbara and Lonnie Tegeler,
Rocking T Chuck Wagon
Chappell Hill, Texas

Rockin' L-H Sourdough Starter

Also called Sourdough Sponge.

2   raw potatoes, peeled and sliced into the
     bottom of a 2-gallon crock jar
1   yeast cake, diluted in 2 cups warm water
2   tablespoons sugar
2   cups all-purpose flour

Combine the potatoes in the crock with the yeast, sugar, and flour, and beat well. It's not necessary to remove any flour lumps since they will dissolve before you are ready to use the starter. Cover with a cloth. (Caution: Do not cover tightly.) Place the crock on a shelf in a warm spot free from drafts. This starter will be bubbling in about 72 hours.

How long will it take? The sourdough starter can be used on the third day, provided that it has started working. But it is better to wait for a couple more days. Add extra fuel each day for the sourdough to work on—a spoonful of sugar along with a couple of spoonfuls of flour. Add warm water if the batter is too thick. Mix well. Cover. Put in a warm spot to work more. In about a week the starter should be filled with a million bubbles. It looks and smells sour, but it has become a rich luscious sourdough starter. If you wait two weeks, the sourdough starter will gain more flavor. Waiting this extra time gives extra flavor, not to be compared with any other batter. By the third week, it will be bubbling so hard that the starter will be trying to climb over the top of the crock. It is now a rich, creamy batter honeycombed with bubbles.

With a wooden spoon, stir the starter smooth, and remember: Sourdough loves to be stirred. Dip out the slices of potato in the bottom, making sure you get them all because there is nothing worse than finding lumps in your sourdough biscuits. Always use a wooden spoon, never metal. A metal spoon will contaminate your sourdough. If the batter sponge seems stiff and heavy, add more water—enough to make a rich, thick creamy sponge. It is best to have the batter thicker since it will thin down while working overnight. If the starter is too thin, throw in extra flour to make a smooth, creamy batter. Cover. Continue to let the starter "work" in a warm place free from drafts.

Allow plenty of room for expansion since sourdough, when "working," can more than double in volume. Keep sourdough starter at a constant room temperature. Extreme cold will cause the sourdough to go "flat." Sudden heat will cause the sourdough to begin to "work" and expand very quickly.

Lee Henry, Rockin' L-H Chuck Wagon
Eufaula, Oklahoma

Crunchy Cowboy Biscuits

1   (7½-ounce) tube refrigerated home-style
     biscuits, separated into 10 biscuits
1   tablespoon melted butter
⅓   cup crushed corn chips

Preheat the oven to the temperature recommended on the biscuit package. Arrange the biscuits in a 10-inch round, greased baking pan. Brush the biscuits with butter. Sprinkle with the corn chips, and then gently press the chips into the dough. Bake at the recommended temperature for 14 to 16 minutes, or until the biscuits are golden brown.

Makes 10 biscuits.

Roy Cooper, rodeo cowboy

Perfect Sourdough Biscuits

Winner of Pawnee Bill's Chuck Wagon Cook-Off, 1999 and 2000.

Shortening for greasing the inside of the Dutch oven
- 4   cups all-purpose flour
- ¾   teaspoon salt
- 3   tablespoons sugar
- 1½   tablespoons baking powder
- ¾   teaspoon baking soda
- ½   cup shortening
- 3½   cups sourdough starter

Using a 14-inch Dutch oven, rub some shortening generously over the inside. Set the Dutch oven by the campfire to melt the shortening and to preheat. Put all the flour in your sifter. On top of the flour, put the salt, sugar, baking powder, and baking soda. Sift them in a bowl all together at one time. Using a fork, cut the shortening into the dry ingredients until blended well. Pour in the starter, and mix until you can't stir the dough any more. Gently knead the dough with your hands (the less you handle the dough, the lighter and fluffier your biscuits will be) until all the dry ingredients are mixed together. The dough should have a slightly wet, sticky feel to it. Spread a small amount of flour on the chuck table. Gently flatten out the dough until it is about 1 inch thick, or about the size of the bottom of your Dutch oven. For man-size biscuits, cut the dough with a tin coffee cup. The size of your biscuits is up to you. When putting the biscuits in the Dutch oven, I like to lay them in the melted shortening, then turn the biscuits over (this will cause the biscuits to brown nicely on top). Crowd the biscuits into the Dutch oven. They are ready to bake over your campfire. You don't have to let these biscuits rise; if you did it right, they will rise as they bake. These biscuits should take 27 minutes to bake at 400°. You should know how to maintain about the right temperature in your Dutch oven. If not, practice makes perfect.

Makes 2 to 3 dozen biscuits.

*Lee Henry, Rockin' L-H Chuck Wagon
Eufaula, Oklahoma*

Renaissance cowboy Kirby Jonas is a Montana native and an Idaho firefighter who has penned more than a half dozen western novels. In 2004 he cowrote *Yaqui Gold* with actor Clint Walker.

Holey Sock Biscuits

- ½   cup shortening (butter-flavored Crisco works great)
- 2   cups all-purpose flour
- 2   tablespoons sugar
- 3   teaspoons baking powder
- 1   teaspoon salt
- ¾   cup milk

Preheat the oven to 425°. In a mixing bowl, cut the shortening into the flour, sugar, baking powder, and salt with a fork until the mixture resembles fine crumbs. Stir in the milk until you have a ball of soft dough. Knead the dough gently, and roll it out (it works best on a lightly floured surface). Roll or pat down gently to ¾-inch thick. Cut to the desired size with a biscuit cutter or a cup. Place the biscuits on an ungreased cookie sheet, about 1 inch apart. Bake for 10 to 12 minutes.

Makes about 12 to 15 biscuits.

Kirby Jonas, writer

Iron Eyes Cody made 130 movies from the 1930s to the 1980s, including *Son of Paleface, A Man Called Horse, Nevada Smith,* and *Sitting Bull*. He was the crying Indian in the "Keep America Beautiful" television ad campaign that ran during the 1970s and '80s.

Trailside Bannock

- 2 cups all-purpose flour
- 1 tablespoon baking powder
- ½ teaspoon salt
- 1 heaping tablespoon lard or bear grease
- ½ cup powdered milk
- 1 cup water (melted snow also works)

Start with a fairly clean skillet, to which you add the flour, baking powder, salt, lard, and powdered milk. Add the water slowly. If you add too much water, you will have a pay streak (doughy center). When the ingredients are thoroughly mixed, set the skillet on the grill and let the dough rise until it looks like it won't rise any more. Take the skillet off the fire, and use a small forked stick to prop up the skillet so it is exposed to the fire. When the top is brown, it should be done. You can slice it or nibble at the edges, whichever you prefer.

Note: If you get a pay streak, just work around it, and for the next batch try to remember what caused it. By the time you get your rabbit or grouse (skinned, not plucked) off the grill, the bannock should be done.

Iron Eyes Cody, actor
Submitted by Victor W. Buck

Lonely Man's Garlic French Bread

1 clove garlic
½ cup softened butter or margarine
French bread

Mash the garlic clove to a pulp, and then blend and cream it well with the butter or margarine. Partially cut the French bread into thick slices, being careful not to cut through to the bottom crust. Spread the garlic butter between the slices. Wrap the loaf in aluminum foil, and place on the grill in a warm spot that is not directly over coals. Turn several times. Keep wrapped until serving time. Enjoy!
　Makes 1 loaf.

Dirk London, actor

Proudly carrying on the family tradition, writer and roper Montie Montana Jr. produces *Buffalo Bill's Wild West Show.*

Pesto Toast
George Russell

Rustle up a batch.

Olive oil
Minced garlic
Chopped olives
Parmesan cheese
Fresh basil leaves
Crushed and dried red peppers
Crusty French bread, sliced moderately thin

In a bowl, combine equal parts of the olive oil, garlic, olives, Parmesan cheese, and basil leaves. Mix in a dash of crushed and dried red peppers. Spread an ample tablespoon of the mixture on each slice of bread. Wrap each piece in foil, and place in the corner of the grill (low to moderate heat) while you're cooking the entrées. Serve as an appetizer, with salad, or with the main course. (For the culinary fearless, the spread mixture can also be used as a dip.)

Buddy Ebsen, actor

Hang 'Em High
Jalapeño Cornbread

1 (6½-ounce) package cornbread mix
½ cup cornmeal
1 (15-ounce) can creamed corn
1 egg
2 tablespoons canola oil
1 cup milk
1 jalapeño chile, cut up fine
1 yellow chile, cut up fine
1 serrano chile, cut up fine
1½ cups shredded pepper cheese
1 tablespoon packed brown sugar
Pinch of salt
1 tablespoon baking powder
2 tablespoons bacon drippings (optional instead of canola oil)
1 handful chopped-up onion (optional; don't screw it up with too much, unless you really like onions)

Mix all this stuff up in a bowl, and then put the mixture in a muffin pan or any kind of a high-sided pan. Be sure to butter the pan, or use some of that spray grease. Preheat the oven to 400°, and cook the cornbread muffins about 20 minutes, or until they turn golden brown or a stuck-in toothpick comes out clean. Eat 'em as soon as they cool off a little. Save the rest of 'em in sandwich bags in the refrigerator, so they don't dry out. These are really good.
　Makes about 6 servings.

Montie Montana Jr.,
roper, writer, and producer

The Sons of the Pioneers seen here include (clockwise from the bottom left) Tommy Doss, Dale Warren, Pat Brady, Karl Farr, and Lloyd Perryman.

Blue Prairie Buttermilk Muffins

    5   cups all-purpose flour
    5   teaspoons baking soda
    2   teaspoons salt
    1   (15-ounce) box raisin bran flakes (about 7
        cups)
    3   cups sugar
    4   large eggs
    1   cup vegetable oil
    4   cups buttermilk
    ¼   cup chopped walnuts

Preheat the oven to 375°. In a large bowl, stir together the flour, baking soda, salt, raisin bran, and sugar. In a bowl, whisk together the eggs, oil, buttermilk, and walnuts. Add the egg mixture to the flour mixture, and stir the batter until it is just combined. (The batter may be made in advance and kept chilled in an airtight container for up to 6 weeks.) Spoon ¼ cup batter into each cup of well-buttered or paper-lined ½-cup muffin tins, and bake the muffins in the middle of the oven for 15 to 20 minutes, or until a tester comes out clean.

Makes about 42 muffins.

Tommy Doss, Sons of the Pioneers

Richard Boone played Paladin, a debonair soldier of fortune, in the classic *Have Gun, Will Travel* series from 1957 to 1963.

Good-Day-for-Mango Bread

- 2 cups all-purpose flour
- 1 cup granulated sugar
- ½ cup packed brown sugar
- 2 teaspoons baking soda
- ½ teaspoon salt
- 1 teaspoon ground cinnamon
- 3 beaten eggs
- 1 cup oil
- 1 teaspoon vanilla extract
- 1 cup chopped nuts (pecans or walnuts)
- ¾ cup raisins
- 2 large, juicy mangoes

Preheat the oven to 325°. Mix the flour, granulated sugar, brown sugar, baking soda, salt, and cinnamon together in a large bowl. Add the eggs, oil, vanilla, chopped nuts, and raisins. Mix well with the flour mixture. Over this mixture slice the mangoes so that the juice drops into the mixture. If the mangoes are not juicy enough, add a little orange juice. The mixture will be thick. Pour into two greased 9 x 5-inch loaf pans. Bake for about 1 hour. Test with a straw after 45 minutes. The bread can be frozen after cooling. Slice and warm before serving. If using as a dessert, add vanilla ice cream.

Makes 2 loaves.

Richard Boone, actor
Submitted by Mrs. Richard Boone, actor

Richard Boone returned to TV in the 1973 series *Hec Ramsey* as a cowboy detective who used forensics to solve crimes. Boone also starred in the western films *The Tall T, Rio Conchos, The Alamo, Big Jake,* and *The Shootist.*

The California Kid's Kaiserschmarren

2   whole eggs
1   egg white
    Pinch of salt
4   tablespoons all-purpose flour
2   to 3 tablespoons milk or cream
2   tablespoons raisins, preferably soaked in
    light or dark rum for 15 minutes, then
    drained
1   plus 1 tablespoons butter
2   tablespoons granulated sugar
    Confectioners' sugar
    Cranberry sauce or berry preserves

Preheat the oven to 400°. Put the eggs and egg white into a mixing bowl. Beat with a wire whisk until well blended and foamy. Whisk in the salt, flour, and milk or cream. Beat well, adding additional milk by driblets until a smooth batter is achieved. Mix in the raisins. In a medium, nonstick, frying pan over medium heat, melt 1 tablespoon of the butter. Pour the batter into the frying pan. When the bottom of the pancake is golden brown, flip it over with a spatula. Immediately place the frying pan in the preheated oven for 4 to 5 minutes. The pancake will puff slightly. Remove the pancake from the oven. Using two rubber spatulas or wooden spoons, tear the pancake into rough, bite-size pieces. Push the pancake pieces against one side of the pan. Place the pan back on a burner over medium heat. In the "empty" half of the frying pan, melt the remaining 1 tablespoon of butter. Sprinkle the granulated sugar over the butter, and allow to bubble for a minute or two. Quickly toss the pancake pieces with the butter-sugar mixture. Turn the pancake pieces out onto serving plates. Dust with confectioners' sugar, and serve with fruit sauce on the side.

Makes 2 or 3 servings.

Governor Arnold Schwarzenegger, actor

Arnold Schwarzenegger played Handsome Stranger, bodyguard to Ann-Margret's Charming Jones and foil to Kirk Douglas's Cactus Jack, in the 1979 horse opera *The Villain*.

Yazoo Spoon Bread

This is the first batter bread I ever tasted. My grandmother "Dandy" taught me how to make this bread when I first started learning how to cook in Yazoo City, Mississippi. It's a batter bread to be spooned onto a plate. It is similar to polenta.

1¾   cups cornmeal
3   cups milk
1   teaspoon salt
2   tablespoons butter
3   eggs, lightly beaten with a fork
2   teaspoons baking powder

Preheat the oven to 300°. In a 2-quart pot, gradually stir the cornmeal into the milk. Let it come to a boil to make a mush. Add the salt and butter, and then add the eggs and baking powder. Bake in a square, oiled, glass baking dish for 35 minutes, or until the top is golden. Spoon the bread right from the baking dish to serve.

Makes 6 to 8 servings.

Stella Stevens, actress

Jimmy Hawkins had a fine time playing cowboys as a teenager. He was Tagg Oakley, brother to sharpshooting sister Annie, in the 1950s TV series *Annie Oakley*. He was also in the western films *Winchester '73, Destry,* and *Savage Frontier.*

Tagg Oakley Special

A peanut butter and jelly sandwich for the kid in all of us.

2   fresh slices white Wonder bread (*Annie Oakley* was sponsored by Wonder bread)
    Skippy peanut butter (another sponser)
    Boysenberry jelly

Just spread a generous portion of fresh-roasted Skippy peanut butter on 1 slice of the Wonder bread. Then spread an equal portion of boysenberry jelly on the other slice. Knotts Berry Farm jelly is really good, but you can choose your own favorite jelly or jam.

Now, slap 'em together. Make sure you have a large glass of cold milk. (Carnation milk—they, too, sponsored *Annie Oakley*.) To top it off, grab a fresh bag of potato chips. (Ahhh, Laura Scudder's—they also were a sponsor.) It doesn't get any better than that. It got me through many a lunch on location when they couldn't start the fire. And it helps build strong bodies eight ways. Boy, did they drill that into us when we did the commercials for the show. Well, what are you waitin' for? Eat up!

Makes 1 serving.

Jimmy Hawkins, actor

GOLD RUSH

Hare-Trigger Special Cake

2 cups sugar
1½ cups light vegetable oil
4 eggs, unbeaten
2 cups self-rising flour
2 teaspoons cinnamon
1 teaspoon vanilla extract
2 to 3 cups grated carrots
½ cup chopped nuts
Cream Cheese Icing (recipe follows)

Preheat the oven to 300°. Grease and flour three 8 or 9-inch-round cake pans. In a mixing bowl, mix in the following order: sugar, oil, eggs, flour, cinnamon, vanilla, carrots, and nuts. Pour the batter into the pans, and bake for about 30 minutes, or until a toothpick inserted into the center comes out mostly clean. Let the cake cool and spread the Cream Cheese Icing on the cake.

Makes 10 to 12 servings.

Cream Cheese Icing:
½ stick margarine
1 (8-ounce) package cream cheese
1 (16-ounce) box confectioners' sugar
1 teaspoon vanilla extract

In a bowl, cream together the margarine, cream cheese, sugar, and vanilla. Add a few drops of milk if the icing seems to be too thick.

Trigger, the smartest horse in the movies (and in the kitchen)

Roy Rogers's faithful canine Bullet has whipped up something special for his favorite equine, Rogers's steed Trigger. But Trigger has a mighty fine carrot cake that should hit the spot for any cowboy with a sweet tooth.

A believer in cowboy logic, singer/fiddler Charlie Daniels, easily identifiable by his bull rider hat and belt buckle, has loved cowboys and cowboy movies since boyhood. He also loves horses and rodeo and continues to be involved with the Murfreesboro Noon Exchange Rodeo, which takes place down the road from his Twin Pines Ranch in Middle Tennessee.

Hazel's Great Chocolate Cake

1   cup butter or margarine
2   cups sugar
2   eggs
1   teaspoon vanilla extract
3   cups sifted all-purpose flour
½   cup cocoa
2   teaspoons baking soda
1   teaspoon salt
2   cups buttermilk
    Chocolate Butter Frosting (recipe follows)

Preheat the oven to 350°. Grease and flour two 9-inch layer cake pans or one large sheet-cake pan. In a large mixing bowl, cream the butter, and then gradually beat in the sugar until fluffy. Add the eggs one at a time. Beat well for about 2 minutes. Add the vanilla. Add the flour, cocoa, baking soda, and salt alternately with buttermilk, using the low speed of the mixer. Pour the batter into the pans. Bake for 35 to 40 minutes. Remove the cake from the pans after a few minutes. Cool on a rack. Frost with Chocolate Butter Frosting.

Makes 10 to 12 servings.

Chocolate Butter Frosting:

1   (16-ounce) box confectioners' sugar
½   cup cocoa
⅛   teaspoon salt
¼   pound butter or margarine (room temperature)
1   teaspoon vanilla extract
5   to 7 tablespoons milk

Mix together the confectioners' sugar, cocoa, salt, butter, vanilla, and milk, and beat on low speed until smooth. This icing tastes better after it sits on the cake for about an hour.

Charlie Daniels,
singer/songwriter and rodeo man

Best-for-Last Chocolate Cake

2 cups sugar
½ cup vegetable oil
2 eggs
1 teaspoon vanilla extract
1 cup buttermilk (or sour milk)
2 cups all-purpose flour
3 heaping tablespoons cocoa
1 teaspoon baking soda
1 cup boiling water
   Fudge Frosting (recipe follows)

Preheat the oven to 325°. Grease and flour 2 (9-inch) cake pans. In a mixing bowl, mix together well the sugar, oil, eggs, and vanilla. Mix in the buttermilk. Add the flour, cocoa, and baking soda, and continue to mix.

Slowly pour in the boiling water, and mix thoroughly. (The mixture will be very runny.) Pour into the prepared pans, and bake for about 30 minutes, or until a toothpick inserted in the middle comes out clean. Turn the cakes out onto a wire rack to cool. After the cakes have cooled, spread them with Fudge Frosting.

Makes 8 to 10 servings.

Fudge Frosting:
1 box Jiffy fudge frosting
1 tablespoon butter

Make the fudge frosting according to directions on the box, but add 1 tablespoon butter.

Jennifer Holt, actress
Submitted by niece Sandie Holt

Jennifer Holt made nearly fifty films and was the heroine in a number of westerns in the 1940s. She was often the leading lady to such good guys as Eddie Dean, Lash LaRue, Johnny Mack Brown, and Rod Cameron. Born into a family of cowboys, Jennifer sits on the fence here with father Jack Holt and brother Tim Holt.

James Drury is one of the few actors to star in a TV series where the main character never had a name. In *The Virginian,* from 1962 to 1971, Drury was the cool and steady lead cowboy who helped run Shiloh Ranch. Drury also starred in the western films *Love Me Tender, Good Day for a Hanging,* and *Ride the High Country.*

The Virginian's Best Chocolate Cake in the West

1   package Duncan Hines chocolate cake mix
1   (3.9-ounce) package instant chocolate
    pudding mix
2   cups sour cream
1   cup butter at room temperature
5   eggs
1   teaspoon vanilla extract
2   cups semi-sweet chocolate chips

Preheat the oven to 350°. Grease a 10-inch Bundt pan. In a mixing bowl, stir together the cake mix and pudding mix. Create a well in the center. Add the sour cream, butter, eggs, and vanilla. Beat on low speed until blended. Scrape the bowl and beat again. Fold in the chocolate chips. The batter will be thick. Pour the batter into the Bundt pan. Bake for 60 to 70 minutes. Let cool 10 to 15 minutes, and then turn out onto a wire rack or plate and cool completely. Then you may sprinkle with confectioners' sugar and drizzle with your own frosting.
    Makes 10 to 12 servings.

Carl Ann and James Drury, actor

Cookie's Chocolate Cake with Strawberry Topping

2½   cups all-purpose flour
1½   cups granulated sugar
½   cup cocoa
2   teaspoons baking soda
½   teaspoon salt
⅔   cup canola or vegetable oil
2   tablespoons vinegar
1   tablespoon vanilla extract
2   cups cold coffee
    Cinnamon and sugar mixture
    Confectioners' sugar
    Strawberries, sliced in half
    Chocolate syrup

Preheat the oven to 350°. In large mixing bowl, mix the flour, granulated sugar, cocoa, baking soda, and salt together with a wire whisk. Then add the oil, vinegar, vanilla, and coffee. Pour the mixture into a 12 x 8-inch baking pan, and spread evenly. Sprinkle the top with about ⅓ cup cinnamon and sugar mixture. Bake for 25 to 30 minutes, or until a toothpick inserted comes out clean. Allow the cake to cool. Sprinkle with the confectioners' sugar. Put the strawberry halves on top, and then drizzle the chocolate syrup over the entire top of the cake.
    Note: This is also good with vanilla ice cream, caramel, or whipped cream. This cake keeps for several days in a refrigerator if sealed with plastic wrap.
    Makes about 9 servings.

Terri "Cookie" Doty, Kedesh Ranch Shell, Wyoming

"It's not a question of who's right—it's a question of what's right."

—Joel McCrea in
Wichita (1955)

Medicine Man's Rum Cake

½   cup chopped nuts
1   package Duncan Hines Butter Recipe cake mix
1   (3¾-ounce) package vanilla instant pudding mix
½   cup rum
½   cup water
½   cup cooking oil
4   eggs
    Rum Glaze (recipe follows)

Preheat the oven to 325°. Place the nuts in bottom of a well-greased Bundt or angel-food-cake pan. In a large bowl, mix the cake mix, pudding mix, rum, water, oil, and eggs for 2 minutes, scraping the bowl continuously. Pour the batter over the nuts, and bake for 50 to 60 minutes or until done. Pour the Rum Glaze over the hot cake, and let cool in the pan for 30 minutes. This recipe is a favorite.

    Makes 8 to 10 servings.

Rum Glaze:
1   cup sugar
½   cup butter
¼   cup water
¼   cup light rum

Mix in a saucepan the sugar, butter, water, and rum, and boil 2 to 3 minutes.

Lazy Hills Guest Ranch
Ingram, Texas

Joyce's Peanut Butter Pie

½   cup sugar
1   (3-ounce) package cream cheese
¾   cup chunky peanut butter
1   (12-ounce) container nondairy whipped topping
1   (9-inch) chocolate graham cracker crust

Cream together the sugar, cream cheese, and peanut butter. Fold in the whipped topping. Pour the mixture into the crust and refrigerate.

    Makes 6 to 8 servings.

Melissa and Dave Stamey,
singer/songwriter

Singer and songwriter Dave Stamey enjoys performing at cowboy gatherings across the West. He has been named male performer of the year by the Western Music Association. His albums include *Tonopah* and *Buckaroo Man.*

Although she was most famous as Superman's girlfriend Lois Lane, Noel Neill was the heroine in such western films as *Abilene Trail, Montana Incident, The Lawless Rider,* and *The Adventures of Frank and Jesse James.* Neill has worked with such cowboys as Jimmy Wakely, Ken Curtis, Whip Wilson, Johnny Mack Brown, and Clayton Moore.

Moonlight Apple Pie (Chuck Wagon Style)

2   gallons apple cider
1   cup whole allspice
1   cup whole cloves
1   nice handful ground cinnamon
1   cup firmly packed brown sugar
2   cups good vodka or 1 cup Everclear

Put the cider, allspice, cloves, and cinnamon in a large pot, and boil hard for 10 minutes. Strain out the cloves and allspice. Stir in the brown sugar. Cool the mixture enough to drink. Add the vodka or Everclear. Store in a crock jug. Drink standing or you won't be able to stand.

The number of servings depends on one's thirst and stamina.

The Moonlight Ranch Shed and Bed
Valley Mills, Texas

Favorite Red Bean Pie Dessert

1   rounded cup cooked and mashed pinto
     beans
1   scant cup sugar
1   cup milk
3   egg yolks, beaten, whites reserved
1   teaspoon vanilla extract
1   teaspoon ground nutmeg
1   (9-inch) unbaked piecrust

Preheat the oven to 350°. In large mixing bowl, combine the pinto beans, sugar, milk, egg yolks, vanilla, and nutmeg, and mix thoroughly. Pour the mixture into the piecrust. Bake for about 30 minutes.

Optional: Make a meringue topping using the egg whites and ¼ cup granulated sugar. Beat the whites and sugar together until stiff peaks form. Spread on the cooled pie, and bake until golden brown.

Makes 8 servings.

Noel Neill, actress

Trampas's Banana Cream Pie

- 8 ripe bananas
- 1 tablespoon lemon juice
- ⅔ cup sugar
- ⅓ cup all-purpose flour
- ¼ teaspoon salt
- ½ teaspoon ground cinnamon
- 2 teaspoons vanilla extract
- 1 (9-inch) unbaked piecrust
- 2 tablespoons butter
  Smidgen of ground nutmeg

Meringue:
- 3 egg whites
- ¼ cup granulated sugar

Thinly slice the bananas into a large bowl. Sprinkle the lemon juice over the top, and stir gently to coat. In a separate bowl, mix together the sugar, flour, salt, cinnamon, and vanilla, and then add this mixture to the bananas, mixing gently. Preheat the oven to 425°. Place the mixture in the pie pastry. Place slivers of butter over the filling, and sprinkle with a smidgen of nutmeg. Make a loose canopy over the pie and crust with aluminum foil, and bake for about 30 minutes. (The canopy's main purpose is to prevent the crust from burning.) Let cool. To make the meringue, beat the egg whites and sugar together until stiff peaks form. Place the meringue on the cooled pie, and brown in a 350° oven for about 10 to 15 minutes to brown.

Makes 6 servings.

Doug McClure, actor

Easygoing, ever-smiling Doug McClure starred in three TV westerns: *The Overland Trail* in 1960; *The Virginian,* in which he played Trampas; and *Barbary Coast.* His films include *Shenandoah* and *Maverick.*

Roberta Shore starred on *The Virginian* TV series as Betsy Garth from 1962 to 1965. She was a guest on such TV westerns as *Lawman, Laramie, Wagon Train,* and *Maverick.*

Betsy Garth's Fresh Pear Pie

Pies are my specialty and this is one of my favorites.

3   to 4 ripe pears, peeled, seeded, and quartered
1   (9-inch) unbaked piecrust
1   cube butter, softened
1   cup sugar
5   tablespoons all-purpose flour
2   eggs, beaten
1   teaspoon vanilla extract

Preheat the oven to 350°. Put the pears in the unbaked pie shell. In a bowl, mix together the butter, sugar, flour, eggs, and vanilla, and pour the mixture over the pears. Bake for 1 hour. Enjoy!
    Makes 6 to 8 servings.

    Roberta Shore, actress

Double-Barreled Peach and Blueberry Cobbler

Filling:
2   pounds fresh peaches, or frozen (thawed and drained)
2   pounds fresh blueberries, or frozen (thawed and drained)
1   cup sugar
3   tablespoons cornstarch
1   teaspoon almond extract

Topping:
2½   cups all-purpose flour
½   cup sugar
1½   teaspoons baking powder
¾   teaspoon baking soda
½   teaspoon salt
1   stick chilled unsalted butter, diced into ½-inch cubes
¾   cup buttermilk
¾   cup chilled whipping cream
    Cinnamon-sugar mix

Preheat the oven to 400°. For the filling, toss together in a large bowl the peaches, blueberries, sugar, cornstarch, and almond extract. Transfer the filling to a 13 x 9 x 2-inch glass baking dish. Bake the filling until the edges start to bubble, about 35 minutes. Reduce the oven temperature to 375°. While the filling is baking, make the topping. Whisk the flour, sugar, baking powder, baking soda, and salt together. Add the butter, and mix with your fingers until the mixture resembles coarse meal. Slowly add the buttermilk and whipping cream until the dough comes together, using a fork (a stand mixer on low speed can be used). Drop the dough by rounded tablespoons over the hot filling to cover. Sprinkle with the cinnamon-sugar. Bake until golden brown, about 30 minutes. Serve with ice cream or whipped cream.
    Makes 12 servings.

    Laughing Water Ranch
    Fortine, Montana

A magnificent showman and the son of the son of a fiddler, Bob Wills is "the King of Texas Swing." Bob Wills and His Texas Playboys made hits across Texas and the nation for years with such tunes as "Take Me Back to Tulsa," "Bubbles in My Beer," "Lily Dale," "Forbidden Love," and "San Antonio Rose." Wills also made about ten western films in the early 1940s.

Year-of-the-Texan Peach Cobbler

My mother dictated this to me over the phone many years ago. My dad loved to have this with some ice cream.

—Diane Wills Malone

½ cup butter
1 cup all-purpose flour
1½ teaspoons baking powder
½ teaspoon salt
1 cup milk
1 cup sugar
2 cups peeled and sliced peaches, juices reserved

Preheat the oven to 350°. Melt the butter in a 13 x 9-inch pan. In a bowl, combine the flour, baking powder, and salt. Stir in the milk and sugar to make a batter. Spoon the batter over the melted butter. Spoon the peaches and any juices over the batter. Bake until the batter is browned and has risen around the fruit, approximately 30 minutes.

Makes 6 to 8 servings.

Bob Wills, singer

TOM MIX
MUSEUM

One of the silent screen's greatest stars, Tom Mix (1880–1940) appeared in more than three hundred movies and remains for many people the epitome of the heroic cowboy. A former rodeo performer, ranch hand, and soldier, Mix did most of his own stunts and insisted on wearing a huge white hat as a distinctive trademark.

The Tom Mix Museum opened in 1968 in Dewey, Oklahoma (where the future movie star briefly served as a lawman), and contains hundreds of original Mix items, including several of his costumes, boots, gloves, saddles, and one of his signature white hats. Original Mix memorabilia, including children's books and cereal prizes, are on display. A small theater shows snippets from surviving films, and a life-size statue of Tony, Mix's equine costar, greets visitors.

But perhaps the most interesting exhibit is "the suitcases of death." Mix died when an unsecured metal suitcase struck the back of his head during a car wreck, and now the fatal piece of luggage (still dented from the actor's skull) and its companion are prominently displayed in the museum.

The suitcases of death are not the strangest Mix items available for public viewing. That honor surely goes to his boyhood outhouse, complete with a crescent moon door, which you can visit at the Tom Mix Comes Home Museum in Driftwood, Pennsylvania (the actor's birthplace).

The Tom Mix Museum is located at 721 N. Delaware Avenue in Dewey, Oklahoma. For more information, go to *www.ok-history.mus.ok.us/mus-sites/masnum31.htm*.

Randy Travis tackled a Montana cattle drive with Roy Rogers for the 1990 TV special *Randy Travis— Happy Trails.* The country singing star also has saddled up for the westerns *Dead Man's Revenge, Frank and Jesse, Texas, The Cactus Kid, Texas Rangers,* and *The Long Ride Home.*

Lib's Quick-'n'-Easy Cobbler

2   cups sliced fresh peaches
¾   plus 1 cup sugar
1   stick margarine or butter
1   cup all-purpose flour
1   teaspoon baking powder
1   cup milk

Preheat the oven to 350°. Combine the peaches with ¾ cup sugar. Let stand for 20 minutes. Melt the butter or margarine in a 1½-quart baking dish in the oven. Sift together the flour, the remaining 1 cup sugar, and the baking powder. Add the milk, and stir briskly. Lumps will remain. Pour the mixture into the baking dish with the melted butter. Top with the peaches. Bake for 45 minutes. Best if served warm with vanilla ice cream.

Makes 4 to 6 servings.

Randy Travis, singer and actor

Kim Darby has been a guest on the TV series *Gunsmoke, Wagon Train,* and *Bonanza* and played Calamity Jane in *This Is the West That Was.* But western fans love best her riveting role as young Mattie Ross in *True Grit* in which she matched wit and tenacity with John Wayne's Rooster Cogburn. Darby stands her ground here with Wayne and Glen Campbell (right).

Desert Dessert Enchiladas

This is one of those emergency dishes that you can throw together when friends drop by unexpectedly.

1   **package small flour tortillas**
    Peanut or corn oil
    Your favorite fruit pie filling
    Cinnamon-sugar mixture

Preheat the oven to 350°. Use a cookie sheet covered with aluminum foil or parchment paper. Soften the tortillas until they roll easily. Brush the oil on both sides of each tortilla. Place a small amount of your favorite pie filling (try peach, cherry, and apple; they are all delicious) in the lower third of the tortillas, and roll up. Place the tortillas seam-side down on the cookie sheet. Sprinkle with the cinnamon-sugar mixture. Bake the enchiladas in the oven until they turn golden and are flaky (the tortillas will puff up in places), about 20 minutes. Serve with your favorite ice cream or with whipped cream.

Note: You must brush both sides of the tortilla with the oil or they won't get flaky. Also, some brands of tortillas are flakier than others—I don't know why—so it might take a couple of tries before you find one that will work.

Kim Darby, actress

Cowboy Kolaches

Many of the Texas cowboys brought their favorite recipe with them from their native country. The kolache remains a favorite today in major Texas cities and on the ranch.

1   cup milk
½   cup sugar
1   teaspoon salt
½   cup butter
1   package active dry yeast
¼   cup warm water
1   egg
2   plus 2 cups all-purpose flour
    Fruit of choice or cream cheese

In a medium saucepan, scald the milk. Add the sugar, salt, and butter. Dissolve the yeast in the warm water. Combine the yeast mixture, milk mixture, and egg, and add 2 cups of the flour. Mix until smooth. Stir in the remaining 2 cups flour to make a stiff batter. Set the batter aside, and let it rise to double the original size. When risen, roll out the dough on a floured board, and cut out circles with a biscuit cutter. Place the kolaches in a pan, and let rise to double in size. Punch down the center of each kolache, and fill with your favorite fruit, such as peaches, plums, or blackberries, or add cream cheese to the centers. Bake in a Dutch oven, or in a conventional oven, at 375° for 15 to 20 minutes. Cool and serve.

Barbara and Lonnie Tegeler,
Rocking T Chuck Wagon
Chappell Hill, Texas

Tippi's Buffalo Chips Pyle

This was one of Denver's favorite snacks, and it is a fitting recipe for cowboy cooking.

2   cups Post Toasties
2   cups oatmeal
1   cup coconut
1   cup chopped pecans
6   ounces chocolate chips
1   cup margarine
1   cup vegetable shortening (Crisco)
2   cups packed brown sugar
2   cups granulated sugar
4   eggs
2   teaspoons vanilla extract
4   cups all-purpose flour
2   teaspoons baking powder
½   teaspoon salt

In a large bowl, mix together the Post Toasties, oatmeal, coconut, pecans, and chocolate chips. In a separate large mixing bowl, cream together the margarine, shortening, brown sugar, and granulated sugar. Add the eggs, vanilla, flour, baking powder, and salt. Mix well, and add to the Post Toasties bowl. Preheat the oven to 325°. Use ¼ cup of the batter for each cookie (6 per cookie sheet). Bake for 15 minutes or until light brown. This recipe makes a big batch of Buffalo Chips for hungry cowboys and cowgirls.

Makes 5 to 6 dozen cookies.

Denver Pyle, actor

Denver Pyle was in hundreds of westerns from TV series to feature films. His movie credits include *Johnny Guitar, The Horse Soldiers, The Alamo, The Man Who Shot Liberty Valance, The Rounders, 5 Card Stud,* and *Winterhawk,* and he was Mad Jack, the narrator of TV's *The Life and Times of Grizzly Adams.*

James Best doesn't seem to want to put his hand anywhere near his gun as he comes face-to-face with Paul Newman's Billy the Kid in *The Left Handed Gun* (1958), directed by Arthur Penn. Historians now believe that the real Billy the Kid was not left-handed after all. But that's O.K. because Paul Newman isn't a true lefty either.

Black Hat Marble Squares

1 (8 ounce) package cream cheese, softened
⅓ plus 2 cups sugar
1 plus 2 eggs
1 stick margarine
¼ cup water
1½ ounces unsweetened chocolate
2 cups all-purpose flour
½ cup sour cream
1 teaspoon baking soda
1 teaspoon salt
6 ounces chocolate chips

Topping:
2 cups sugar
1 stick margarine
½ cup milk
2 cups unsweetened chocolate chips

Grease a 16 x 11-inch pan. In a large bowl, combine the cream cheese, ⅓ cup sugar, and 1 egg. Mix well. In a saucepan, combine the margarine, water, and unsweetened chocolate, and bring to a boil. Remove from the heat. Preheat the oven to 375°. In a separate bowl, combine the flour and the remaining 2 cups sugar. Stir in the chocolate mixture. Add the remaining 2 eggs, sour cream, baking soda, and salt. Mix well. Pour the mixture into the prepared pan. Spoon the cheese mixture over the batter. Cut through with a knife to give a marbled effect. Sprinkle with the chocolate chips. Bake for 25 to 30 minutes. Prepare the topping: In a saucepan, combine the sugar, margarine, and milk. Bring the mixture to a boil. Remove from the heat, and add the chocolate chips. Stir until the mixture starts to thicken. Spread the topping over the baked dough, swirling through with the knife to mix the chips in better. Cut into squares to serve.
Makes 12 servings.

Dorothy and James Best, actress and actor

Gene Autry was always "back in the saddle again" on his horse Champion. His *Melody Ranch* radio show ran for sixteen years on CBS. During the course of his career, Autry sold more than forty million records.

Gene Autry's Hearty Western Chocolate Chip Cookies

1	cup vegetable shortening (Crisco)
½	cup butter
1⅓	cups granulated sugar
1	cup packed brown sugar
4	eggs
1	tablespoon vanilla extract
1	teaspoon lemon juice
2	teaspoons baking soda
1½	teaspoons salt
1	teaspoon ground cinnamon
½	cup rolled oats
3	cups all-purpose flour
2	(12-ounce) packages semisweet chocolate chips
2	cups chopped walnuts

Preheat the oven to 350°. In a large bowl, beat the shortening, butter, and both sugars together for 5 minutes. Beat in the eggs one at a time. Add the vanilla extract and lemon juice. In a separate bowl, combine the baking soda, salt, cinnamon, oats, flour, chocolate chips, and walnuts. Fold the two mixtures together. Spoon out the dough, approximately 1 to 1½-teaspoon-size at a time, onto a cookie sheet. Bake for 16 to 18 minutes.

Makes 4 to 5 dozen cookies.

Gene Autry, singer and actor

GENE AUTRY'S
COWBOY CODE OF HONOR

A cowboy never takes unfair advantage—even of an enemy.
A cowboy never betrays a trust. He never goes back on his word.
A cowboy always tells the truth.
A cowboy is kind and gentle to small children, old folks, and animals.
A cowboy is free from racial and religious intolerances.
A cowboy is always helpful when someone is in trouble.
A cowboy is always a good worker.
A cowboy respects womanhood, his parents, and his nation's laws.
A cowboy is clean about his person in thought, word, and deed.
A cowboy is a patriot.

Smiley Burnette (as Frog Millhouse, left), and Gene Autry dig
into a turkey feast. That goes ditto for Frog's young nephew,
Tadpole (Joe Stauch Jr.).

GENE AUTRY
Oklahoma Museum

O.K., follow us on this one. The Gene Autry Oklahoma Museum does not honor Gene Autry per se. Its purpose is to honor the singing cowboys of Hollywood history, including Rex Allen, Tex Ritter, and all the others.

The museum derives its name from the town itself. In 1941, the citizens of Berwyn, Oklahoma, decided to honor their most famous resident, who owned a ranch in the area, by officially renaming the town Gene Autry.

The museum is located in an eight-room former schoolhouse and boasts several original items that once belonged to Autry, including a pair of his boots, a business suit, and a U.S. flag–emblazoned shirt that Autry often wore during performances.

Plenty of movie memorabilia and Autry collectibles are on display. Probably the most interesting of these are the hard-to-find Monarch bicycle and tricycle, millions of which were sold during Autry's heyday. A guitar sold by Sears & Roebuck that features Autry's image is another popular item.

The Gene Autry Oklahoma Museum is located at 47 Prairie Street in Gene Autry, Oklahoma. For more information, go to *www.cow-boy.com/museum.htm.*

Pistol Peanut Butter Bars

This is one of the favorite snacks of our guests and staff. It is very quick and easy to make.

1   cup softened butter
2   cups chunky peanut butter
2   cups graham cracker crumbs
3   cups confectioners' sugar
2   cups semisweet chocolate chips

Cream the butter and peanut butter. Add the graham cracker crumbs and confectioners' sugar. Mix well. Press into a 9 x 13-inch greased cake pan. Melt the chocolate chips in the microwave for 2 minutes, or until just melted. Spread the melted chips over the mixture in the pan. Smooth out the chocolate topping with a spatula. Chill until the chocolate is set. Cut into small squares. Keep refrigerated when not being served.

Makes 24 servings.

Grapevine Canyon Ranch
Pearce, Arizona

Famous for his deputying days in Mayberry, Don Knotts played like a gunfighter in the western comedy *The Shakiest Gun in the West*. He also carried bullets in two *Apple Dumpling Gang* movies and *Hot Lead and Cold Feet*.

Shakiest Campfire S'mores in the West

4   ounces Hershey's chocolate candy bar (milk or dark chocolate according to preference)
8   cookies (oatmeal ones work well)
16 marshmallows

Have someone begin to tell a ghost story (one involving a man searching for his missing golden arm is always good). Grease the grid over your campfire, and get the campfire coals worked up to a high temperature without too much flame. Place 1 ounce of chocolate on the bottom side of one of the cookies. An oatmeal cookie is usually a good size and consistency, but a large chocolate chip cookie gives you that much more chocolate to enjoy. Put two marshmallows on a stick and roast them. Turn the marshmallows, trying to shake only a little while listening to the ghost story, to get them nicely melted and golden brown. Put the roasted marshmallows onto the chocolate, and top them with another cookie (bottom side down) to make a sand-wich. Using a metal spatula, place the S'more sandwich on the campfire grid for just a few seconds to melt the chocolate just a little bit more. Remove the S'more, and serve on a cowboy-style plate. Repeat the procedure three more times.

Variation: You can improvise this recipe by using a fireplace and an oven at home. If so, maybe switch the ghost story to one about a haunted house to maintain the desired amount of shaking.

Makes 4 servings.

Don Knotts,
actor and self-reputed fast-draw expert

Director Earl Bellamy worked on so many TV series that it would be hard to count 'em all (more than fifteen hundred episodes), but among his many westerns were *The Lone Ranger, Annie Oakley, The Adventures of Rin Tin Tin, Wagon Train, Tales of Wells Fargo, Rawhide, Laramie,* and *The Virginian.*

Dark Canyon Chocolate Mousse Cups

Earl's motto, other than "no strain," was, "Life is short. Eat dessert first." Believe me, he would have loved to have done that at every meal. So, of course, I am sending a dessert that he really loved.

—*Gail Bellamy*

¼ cup sugar
⅛ cup water
1½ cups heavy cream
6 ounces semisweet chocolate chips
3 egg yolks
3 tablespoons amaretto
½ cup toasted almonds
   Chocolate Cups (optional; recipe follows)

For the mousse mixture, combine the sugar and water in a pot, and boil for 3 minutes. Whip the cream. In a food processor with a metal blade, process the chocolate chips by pulsing for 15 to 20 seconds. Continue processing and gradually pour in the hot sugar-syrup, egg yolks, and amaretto. Add the almonds, and process for about 20 seconds. Pour the mixture into the whipped cream and fold together. Pour into the Chocolate Cups or serving glasses (this recipe makes twice as much filling as you need for the cups).

Makes 6 servings in cups with extra mousse leftover, or makes 6 larger servings in glasses.

Chocolate Cups:
6 ounces semisweet chocolate chips
1 tablespoon shortening
1½ cups finely ground nuts

In a small microwave-safe bowl, melt the chips and shortening in a microwave on high for 2 minutes. Add the nuts. Spread the mixture evenly on the sides and bottoms of cupcake cups. Place the cups in a cupcake pan, and put in the refrigerator to harden. Tear off the paper when hard.

Makes 6 cups.

Earl Bellamy, director

Singing and songwriting cowboy Curly Musgrave was the Western Music Association's male performer of the year and songwriter of the year in 2002 and 2003. In 2003, he notched the Academy of Western Artists Will Rogers Awards for male performer of the year and entertainer of the year. His solo CDs include *Born to Be a Cowboy, Cowboy True, The Heritage,* and *Range & Romance.* Musgrave often performs in tandem with Belinda Gail.

Curly's Love

In our family desserts were rare and a treat. My mom taught me to make this. Every once in a while, I'll whip some up just to remember how good my mouth felt as a kid when I'd squish all that sweet "Love" around in there.

A little aside—my mom was a real character. She loved to tease and kid. She and my new bride were chatting and she asked, "Has Jim made Love yet?" Aghast at my mom's intrusive question, Kathi said, "What?!" Mom repeated the question several times until the embarrassment was complete, and then she said, "You know, Love, the dessert." She told Kathi how it (the dessert) was made, and Kathi still giggles and gets red-faced when she recalls that incident. Anyway, here's how to make Love.

1   (6-ounce) package Jello gelatin (your
    favorite flavor)
2½ to 3 cups boiling water
1   (12-ounce) can evaporated milk
    Any variety of fruit, sprinkles, or other
    toppings, for fun and taste

Add the boiling water to the Jello, and put it in the freezer to quick-chill it and start it setting up. Put the can of milk in the freezer, and leave it for about 45 minutes until it's good and cold, but not frozen. Blend the milk into the Jello and whip. Immediately stir in your fruit of choice. (Fresh blueberries or raspberries are a personal favorite.) Place in the refrigerator. Because the ingredients were cold to start with, it'll set up in minutes. I sprinkle some chopped nuts or my favorite cereal on top and can't resist a shot of whipped cream.

It'll serve about 8 polite folks, but I usually eat it all myself. 'Course I sometimes will share it with a best friend, but my horse ain't partial to gelatin desserts for some reason. So, I have to eat his, too. I love Love.

Curly Musgrave, singer/songwriter

Second Banana Pudding

¼   cup sugar
2   tablespoons cornstarch
     Pinch of salt
2   cups milk
4   egg yolks, beaten
1   teaspoon vanilla extract
1   cup freshly whipped cream
     Vanilla wafers
5   ripe bananas, sliced

Mix the sugar, cornstarch, and salt in a dou-
ble-boiler. Slowly add the milk, and cook,
covered, over boiling water without stirring
for 9 minutes. Uncover and cook, stirring, for
9 more minutes. Add the egg yolks. (Hint:
Spoon in some milk mixture to the eggs
before adding the eggs to the mixture in
order to bring the eggs to the milk's temperature.) Stir while cooking for 2 more minutes. Let cool and then add the vanilla. Fold
in the whipped cream. Line a casserole dish
with the vanilla wafers. Fill with alternating
layers of pudding and bananas. Begin and
end with pudding.
    Makes 6 to 8 servings.

George Lindsey, actor

Known around the world as Mayberry's beloved
mechanic Goober Pyle, George Lindsey saw how
the West was won as a guest star on the TV
series *Death Valley Days, The Rifleman, Daniel
Boone,* and *Gunsmoke.*

With the sun at his back, George Lindsey may have at least one edge in this test of his quick-draw in a
1963 episode of *Temple Houston* titled "The Guardian."

Frankie Laine's world has always been filled with song.

O.K. Corral Panne Cotta

A deceptively rich Italian dessert.

- 2   cups heavy whipping cream
- ¼   cup sweetened condensed milk
- 1   vanilla bean, split lengthwise
- 1   (¼-ounce) envelope plus ¾ teaspoon
       unflavored gelatin

Combine the cream and condensed milk in a 4-cup saucepan or in a microwave-safe measuring cup. Add the vanilla bean, and sprinkle the gelatin on top. Let stand at least 5 minutes. Simmer the mixture over medium-low heat until small bubbles form around the edges, stirring often. If using a microwave, microwave on high (100 percent power) for 3 minutes. Discard the vanilla bean. Strain the mixture. Pour into six individual custard cups or molds. Cover with plastic wrap, and refrigerate at least 4 hours or for up to 3 days. To remove from the molds, run a small spatula around the edge of each cup. Place a serving plate over the top, and invert, inserting a metal spatula into the side between the panne cotta and the cup to create an air pocket. This pudding can be served plain or topped simply with a strawberry, or add a raspberry sauce.

Makes 6 servings.

Frankie Laine, singer/songwriter

Thrill-of-the-Grill Strawberries

6   (9-inch) squares heavy-duty aluminum foil
1   quart fresh strawberries
1   cup superfine sugar
6   tablespoons cognac, rum, or orange juice
    Whipped topping or ice cream

Press each square of foil over the bottom of a glass to make a cup shape. Set the foil cups in a shallow pan. Remove the hulls from the strawberries, and then wash and drain them. Slice the strawberries into the foil cups, dividing them equally. Sprinkle the sugar over the sliced berries. Let stand for at least 30 minutes. At grilling time, have the grill on low heat. Add 1 tablespoon cognac, rum, or orange juice to each cup. Gather the foil together and twist to close, making small bundles. Lift the bundles from the pan onto the grill. Allow the berries to heat thoroughly. Serve with whipped topping or over ice cream.

    Makes 6 servings.

Carolina Cotton, singer and actress

John B. Stetson first made his famous hat in 1865 in Philadelphia. By the end of the 1800s, his company was producing two million Stetsons a year.

A real southern belle, singer/actress Carolina Cotton made about ten westerns with such leading guys as Charles Starrett and Gene Autry, including a series of hoedown-style westerns that starred Ken Curtis. She's seen here in the 1952 film *Apache Country*.

Cimarron Strip Grilled Bananas

This wonderful and very special dessert comes from the South American cowboys working their banana plantations. It's a very simple—yet elegant—dish, to be served warm with vanilla ice cream or fresh pineapple slices.

6   bananas
½   stick butter
3   tablespoons packed brown sugar
¼   cup chopped pecans or walnuts
    Vanilla bean or vanilla bean extract
    Ground cinnamon stick or shakes of ground cinnamon
    Ground nutmeg
    Pinch of salt for good luck

Place a bunch of bananas on a warm fire, about 350° to 400°. (*Note:* Buy them as a bunch and do not cut them apart; this will help dramatically while grilling, since you want them upright so the juices don't drain.) Take your buck knife, and make a 1 to 1½-inch slice down the top/belly of each banana on one side only. Meanwhile, in a wrought-iron skillet, melt the butter and brown sugar. Add the nuts and stir. Once the nuts are golden brown and the butter is bubbling slightly, throw in the shakes of vanilla, cinnamon, nutmeg, and salt. When the bananas are 100 percent black and the juices are bubbling inside the slices, place them onto a platter. Slowly pour the butter mixture into the slices. Continue pouring onto the ice cream, and serve immediately so that your guests experience the true delight of this dessert—the contrast of hot and cold.
  Makes 6 servings.

  Stuart Whitman, actor

Simply Grape Dessert

It's a wild bunch.

1   pound seedless grapes

Wash the grapes and remove the stems. Dry them in a towel. Put them in a bowl in the freezer for 1 hour. Remove and serve.
  Makes 4 to 6 servings.

  Ivan Cury, radio cowboy

Grapevine Homemade Ice Cream

A ranch favorite.

4   cups heavy cream
¾   cup granulated sugar
    Pinch salt
2   teaspoons vanilla extract

Mix the cream, sugar, salt, and vanilla together until the sugar is dissolved. Freeze in an ice cream freezer.

Variations:

Butterscotch: Cook the sugar with 2 tablespoons of butter until browned. Heat the cream and dissolve the sugar in it. Add the remaining ingredients and cool before freezing in the ice cream freezer.

Coffee: Add 2 tablespoons of instant coffee to the mix.

Strawberry or fruit: Add 3 cups of puréed strawberries or fruit per quart of ice cream.
  Makes 10 servings.

  Grapevine Canyon Ranch
  Pearce, Arizona

Hugh O'Brian starred in the title role of *The Life and Legend of Wyatt Earp,* a topnotch TV western from 1955 to 1961. His western film credits include *The Shootist, Little Big Horn, The Cimarron Kid,* and *The Lawless Breed.*

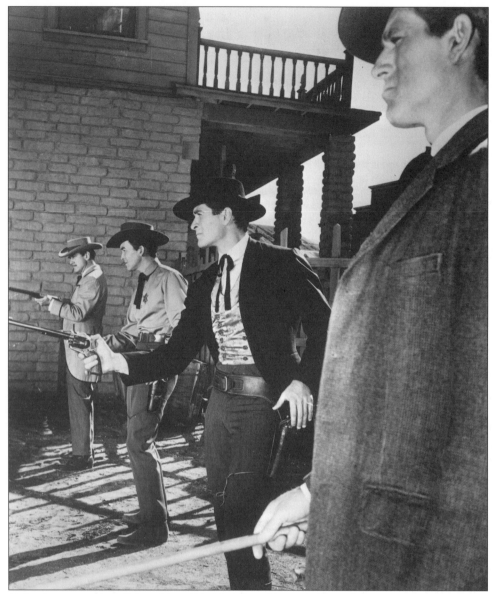

At the shoot-out at the O.K. Corral from TV's *The Life and Legend of Wyatt Earp* are (left to right) Douglas Fowley as Doc Holliday, Dirk London as Morgan Earp, Hugh O'Brian as Wyatt Earp, and John Anderson as Virgil Earp.

Wyatt Earp's Cowboy Dessert

It's better than O.K.

2   scoops lemon sorbet
4   tablespoons tequila
1   tablespoon margarita mix
     Dash of salt
1   sprig fresh mint
1   pinwheel slice lime

Start with a chilled martini or margarita glass. Scoop the sorbet into the glass. Drizzle the tequila and margarita mix over the sorbet. Sprinkle with the salt and top with a sprig of mint. Add the lime slice to the edge of the glass. Serve with a chilled spoon.
  Makes 1 serving.

  Hugh O'Brian, actor

WANTED POSTERS

Here are Web sites for many of the cowboys and cowgirls who contributed recipes to this cookbook. We like to think of the Web as a modern-day Pony Express for learning the latest information about some of our favorite stars.

Rex Allen: *www.pinkbanana.com/rex*
Rex Allen Jr.: *www.rexallenjr.com*
Lynn Anderson: *www.lynn-anderson.com*
Gene Autry: *www.autry-museum.org*
James Best: *www.jamesbest.com*
Baxter Black: *www.baxterblack.com*
Clint Black: *www.clintblack.com*
William Boyd: *www.hopalong.com*
Peter Brown: *www.peterbrown.tv*
Ed Bruce: *www.edbrucemusic.com*
Smiley Burnette: *www.smileyburnette.org*
Tracy Byrd: *www.tbyrd.com*
Glen Campbell: *www.glencampbellshow.com*
Harry Carey Jr.: *www.harrycareyjr.com*
Johnny Cash: *www.johnnycash.com*
Don Collier: *www.doncollier.com*
Clay O'Brien Cooper:
    www.cactusropes.com/team/claycooper.htm
Barry Corbin: *www.barrycorbin.net*
Cathy Lee Crosby: *www.cathylee.com*
Charlie Daniels: *www.charliedaniels.com*
Michael Dante: *www.michaeldante.com*
Kim Darby: *www.kimdarby.com*
Gail Davis: *www.tvsannieoakley.com*
James Drury: *www.thevirginian.net*
Don Durant: *www.johnnyringo.net*
Buddy Ebsen: *www.buddyebsen.com*
Don Edwards:
    www.somagency.com/DonEdwards
Dale Evans: *www.royrogers.com*
Rhonda Fleming: *www.rhondafleming.com*
Glenn Ford: *www.glennfordonline.com*
Belinda Gail: *www.belindagailsings.com*
Mickey Gilley: *www.gilleys.com*
Stuart Hamblen:
    http:/members.aol.com/HamblenMC
R. W. Hampton: *www.rwhampton.com*
Ty Hardin: *www.tyhardin.com*
William S. Hart: *www.hart-friends.org*
Jimmy Hawkins:
    http://home.earthlink.net/~xka
Robert Horton: *www.roberthorton.com*
Bob Hoy: *www.thehighchaparral.com*
Herb Jeffries: *www.herbjeffries.com*
Waylon Jennings: *www.waylon.com*

Kirby Jonas: *www.kirbyjonas.com*
Don Knotts: *www.donknotts.tv*
Frankie Laine: *www.frankielaine.com*
Chris LeDoux: *www.chrisledoux.com*
Johnny Lee: *www.johnnyleefanclub.com*
George Lindsey: *www.lindseyfilmfest.com*
Leonard Maltin: *www.leonardmaltin.com*
Janet McBride:
    www.heroeswest.com/yodelqueen
Denny Miller: *www.denny-miller.com*
Montie Montana and Montie Montana Jr.:
    www.buffalobill.com
Patsy Montana: *www.patsymontana.net/*
Roger Moore: *www.roger-moore.com*
Audie Murphy: *www.audiemurphy.com*
Ty Murray: *www.tymurray.com*
Paul Newman: *www.newmansown.com*
Hugh O'Brian: *www.hughobrian-wyattearp.com*
    and *www.hoby.org*
Fess Parker: *www.fessparker.com*
Debbie Reynolds: *www.debbiereynolds.com*
Riders in the Sky: *www.ridersinthesky.com*
Kenny Rogers: *www.kennyrogers.com*
Roy Rogers: *www.royrogers.com*
William Sanderson: *www.williamsanderson.net*
William Smith:
    www.williamsmith.org/index.html
Dave Stamey: *www.davestamey.com*
Red Steagall: *www.redsteagall.com*
Stella Stevens: *www.stellavisions.com*
Steve Stevens: *www.celebhost.net/stevestevens/*
George Strait: *www.georgestrait.com*
Bob Tallman: *www.bobtallman.com*
The Texas Trailhands:
    www.texastrailhands.com
Hank Thompson: *www.hankthompson.net*
Randy Travis: *www.randy-travis.com*
Tanya Tucker: *www.tanyatucker.com*
Clint Walker: *www.clintwalker.com*
John Wayne: *www.pilarwayne.com*
Guy Williams: *www.zorrofx.com/welcome.htm*
Bob Wills and the Texas Playboys:
    www.texasplayboys.net
Morgan Woodward: *www.morganwoodward.com*
Sheb Wooley: *www.shebwooley.com*

HOMES ON THE RANGE

The following guest ranches and chuck wagons have contributed recipes to this cookbook. They all invite you to share their brand of western hospitality.

Bar E Ranch
P.O. Box 5
Clinton, AR 72031
501-745-8885
www.cowboycooking.com

Circle Double D Chuck Wagon
8613 Oxbow Lane
Neosho, MO 64850
417-451-6598

Grapevine Canyon Ranch
P.O. Box 302
Pearce, AZ 85625
520-826-3185
www.gcranch.com

Hidden Valley Guest Ranch
3942 Hidden Valley Road
Cle Elum, WA 98922
1-800-526-9269
www.ranchweb.com/hiddenvalley

Kedesh Guest Ranch
1940 Highway 14
Shell, WY 82441
307-765-2791
www.kedesh.com

Laughing Water Ranch
P.O. Box 157
440 Curtiss Road
Fortine, MT 59918
1-800-847-5095
www.lwranch.com

Lazy Hills Guest Ranch
P. O. Box G
Henderson Branch Road
Ingram, TX 78025
1-800-880-0632
www.lazyhills.com

Moonlight Ranch Shed and Bed
136 CR 3196
Valley Mills, TX 76689
254-932-5321

Rocking T Chuck Wagon
5400 Wonder Hill Road
Chappell Hill, TX 77426
979-836-8100

Rockin' L-H Big Red Chuck Wagon
21 Asparagus Lane
Eufaula, OK 74432
1-800-682-3881
www.castironkettlecookout.com

U2 Chuck Wagon
192 A Street
Vale, OR 97918
541-473-3753

Wapiti Meadow Ranch
1667 Johnson Creek Road
Cascade, ID 83611
208-633-3217
www.guestranches.com/wapiti

One of the best sources for information about dude and guest ranches is

The Dude Ranchers' Association
1122 12th Street
P.O. Box 2307
Cody, WY 82414
307-587-2339
www.duderanch.org

And for online information about chuck wagons and their lore, visit

The Chuck Wagon Registry
www.lonehand.com/chuck_wagon_registry.htm

INDEX OF COWBOYS

INDEX OF RECIPES

ABOUT THE AUTHORS

Cheryl Rogers-Barnett, daughter of Roy Rogers and Dale Evans, grew up in the San Fernando Valley where Trigger was her pet. Today, she and her husband, Larry, travel the United States in their RV making appearances at major western film and music festivals. She is the author of *Cowboy Princess*.

Ken Beck and **Jim Clark** are freelance writers who have written numerous books, including *Aunt Bee's Mayberry Cookbook* and *The All-American Cowboy Cookbook*. Ken is an editor for *The Tennessean* and lives in Watertown, Tennessee. Jim is founder of the Andy Griffith Show Rerun Watcher's Club and lives in Nashville.